AMERICA'S DEADLIEST ELECTION

★★★

AMERICA'S DEADLIEST ELECTION

★★*★*★*★*★*★*★*★*★*★*★*★*★*★*★*★*★*

THE CAUTIONARY TALE OF THE MOST
VIOLENT ELECTION IN AMERICAN HISTORY

★★*★*★*★*★*★*★*★*★*★*★*★*★*★*★*★*★*

CNN CHIEF POLITICAL CORRESPONDENT

DANA BASH

WITH DAVID FISHER

HANOVER
SQUARE
PRESS

HANOVER
SQUARE
PRESS™

Recycling programs
for this product may
not exist in your area.

ISBN-13: 978-1-335-08107-0

America's Deadliest Election

Hanover Square Press
22 Adelaide St. West, 41st Floor
Toronto, Ontario M5H 4E3, Canada
HanoverSqPress.com

Printed in U.S.A.

AMERICA'S DEADLIEST ELECTION

INTRODUCTION

All the grand pronouncements about elections that you hear every campaign season about how fundamental they are to a free society are all true: elections are the lifeblood of democracy, the heartbeat of freedom. An election is the structure through which a free people can determine their future, and usher in a peaceful and civilized transfer of power.

It is also true that we cannot take any of that for granted.

We in modern America are painfully aware of this now, but there have been other times in US history when elections were flagrantly undermined and manipulated by the very people asking citizens for the honor to lead them.

This is the story of one of those elections and how it changed American history.

When I first caught the political bug while attending The George Washington University in the early 1990s, I wasn't sure if I wanted to participate or report on them. I quickly realized that my passion was not any one ideology or political philosophy, but rather learning about all of it. I was deeply curious about the different points of view about government and how big or small it should be, and also the fascinating characters running for and holding elected office.

Since then, I've reported on campaigns and elections—mostly for national government but also countless gubernatorial and mayoral races across the country.

I have witnessed the best and the worst of the process, from standing on the press riser and watching the nobility of John Mc-Cain's 2008 concession speech, to the chaos of 2020. I've been privileged to interview a great number of notable candidates, serve as a moderator for multiple significant debates over the years, and now anchor and coanchor two programs on CNN.

My feelings about covering elections haven't changed at all. I still love it. Maybe even more than ever before. That is certainly one reason the election we write about in this book resonated so strongly with me.

While the structure is the same, every election has its own set of issues that appeal to or repel voters, personalities that captivate the public, and general rhythms and cadences defined by both the calendar and the world around us.

But few elections are as unique or have had the lasting impact on America as Louisiana's 1872 gubernatorial election.

Until we began our research, I am embarrassed to say that I knew virtually nothing about this incredibly consequential election that took place a century and a half ago. It turns out that few people do. But as I began learning the details, it brought me new understanding to the most memorable interview I have ever done.

In 2018, I spoke with legendary civil rights leader John Lewis as we stood on the Edmund Pettus Bridge in Selma, Alabama. On that bridge more than fifty years earlier, Lewis was beaten almost to death during the historic march to Montgomery in a quest to earn the most basic fundamental right for African Americans—the right to vote.

While I certainly didn't know it at that time, there exists a direct connection between this long-forgotten 1872 election in Louisiana and the inspirational life of John Lewis. The election in question had a negative impact on the lives of Black voters all across the South who had a chance for real freedom after the Civil War and Reconstruction that followed, but instead became disenfranchised and systemically discriminated against for more than a century.

Its echoes are still felt today.

Louisiana's 1872 gubernatorial election is also a cautionary tale because of the astonishing parallels between that election and some of the events, players and words used in American politics today.

There are direct quotes on these pages, statements made more than a hundred and fifty years ago, that easily could have been spoken by today's politicians. But those parallels only tell half the story; it is what happened afterward that is chilling.

The events that took place in the four years following the 1872 election not only escalated into a national dispute that resulted in the controversial presidential election of 1876, an election literally decided by one man, it also led to the Supreme Court decision that essentially ended Reconstruction and legalized the segregated society that would bring John Lewis to the Edmund Pettus Bridge more than a century later.

Democracy has often been referred to as an experiment. This is the story of what happened—and what can happen again—when that experiment fails.

Dana Bash

1

A person might quickly run out of adjectives trying to describe New Orleans. In the fall of 1872, it seemed as if all the rivers of history had flowed together to create a place unlike anywhere else in the world. The city's contradictions gave it a unique and colorful character: big and loud and majestic; dirty and dangerous and chaotic. It was melodious and raucous; the music never stopped, but neither did the violence. It was renowned for its continental sophistication, boasting theater, opera and masked balls, yet it had only four paved roads, and sewage flowed through the streets.

The mighty Mississippi had made New Orleans and with it Louisiana an economic powerhouse, supplying almost half of the nation's cotton, yet the state was many millions of dollars in debt. Before the Civil War, the city's location made it the doorway from the Gulf of Mexico to the American midlands and thus America's largest slave market, but it also was home to the greatest number of free Black citizens and freed slaves in the South.

Since Europeans first claimed it in 1717, the Louisiana Territory had been under French, Spanish and British rule before finally being purchased by the United States in 1803. As a result, its population was an extraordinary mix of French, Spanish, English, German, Scottish, Native American, Creole and African. It was Black and white and brown, Protestant and Catholic and Jewish with just a touch of *vodou*. It was a place of endless possibilities; the boldest dreamers had always come there, but so had the ruthless schemers.

It often was hard to tell the difference.

For much of the Civil War, Louisiana was an occupied Confederate state. It had seceded in January 1861, but slightly more than a year later a Union fleet led by Admiral David Farragut fought through Rebel strongpoints along the Mississippi to capture New Orleans. Loyalties in the city and state remained divided throughout the rest of the war. Both sides sent thousands of soldiers to fight. For a time, Louisiana had two capitals: the Union occupied territory was governed from New Orleans, while a Confederate government was set up in Shreveport.

In the aftermath of the war, as victorious northerners debated the fate of the former Confederate states, Louisiana remained an occupied territory, part of the Fifth Military District under the harsh command of General Philip Sheridan. It was a place ripe with opportunity for clever men, and thousands of northerners raced south carrying five-dollar carpetbags to stake their claims.

Among them was handsome, charismatic, twenty-two-year-old Henry Clay Warmoth. A lieutenant colonel in the Union Army, he had first been sent there personally by General Ulysses Grant in February 1864. Originally a Missouri lawyer, Warmoth was clever, personable and well-connected, but mostly very ambitious, and he immediately recognized a place where he might build a prosperous future.

Warmoth fit well. He was also a man of flexible values. While being tested for his law license, he was asked a complicated question about property rights. After the facts were stated, he was asked, "To whom does the property of the defendant belong?"

His glib response reflected his intentions—and his character. "To the lawyers, of course."

As the war ended and Reconstruction began, he settled in New Orleans. Congress was trying to find the means to heal the nation. Smart lawyers would be needed to shape the future. Warmoth's wartime post as a judge on the military's provost court had allowed him to become known—and connected—in the legal community. The proverbial pot of gold was there for him; all he had to do was scoop it up.

Instead of returning to the law, he decided to pursue a potentially much more lucrative profession: politician. He was suited for politics, not being bogged down by cumbersome principles. He rose quickly in the chaotic years after the war ended. By the time he was elected governor in 1868, the violence and murders had already begun. In office, he was loud and divisive. Although he claimed to appoint "the best men in the State...the most representative and capable" to official positions, in fact, as the *New York Times* reported, "It is difficult to exaggerate the evils...he has brought on the state." Other newspapers called him "a despot," "a demagogue" and "a tyrant."

The more they attacked him the stronger his support grew, especially among carpetbaggers and Black voters. He built and retained an almost cultlike following. And made himself a very wealthy man.

Warmoth's divisive, controversial and corrupt policies would lead eventually to his impeachment by his political opponents. In his defense, he angrily told journalists, "I have been the best abused man...in the Union, but have seldom felt it necessary to reply to the wild and baseless charges that have been made against me...

"Every one [of several] investigations has been prompted by the most determined hostility; has been aided by ablest legal tal-

ent and has been carried on with the most unrelenting vigor...
but with all the charges made against me, no man has ever produced a scintilla of evidence implicating me in a single act of
official corruption or dishonor."

During his term in office, blood would flow freely in Louisiana, from the crowded streets of New Orleans to the cotton fields of the old plantations, along the rivers and in the
swamps, leading to what remains arguably the most complicated,
contentious and deadliest election in American history. More
than a century and a half later the consequences of Louisiana's
1872 gubernatorial election would continue to reverberate in
American politics.

Warmoth's political career began in November 1865, only
seven months after the end of the war, when the newly organized
Union Republican party elected him to represent Louisiana as
a nonvoting member of Congress. This was the first election in
the state's history in which Black men were permitted to vote.
Many of them even contributed a few cents to a fund established
to defray Warmoth's expenses in Washington, which eventually
raised an amazing $15,000—nearly $300,000 today—and gave
a hint of what was to come. As Warmoth pointed out proudly,
he received 19,396 votes, although he failed to mention he ran
unopposed.

He was cast perfectly for the role, with a pleasantly large
nose, "keen measuring eyes, a superb mustache," high, round
cheekbones and a firm chin that might have been chiseled from
marble. He was almost as tall as President Lincoln, although, as
he was known to point out, not when the president was wearing his top hat.

Warmoth was comfortable with powerful people and often
found himself in the middle of history: he had literally walked
down the great staircase in the White House next to Lincoln
and been present for his second inaugural address. Less auspi-
ciously he had met with General Grant only hours before Lin-

coln's assassination and then stood in the parlor of the Kirkwood
Hotel as Chief Justice Salmon P. Chase administered the oath of
office to President Andrew Johnson. And he had helped make
the arrangements for Lincoln's funeral, traveling with the cor-
tege to New York City.

His words were as smooth and reassuring as his appearance.
Supporters admired him for his refreshing candor; opponents
found him loud and abrasive. His strength as a politician lay in
his claim that he was not a politician. He successfully forged an
image as the honest representative of the common man, which
was why, he contended, powerful politicians continually attacked him. As he once told a *Chicago Tribune* reporter, "I don't
pretend to be honest... I only pretend to be as honest as anybody in politics. And more so than those fellows who are opposing me now."

While he made the politically correct promises after his election, claiming he was not a partisan, pledging to uphold the law
and order for all people, his election stunned and terrified white
Louisianians. While the result was never in question, the turnout
was astonishing. Nineteen thousand votes with no opponent?
It was a warning, a harbinger of future elections. If those Black
voters formed a coalition with the carpetbaggers who were just
beginning to show up in large numbers throughout the South,
they easily would gain control of the state government. While
the defeated Confederates understood and accepted that they
would pay a price for waging war, they were now realizing that
their genteel society had been turned upside down. Their future was going to be determined at the ballot box. Unless they
acted, their enemies and former slaves would be making—and
enforcing—the laws.

They had to be stopped. Whatever it took, this new voting
bloc had to be stopped.

The concept of voting for leaders can be traced back to ancient Greece, where male landowners cast ballots on shards of

broken pottery to determine which—if any—politicians should be exiled. The first election in America was held in 1607, when six white male colonists in Jamestown, Virginia, elected Edward Maria Wingfield president of the governing council. Historically, the right to vote had been restricted to white male property holders, people who paid taxes and aged at least twenty-one years, the idea being that people who had a "stake in society" would be harder to influence. Voting rights remained a contentious issue after the American Revolution. John Adams railed against extending suffrage, writing, "...every man who has not a farthing, will demand an equal voice with any other in all acts of state," and as a result it would "confound and destroy all distinctions, and prostrate all ranks to one common level."

But Benjamin Franklin disagreed. "Today a man owns a jackass worth fifty dollars," he proposed, "and he is entitled to vote, but before the next election the jackass dies. The man in the meantime has become more experienced, his knowledge of the principles of government and his acquaintance with mankind are more extensive, and therefore he is better qualified to make a proper selection of rulers—but the jackass is dead and the man cannot vote. Now, gentlemen, pray inform me, in whom is the right of suffrage? In the man or in the jackass?"

Each colony and later each state held the power to determine who was allowed to vote in its elections. Qualifications for voting had not been mentioned in the original Constitution. There were no national voting standards, even when electing federal government officials. Over time most of the economic tests, like having to own property or pay taxes, had disappeared. But despite a few rare instances in which the right to vote had been extended to propertied women, free Black people and even Native Americans, for the most part it had remained restricted to white men. Sometimes only to white Christian men. Although a rabble-rousing New York abolitionist named Susan B. Anthony was leading a movement to extend the right to vote to women and Black Americans, her suffrage organization had gained limited support.

Throughout the former Confederacy, especially in states such as Louisiana, Alabama and Mississippi, the former Rebels were organizing—preparing to fight to diminish the impact of northern Reconstruction policies. The most notable of these groups, the Ku Klux Klan, had been formed in Pulaski, Tennessee, in December 1865 by six former Confederate officers. A secret social fraternity, based loosely on existing social organizations like the Masons, its name supposedly was derived from the Greek word *kuklos*, meaning circle. The kuklos clan, or tightly knit familial group, quickly became known as the Ku Klux Klan.

Like other fraternities, its members created secret rituals and adopted distinctive costumes—in this case long multicolored robes and a pointed hat with eye slits cut into it. By disguising their identities, the regalia provided protection for members— as well as adding an aura of danger. While the Ku Klux Klan had not been formed specifically to intimidate people, when its members discovered their garb had that effect, the costume spread quickly throughout the South.

A local version of the Klan came to Louisiana in early 1867, when former Confederate Colonel Alcibiades DeBlanc founded a militia known as the Knights of the White Camelia. Rather than keeping their identities secret, armed members of the White Camelia marched boldly through the streets of New Orleans or patrolled dark roads at night, threatening freedmen and their white supporters.

The War Between the States, as Southerners were already referring to it, was done, but the resistance was just beginning. Violence erupted again soon after. In New Orleans on Monday, July 30, 1866, a glorious summer day, a convention to create a new state constitution was scheduled to meet at noon.

In an editorial published that morning, the conservative *New Orleans Times-Picayune* lauded the city's Black population, claiming that in New Orleans there had always been "a feeling of the most kindly and friendly character" between the races. But in a formal proclamation, the city's mayor, Democrat John T. Monroe, bluntly warned delegates not to meet. He was mostly ignored. A large group of Black men marched through the streets to celebrate the day when the constitutional convention reconvened to draft a far more radical document that granted full citizenship, including voting rights, to all Black men.

A mob of mostly ex-Confederate soldiers armed with guns, clubs and knives, organized by Mayor Monroe, was waiting for the demonstrators when they reached the Mechanics Institute, the large building in which the legislature was meeting. Seconds later the first shot was fired. The marchers rushed into the massive building for protection. But it was hopeless. Police officers joined the attackers, breaking windows and firing into the building.

It was a massacre.

THE HISTORIC NEW ORLEANS COLLECTION, 1974.25.3.271

The Mechanics Institute, the seat of Louisiana's government, had been the site of an 1866 attack by white rioters trying to prevent a new state constitution from being enacted. As many as two hundred Black freedmen were killed and more than one hundred were wounded in the riot.

As many as two hundred Black men were killed and many more injured. Several men who raised their arms to surrender were shot in cold blood. Those wounded were stabbed and clubbed to death. Others were killed as they prayed. Black men just passing by were pulled off streetcars and beaten or murdered.

It took more than an hour before federal troops arrived to stop the carnage. By then the floor of the Institute was caked in blood.

Dozens of men, both white and Black, were arrested but later released. The real instigators of the massacre, reported the *Times-Picayune*, were "reckless and unprincipled" men attempting to "regain offices and patronage which they had lost since the close of the war, by which they had raised themselves from poverty and obscurity to comparative wealth and partisan notoriety." No one knew who had fired the first shots, but the paper alleged without any evidence it had been fired by a Black man who shot an innocent white man "standing quietly at the curbstone."

There is no record that anyone was prosecuted for the crimes committed that day. Battle lines were being drawn. But that Monday morning it became clear that protecting democracy would require far more than an expansion of voting rights, and that more people were going to die in that fight.

The primary question that had to be answered was under what terms would the union be reconstructed? How much power would the national government have to impose laws that under the Constitution had been granted to the individual states, for example? There was no simple answer, no model on which to base decisions. Louisiana would serve as the testing ground for policies that might be applied to the rest of the Confederacy.

As one of the few people representing Louisiana's interests in Washington, Henry Warmoth found himself in the middle of the debate, trying to help forge a political compromise that would prevent more bloodshed while furthering his own career.

Slavery would be outlawed, that was certain, but beyond that there was little consensus about other conditions. According to the *Times-Picayune* there was considerable evidence that shortly before he was assassinated, "Mr. Lincoln seriously inclined to the restoration of recognized states, administered by their own citizens with no other conditions than that of full fealty to the constitution." Any "punishments and proscriptions...were few, and dictated by policy rather than revenge." It was an extraordinary claim, and the paper offered no evidence to support it.

His successor, Democrat Andrew Johnson, who had been raised in the secessionist state of Tennessee, had very different views. His plan required the Confederate states to abolish slavery, pay their war debts and swear allegiance to the Union. In return they would retain their rights to determine how to rebuild their laws—including who would be granted the right to vote—and their economy. But under his plan, freed slaves would not receive General Sherman's promised "forty acres and a mule," and landowners would regain the properties they owned before the war.

Territories rejoining the Union would be bound by the three constitutional Amendments—the 13th, 14th and 15th—which formed the political foundation of Reconstruction. The Thirteenth Amendment, which had been passed by Congress in January 1865, outlawed slavery, stating, "Neither slavery nor involuntary servitude, except as a punishment for crime whereof the party shall have been duly convicted, shall exist within the United States, or any place subject to their jurisdiction."

The Fourteenth Amendment was passed after states began instituting black codes to lessen the impact of the Thirteenth Amendment. It granted citizenship to every person born in the United States and prohibited states from making or attempting to enforce "any law which shall abridge the privileges or immunities of citizens of the United States; nor shall any State deprive any person of life, liberty, or property, without due process of law; nor deny to any person within its jurisdiction the equal protection of the laws."

The Fifteenth Amendment extended the right to vote to former slaves, stating it "shall not be denied or abridged by the

United States, or by any State, on account of race, color, or previous condition of servitude." But it was intentionally loosely worded so as to allow the states to establish their own qualifications. States were still free to prevent women from voting or institute a variety of fees, tests and other hurdles to make it difficult or almost impossible for Black men to vote.

While Congress was amending the national constitution, in New Orleans, Louisiana's legislature was slowly drafting a new state constitution. In 1864 Louisiana had become the first southern state to adopt a conciliatory constitution—although it applied only to the thirteen occupied parishes around New Orleans and Baton Rouge. It was a small first step toward rejoining the Union. In accordance with the Emancipation Proclamation, slavery was abolished without any compensation to slaveholders. Additionally, the legislature was authorized—but not compelled—to extend voting rights to Black men who had fought for the Union, owned property or were literate.

Confederate supporters organized to fight back against these radical changes. They successfully elected a Democratic mayor and legislature in New Orleans. And then they picked up weapons. July 30th's murderous attack at the statehouse sent a message heard by every politician, every northerner, every person, Black or white. In the South, Black men could be killed with impunity.

Congress finally was forced to act, passing the Reconstruction Act of 1867. There no longer was any attempt at compromise. It granted the right to vote to Black men and prohibited ex-Confederates from holding office. President Johnson vetoed it, warning it would "operate against the white race." Congress overrode the veto. Union General Philip Sheridan was put in command of the Military District of the Southwest, which included Louisiana and Texas, until a new civilian government could be elected. Sheridan ordered a massive effort to register all legal voters, then scheduled a convention to draw up a new state constitution.

Eighty thousand voters—among them an estimated seventy

thousand newly registered Black voters—elected ninety-eight delegates to that convention. Almost half of those delegates were Black, ninety-six of them were Republicans.

There was no longer any need or desire to find a compromise. The Confederacy had lost the war and with it a way of life. The new state constitution reached much further than the end of slavery, imposing a new social order on the South: it granted full citizenship to Black men and outlawed segregation on public transportation and in restaurants and classrooms.

The Confederacy's greatest fear had become reality: their former slaves had won the right to vote and the beginnings of equality had arrived. As the Black-owned *New Orleans Tribune* wrote, "We want to ride in any conveyance, to travel on steamboats, dine in any restaurant or educate our children at any school."

In April 1868, as the attempt to impeach President Johnson for his lenient Reconstruction policies was underway in Washington, a massive majority of primarily Black Louisiana voters ratified the state constitution and elected twenty-five-year-old Republican Henry Warmoth the new governor.

HERITAGE IMAGES/HULTON ARCHIVE/ GETTY IMAGES

Young, charismatic carpetbagger Henry Warmoth set in motion incredible and deadly events that would cast a shadow over America for a century.

The fact that Warmoth had been indicted in Texas several years earlier for embezzling $21,000 did not seem to bother voters. His support for the Union and Black suffrage was sufficient for most supporters.

Oscar James Dunn, a Black plastering and painting contractor who had been born into slavery and rose to become a business owner and city councilman, was elected lieutenant governor.

Warmoth's opponent, the former Confederate governor, Henry Allen, received 9,000 votes, even though he had fled to Mexico to avoid prosecution for his role in the rebellion.

Within days the conservative media began reinforcing the rapidly spreading belief that the election had been rigged. At that time the secret ballot did not exist. Originally, Americans had voted out loud—*viva voce*, it was called. After swearing on the Bible that they were who they claimed to be and that they hadn't already voted, they told the clerk which candidate they supported, and their vote was recorded. That had evolved into a written ballot, occasionally handwritten by a literate voter, but more often conveniently preprinted by a political party listing the names of all its candidates or by a candidate himself. These "tickets" were published in newspapers or handed out to voters at the polls who then put them in a sealed ballot box. Tickets often were cleverly designed or brightly colored, so observers could see how a person had voted, and reward or penalize him for that vote.

The election was bitterly fought. According to the *Monroe Telegraph*, for example, Black voters had been warned, "Unless they voted (for Warmoth) they would be put back in slavery..."

The Democratic *Ouachita Telegraph* wrote that voters were marched to the polls from a nearby plantation "in military style by a leader who gave commands and were voted in solid [unity] for the Warmoth ticket."

In Plaquemines Parish, the local conservative paper reported the ballot box was unlocked and unsealed, and people not registered in that district were permitted to vote. The box was guarded by three Black men holding clubs whose presence intimidated white voters, and who inspected each ballot and rejected any Democratic vote.

Anyone who objected was threatened "with arrest or with shackles." An "old and respected freedman," intending to vote for the Democratic candidate, "was dragged off his horse, assaulted, beaten and threatened with immediate death..."

There were a lot of newspapers in Louisiana competing for readership. Telling people what they wanted to hear was good business. It wasn't a new tactic: partisan journalists had always played a role in elections. As far back as 1789 the Federalist *Gazette of the United States* set the standard with its motto, He That Is Not for Us, Is against Us. Facts often were slanted or ignored to support a party or candidate. As a result, passions were aroused, and a hostile climate was created, which sold even more papers. And Henry Warmoth's propensity to speak out bluntly made him an easy target. The man knew how to attract attention.

Warmoth had won an almost impossible position, he complained, and only a man of his talents could deal with it. "With the taxpayers, the press and the National Administration against me," he said later, "I was at once encumbered with embarrassments calculated to appall a timid man, and to require all the nerve, patience and forbearance I could summon to assure peace and to effect even a tolerable administration."

In addition to the unrest created by the embittered Confederates, he faced other issues as well. The state was pretty much destitute; the government had barely collected any taxes during the war and could not pay its debts; the levees that protected New Orleans had been neglected and needed millions of dollars in repairs; the railroad system was broken; and even the penitentiary system had been dismantled. On the day Warmoth was inaugurated a rainstorm flooded the city, making streets impassable and emphasizing the lack of a decent sewer system.

And Warmoth had to solve these problems while dealing with an inexperienced, inept and corrupt legislature.

But worse than any infrastructure or fiscal problems was the racial strife the city, the state and the nation were facing. It impacted every decision. Two constituencies with competing and seemingly irreconcilable needs, interests and desires somehow had to be satisfied.

Had there been a period of time during which Warmoth could lay the groundwork for a rough form of reconciliation, he might have been able to find at least the beginning of a compromise. But there wasn't. Louisiana had been readmitted to the Union in June. A presidential election was taking place in November.

For the first time, the reunited nation would vote on the Reconstruction. Politicians made all the usual campaign promises, but what the election really came down to was racial equality. How was the country going to deal with almost four million new citizens? How were the former slaves going to be protected? The myriad other problems—for example, who was going to pay for rebuilding destroyed Southern cities—were complicated, but there were established ways of dealing with them. People could discuss fiscal policy. They could debate how much power the federal government had under the Constitution in a rational manner. But race? Racial equality was different. The concept was an emotional issue that had already shown it could tear the nation to pieces.

The two major political parties staked claims on opposite sides of the issue. Lincoln's Republican party rejected President Johnson's policies of reconciliation, which they believed were too soft on the defeated South. Too many parents had lost their sons in the war to forgive so easily. Instead of Johnson, the party nominated war hero Ulysses S. Grant for president. No one could ever accuse General Grant of being too soft on the Rebels. The respected speaker of the house, Schuyler Colfax, was selected to run as his vice president.

The Democrats campaigned against Republican policies that had granted political power to the former slaves. Their choice for president was New York's popular governor, Horatio Seymour, the chairman of the party's convention. Seymour advocated limiting the powers of the federal government and opposed the Republican Congress's Reconstruction policies. His campaign slogan was simple and direct: This Is a White Man's Government. For vice president, the convention nominated another Union war hero who also advocated white supremacy, Major General Frank Blair of Missouri.

There had been twenty previous presidential elections. In every one of those elections white men had gone to the polls on election day and freely cast their ballots. There had been some shenanigans, attempts at bribery, celebratory drinking, but rarely had anyone dared interfere with the right to vote. That was what made America so inspiring to the rest of the world. Citizens could freely elect their leaders. By their choices, voters had shaped the future of the young nation. Eight years earlier the American people had stood defiantly against the threatened rebellion, voting for Lincoln even knowing war might follow. More than six hundred thousand men had died because of that decision.

But the election of 1868 was different. It would be, as Warmoth predicted, "The most bitter election in American history… The whole question of Reconstruction was to be settled by this election." There was little doubt about the outcome—Grant would win easily—if the emancipated slaves were allowed to vote.

If.

Legally, there was little conservative Democrats could do to stop them. The party represented a minority. But as they had learned the past few years, there were other measures they could take, actions that had worked in local elections to keep people away from the polls. So rather than being a referendum on the issues, the election would be decided by who was allowed to vote. The viability of the system itself was the issue. Could it be protected? Could it be trusted?

Warmoth's election only a few months earlier had proven that at least some voters could be kept from the polls through violence or intimidation. They could be scared away. But if they still were not dissuaded from voting, then the system itself had to be attacked. Whatever it took, those ballots could not be counted. There were numerous different ways of accomplishing that, both overt and subtle.

But violence was most effective. The Democrats began by taking control of the media. Vigilantes attacked most of the seventy-three Republican newspapers in the state, ransacking their offices and destroying their presses. Several publishers were forced to flee Louisiana.

Among those who resisted was the eighteen-year-old editor of the *St. Landry Progress*, Emerson Bentley, a white carpetbagger from Ohio who had come to Opelousas, Louisiana, to fight for civil rights. Opelousas, about a hundred and fifty miles northwest of New Orleans, was the largest city in the sprawling St. Landry Parish. Throughout the summer there had been periodic attacks on Black families in the city. Innocent people had been murdered. In an attempt to stop the violence a meeting was held between Black and white community leaders. Among the agreements made was that the *Progress* would be allowed to continue publishing—but only after its editors agreed to refrain from printing any incendiary comments about Democrats.

In late September Bentley broke that promise, writing that, unlike Democrats, Republicans "do not plot in the dark; we do not assassinate inoffensive citizens or…seek the lives of political opponents…"

Days later he was teaching a class of sixty young Black students in the local Methodist church when three members of a white supremacist group, the Seymour Knights, burst into his classroom. Among them was a judge and the local constable. After forcing him to sign a retraction they began brutally whipping him. The children ran screaming from the church.

It was believed that Bentley had been killed, although he actually had managed to escape into a barn behind the newspaper office. No one knew if he was dead or alive. Black Republicans began organizing for their own self-defense. But the rumor spread in the white community that Black people were planning retaliation. According to the Democratic newspaper *Opelousas Courier* they intended to "reduce our town to ashes." Supposedly a white man had been shot while searching a home for weapons, and in response "parties of mounted [white] men were sent out in different directions…to procure reinforcements…

"As soon as it was known that the negroes had commenced the fight, and spilled the first blood, the excitement became deep and strong, men rapidly made up their minds that the hour of trial had come."

These stories stirred the violence. The specter of a Black uprising had been used for decades to terrify white residents. Stories of deadly slave uprisings in places like Santo Domingo and Virginia were well-known. Now hundreds of well-armed white men raced to Opelousas.

On September 28th the massacre began.

Twenty-nine Black men were captured that day and twenty-seven of them were killed. The next several weeks were hunting season for vigilantes. Black men and women and white Republicans were murdered, many of them buried in shallow graves, others left where they were killed. They were shot in the streets and in their homes. Those trying to flee were chased into the woods and swamps and lynched. Bentley's coeditor of the *Progress*, C. E. Durand, was among the first victims; his body was left hanging in front of the Opelousas drugstore. "Each day," reported the *New Orleans Advocate*, "new victims fell."

The total number of people killed or wounded was never known. Democrats estimated there were between twenty-five and thirty deaths. Republicans claimed at least 200 dead, and a later government investigation reported 233 victims.

Bentley survived, and three weeks later arrived safely in New Orleans. But the Democrats' goal of destroying the Republican party in one of the state's largest parishes had been accomplished. The *Franklin Planter* reported Republican "clubs have been broken up, the scallywags have turned Democrats and the carpetbaggers have been run off, and their carpet-bag press and type and office have been destroyed."

Throughout the state, the use of violence to intimidate Republicans continued right up until the election. Robed white men rode through towns and villages. In the hamlet of Holloway's Prairie two men and a woman were taken out of an evening church service and hanged. The *New Orleans Republican* reported that a riot in the streets of New Orleans, "one of those scenes of bloodshed and violence which are getting more frequent day by day," ended with four men killed.

A federal legislative committee eventually estimated that a thousand Black and white Republicans had been killed in the months before the election, and hundreds more injured and threatened.

Newspapers like the *Louisiana Democrat* spread the terror, warning, "Let the colored voter remember [the violence] and let him cut loose forever from Radical carpetbaggers and scalawags. His only safety lies in voting the Democratic ticket."

The strategy worked. In Black churches, ministers urged their congregations to stay away from the polls for their own safety. Outside New Orleans few white Republicans dared to vote. As one rural voting-registration supervisor admitted, "I am fully convinced that no man on that day could have voted any other than the Democratic ticket and not been killed inside of 24 hours."

In the parish in which Opelousas was located Grant and Colfax didn't get a single vote; only a few months earlier 2,200 people there had voted for Warmoth.

Even when people did vote, returns were manipulated; ballot boxes were opened and stuffed or simply disappeared when being transported. Tallies were changed or inaccurately reported. There was little Governor Warmoth could do to ensure an honest election, and there is no indication that he tried.

The Democratic candidate for president easily carried the state. Grant received 33,000 votes, about half the total number cast for Warmoth only seven months earlier. Horatio Seymour won with 70 percent of the votes. Seven parishes reported that he had received 100 percent of the votes, in eight others he got only 99 percent.

Louisiana's seven electoral votes made no difference in the outcome. Grant won the election by 134 electoral votes. Even the Democratic *Times-Picayune* admitted there had been considerable fraud in the election—although that paper claimed it had been committed by Republicans. "Seymour came near beating Grant," the paper claimed, adding, "Had there been fair registration and honest voting throughout the South, Grant would have been beaten."

The results sent a strong message: violence, intimidation and fraud worked. Four years later, that lesson would be remembered.

2

"New Orleans was a dirty, impoverished and hopeless city, with a mixed, ignorant, corrupt and bloodthirsty gang in control," wrote Henry Warmoth, describing the situation when he was elected governor in 1868. "It was flooded with lotteries, gambling dens and licensed brothels. Many of the city officials, as well as the police force, were thugs and murderers. Violence was rampant..."

The situation was dire, he continued. Most of the plantations were in ruin. The state was bitterly divided between Democrats and Republicans, rural and city, and there was no money in the state treasury. There were no cotton mills or other industries, few wharves or warehouses. The levees were in a deplorable condition. The state's drinking water was polluted. Waste from the slaughterhouses was drained into the Mississippi. Yellow fever epidemics killed a large number of people each year. Transportation and communication between population centers were essentially nonexistent, as there was not a single hard-surfaced road and less than two hundred miles of usable railroad tracks in the entire state, and there was only limited access to the telegraph.

For an ambitious man like Henry Warmoth, it was a dream come true. By painting the bleakest possible picture of the state when he entered office, there was almost nothing he could do that would make things worse, while he would receive credit for any progress that took place whether he was responsible for it or not. To save the state, he made clear, he needed far more power than traditionally given to the governor. He needed control over the machinery of state.

And he set out to take it.

Warmoth was young and inexperienced but instinctively understood the mechanics of politics: being a successful politician required the accumulation of power. And patronage is the source of political power. He began rewarding his base, sprinkling loyalists throughout the government. At his direction, the Republicans who controlled the legislature created eight new parishes, allowing him to appoint a substantial number of new judges, district attorneys, constables, sheriffs, clerks, recorders and all the other officials who made the government function. He interpreted a newly passed state law to mean he was empowered to fill existing vacancies when the State Senate was not in session without its consent. It was a complicated, controversial and legally dubious approach, but it eventually enabled him to stack half of New Orleans city council with his supporters among other plum positions.

Next, he had to get rid of potential restraints on his use of power. Like countless people before him, as well as those who would follow him into politics after, Warmoth didn't believe the laws applied to him. As far as he was concerned, laws were more a suggestion than a rule. They should be subject to common sense, as he judged it, and "the great law of necessity."

"As Chief Executive," he once explained to a legislative committee, "the Governor has the power to do anything which, in his judgment, is necessary in seeing that the laws are properly executed...

"There is a distinction between laws being interpreted and laws being executed."

He meant it too. According to a popular story being told in New Orleans, when the grand duke of Russia, Alexei Romanov, had visited the city he said to Warmoth, "Governor, they tell me you have as much power as my father."

"Your father? Hell," Warmoth supposedly responded, "your father's power is not a circumstance to mine."

He'd learned how to slip around the law early; ironically, he had become a lawyer when he was only eighteen years old, lying about his age to be admitted into practice. As governor, in addition to controlling the courts through his appointments, he wanted to be able to enforce his interpretation of the law. Citing the need to stop the violence that had plagued the state prior to the election, with the acquiescence of the newly constituted city council, he created a new five-hundred-man police force. The new Metropolitan Police, consisting almost entirely of Black veterans of the Union army, supposedly was formed to assist sheriffs in keeping the law but in fact acted as Warmoth's militia. Clad in black-and-red uniforms they became highly visible in the streets of New Orleans and surrounding areas.

He asserted his authority by firing state officials. "As the Chief Executive of the State, I have control of all the militia, of all the sheriffs, of all the constables and of all the police forces organized in the state, and they are under my orders whenever, in my judgment, it is necessary to use them," he testified in a hearing challenging his dismissals. And then he added, "That is my interpretation of the (state) constitution."

The attorney questioning him noted, perhaps sarcastically, "Now we understand what your powers are."

Warmoth disagreed. "I haven't told you half of them yet," he responded.

The law, he made clear, was whatever he said it was. Then he proceeded to act that way. He claimed he had the right to issue a writ compelling sheriffs to arrest anyone he believed should be arrested. At one point, he requested and signed a clearly unconstitutional bill permitting police to clean up the streets of New Orleans by arresting vagrants. At another time, he suspended the district attorney of Natchitoches Parish, even though he did not have power over the judicial branch of the government.

Inevitably, there was opposition to his actions. In a front-page story, the *Times-Picayune* described him in headlines as "A Governor Who is Above the Law," who "is the very essence of despotic rule." In response, Warmoth attacked the "venal and subsidized" media: "I told the people that if half the lies the newspapers had told about me were true, I ought to be in the penitentiary for life, thereby depriving them of the services of the best Governor the state has ever had in its history."

The relationship between the media and politicians has always been symbiotic, but complex and difficult. The actions of politicians affect every citizen, so it is the obligation of the media to report them. Newspaper publishers and editors like New York's Horace Greeley, for example, even went into politics.

How the media cover them becomes the question. It often pays to be supportive, figuratively and literally. Those outlets providing positive spin may get exclusive interviews and early access to stories. And there is a lot of money to be made. By law, states are required to publish a significant amount of material, ranging from legislative actions to notices about elections, and the newspapers awarded those contracts can count on reliable government payments. After taking office Warmoth had a law passed setting fees for publishing official state information, raising the normal rates in some cases as much as 500 percent and establishing a printing commission to designate those newspapers that would get the business. About thirty-five papers around the state received state revenue, and in several situations those funds supported their entire business.

The three members of that commission were Warmoth, Lieutenant Governor Dunn and the Republican speaker of the house.

The commission also selected the *New Orleans Republican* to be the state's official journal. The fact that Warmoth owned 250 of the 1,100 issued shares in the paper, allowing him to share in the profits, apparently was not revealed in the journal.

But opposition papers, especially the popular *Times-Picayune*, furiously attacked him, claiming, "In that position (as head of the printing commission), he has voted his own printing company the fattest of the subsidies. Under this system about a half million dollars has been appropriated to a fungous and mercenary press, which has earned its infamous wages by calumniating a people who were robbed and oppressed that it might flourish in insolence and impunity."

The ambitious Warmoth also had to secure his own political as well as financial future. Having been elected the second youngest governor in American history, his prospects were seemingly endless. He already was gaining national attention. His handling of the election riots in October 1868 had received substantial coverage. A young Midwesterner acceptable to the South, who could claim support from both Black and white citizens, was definitely an intriguing prospect. When assessing candidates for the 1870 Senate race in Louisiana, the *New York Herald* included him near the top, despite the fact that "Governor Warmoth is too young to enter the lists, his age not reaching the required thirty summers."

As promising as his future might be on the national stage, before any of that could happen he had to protect his political future within the state. That was a problem. Louisiana law limited its governors to a single term. That law would have to be changed to suit Warmoth's interests. In March 1870, buried beside the news that thirty states had ratified the Fifteenth Amendment was the news that the legislature had proposed four amendments to the state constitution to be voted on the following November.

One of them restored the right to vote to all Confederate soldiers. That was certain to be popular with the opposition party. But the last one would not be, though it was the key to Warmoth's future. It removed Article 50, "which provides that the Governor shall be ineligible for reelection at the end of his four year term," from the constitution.

In addition to the Democrats' opposition, several Republicans who had been planning to run for the post objected to this power grab. Among them was the Black lieutenant governor, Oscar Dunn. It caused a crack in the party, a hint of the split that would soon follow.

As it turned out, far more important than the proposed amendments were several bills changing the electoral system. The Constitution grants states the power to determine "The Times, Places and Manner of holding Elections." While the right to vote became subject to federal laws following the Civil War, no laws dictate how each state counts the votes. And throughout American history, the manner in which votes are counted—and who does the counting—has made all the difference.

The system hadn't changed much in half a century. After the polls closed, the boxes were opened and the votes were counted by hand. The "returns" from each box were reported to a central location and added together.

Although, changes were on the horizon. A year earlier, in 1869, a young inventor named Thomas Edison had received his first patent, for a mechanical voting machine to be used to tally votes in Congress. Still, it would be decades before the appearance of lever-operated voting machines.

Few voters knew how the system worked. They cast their vote and went home. Several days later newspapers reported the result. Politicians relied on that lack of interest. So few voters paid attention when the legislature changed the registration and election laws.

But politicians did. They recognized that the new laws gave Warmoth significant control over the electoral system.

Under these new laws, the governor appointed the chief election officer and the supervisor of voters in each parish. Supervisors fixed the day, time and places the polls would be open. They also were empowered to name a commissioner of elections at each polling place to oversee conduct of the voting and return the boxes to the state. Registrars also were responsible for registering potential voters and supplying lists of legally registered voters to the poll commissioners.

A supervisor's decision was final and could not be appealed to the courts.

Most importantly, although almost no one realized it, was a law that established a Returning Board, which made the final determination about the election. The board had the power to settle all disputes; its members were authorized to examine claims of fraud or irregularities and could simply throw out the results in any precinct or parish that in their sole opinion had been unduly influenced by fraud or violence. It gave them the power to discard returns for just about any reason.

The five-man board was composed of Warmoth and Dunn, the secretary of state and two Republican senators.

These new election laws put Warmoth in control of the entire process, from registration through vote counting, virtually assuring his own reelection as well as the fate of other candidates. Elected representatives recognized his power and were careful not to attack him. As one assembly member said when asked his opinion, "Not that I have anything against the governor himself, but I think it improper to give such extraordinary power to any man, were he an apostle."

Another member added cautiously, "Although I would have the greatest confidence in whatever he reported."

There had never been a politician quite like Warmoth. He was an outsider who had succeeded by gaining the support of

other outsiders, people who previously had been excluded from
the process, people who felt they were powerless. He told them
what they wanted to hear. He made them feel good about themselves. And he took action to defend their rights, creating and
heavily arming a state militia that would protect not only him
but Black citizens. And if he wasn't always truthful or even accurate, his supporters didn't seem to care. He understood another fundamental rule of politics: many people won't care if
you're dishonest, as long as you're fulfilling their demands with
your dishonesty.

For newly enfranchised Black voters he was a revelation. Most
previous state government officials had supported slavery, so
whatever Warmoth did—and how he did it—was a significant
improvement.

He also was personally appealing. Supporters and opponents
alike agreed he was charming; he was young, good-looking,
well-spoken and very publicly single. The bachelor Warmoth
cut a dashing figure in New Orleans. He had a great backstory;
he had come to Louisiana as a poor lawyer, his entire fortune
a twenty-dollar gold piece in his pocket, and he had once been
thrown out of an office-apartment for failing to pay the rent,
but he had worked hard and been successful. Like the rags-to-
riches hero of Horatio Alger's *Ragged Dick*, which had just been
published, he was a self-made man of the people. They looked
at him and saw what was possible for themselves or their children. And so they turned out to vote for him.

The four amendments were on the ballot the following November. That election, he later said, "was admitted by everybody in the state...the quietest and fairest election ever held in
Louisiana up to that time."

The facts were different. There were widespread allegations
of fraud on both sides. According to Republican reports, "in
at least a dozen parishes [Black] men were intimidated from
voting." And according to Democratic newspapers, newly ap-

pointed parish supervisors set up registration centers thirty to fifty miles from Democratic areas and did not keep them open for regular hours. The canniest among them was Bossier Parish supervisor Daniel Cady Stanton, the son of abolitionist and women's rights leader Elizabeth Cady Stanton. Carpetbagger Stanton had arrived in Bossier only two months earlier. In addition to limiting the opportunities to register, he opened only four polling stations and kept no list of registered voters in two of them, so no one knew who or how many people had voted. On election day voters discovered that Stanton himself had replaced another candidate on the ballot.

Not surprisingly, he was elected to the state legislature.

While Republicans controlled the voting, Democrats tried to gain control of the counting. In Baton Rouge, as Republican supervisors were opening the ballot boxes, the doors burst open, and the intruders began shooting. Four Black men were killed, and about twenty more people were wounded. Only the arrival of federal troops prevented more deaths. In Donaldsonville, a town several miles outside Baton Rouge that had elected America's first Black mayor only two years earlier, armed Democrats surrounded the courthouse where the ballot boxes were being opened. Fearing violence, the supervisor decided to take the boxes across the river where federal troops offered protection. As they began moving the boxes, members of the mob opened fire, killing one man and wounding several others.

The election officials retreated to the courthouse.

The stalemate was broken the next morning when Warmoth's Black militia arrived, threatening to burn down the town unless the ballot boxes were given to them. After several more people were shot on both sides, the militia marched into town and the ballot boxes were handed over.

As expected, when the votes finally were counted, all four amendments had been approved. Warmoth no longer faced term limits. Republicans won all the Congressional races, retained control of the state legislature and took control of New Orleans's city government. It was an overwhelming victory—and naturally, the Returning Board approved all the results.

Warmoth had become a political force. He had, complained his detractors, "with his bold and efficacious measures" made himself the center of state government. The South had never seen a politician like him. Ulysses Grant invited him to the White House, where he dined privately with the president and his family. He was only twenty-eight years old.

Grant needed all the Republican supporters he could gather. He intended to run for reelection in two years, and the Republican party was split while Democrats were united against him. The Civil War was over but there was no real peace. North and South were battling over the country's future. "At the North," explained the *New Orleans Republican*, "the South is represented as a desperato, with a slouched hat and a revolver. At the South the North is pictured as a burglar with a slouched hat and a revolver."

The *Times-Picayune* was far blunter. In response to a *New York Times* editorial, it presented the Southern position, writing that the *Times* "has reasons in abundance to justify the hate of the North against the South. The fact that this hate does exist has produced a corresponding hatred of the South toward the North. The North commenced the work of hate. It invaded the Southern states. It has killed half a million or so of its people and for six years has carried out its hate in measures unsurpassed for their tyranny and malignity...

"We hate the people of the North as they hate us."

Throughout the South, the president's Reconstruction policies were failing to take hold. Now that they had been brought back to the Union, the Southern states were demanding the decision-making rights granted to them in the Constitution. They focused hard on the words *the consent of the governed* while resisting attempts to expand suffrage to all. But having tasted freedom, Black Americans were not taking a step back. Grant was trying desperately to satisfy both sides. "The Southerners are passionate," he explained. "It is absolutely necessary to give political passions a sufficient time to pass away. The young generation comprehends its duties and interests better..."

But recognizing the rise of the KKK and other white supremacist organizations, he authorized the newly created Department of Justice to send troops into the South to protect Black citizens.

Southern leaders continued to insist that the federal government had limited authority, if any, over the states, even while Grant was imposing new laws.

Somehow Warmoth had been able to stake out a middle ground. While he relied on Republican support, he portrayed himself as a politician above the party fray, demonstrating his independence when votes were at stake. During his first two years in office, he vetoed thirty-nine bills sent to him by the legislature, claiming many of them were fiscally irresponsible. He declared himself the guardian of the pocketbook, vowing not to spend taxpayer money on folly, and angering legislators by turning down funding requests for their local projects. He refused to sign legislation directing St. Charles Avenue in New Orleans to be paved with wooden blocks at a cost of $1,500,000. He vetoed a bill handing control of the city's practically nonexistent drainage system to a new private company and amended the state constitution to set debt limits. Many of the bills he did sign benefited Louisianians of both parties. His promises to "bring railroads, open natural watercourses and facilitate ocean commerce" proved popular. He provided funds for the restoration of the levees and the expansion of railroads throughout the state and into Texas. He supported increased funding for public education, granted people who owed back taxes additional time to repay and removed the final restrictions on men who had fought for the Confederacy.

He made attempts to appease Democrats in his political ap-

pointments, putting numerous Confederate veterans in state offices, including making General James Longstreet commander
of the state militia and General Jeff Thompson chief state engi-
neer. When Republicans objected, he tried to mollify them by
appointing Black men to well-paying positions as well.

But despite his efforts, there was no middle ground on race.
The majority of Republicans were Black; the Democrats were
almost all white. Republicans demanded civil rights be extended
and protected, while Democrats were terrified Black politicians
would take control of the state. Every attempt Warmoth made to
satisfy one side angered the other. Once, a Black Democrat was
addressing a Canal Street rally when Black Republicans arrived
to confront him. He was, they said, a traitor. There was a real
chance that violence would erupt.

This was a chance to remind Black voters that the governor was defending their rights, even in an unpleasant situation.
Warmoth rushed to the scene and "fearlessly," according to the
Democratic papers, got up on the platform and told the Republicans, "I come here to ask that freedom of speech, which,
as Republicans we demand for everybody. This Black citizen
of Louisiana has as much right to his own opinions as you or I
have to our own... He must be permitted to speak when and
where he pleases..."

The Republicans dispersed.

But his own powers of persuasion could not work in every
case, and there seemed no possible compromise when the legislature passed a civil rights bill and sent it to him for signature.
The bill made it a crime to deny any citizen equal accommoda-
tions on a railroad, streetcar or steamboat, or in a hotel or theater. The bill had been proposed by Pinckney Benton Stewart
Pinchback, a Black Union officer elected to the State Senate in
1868, who had declared that Black citizens would no longer accept being "refused a drink of common whisky in a common
grog-shop." His bill would essentially integrate the state. To

Democrats it was an anathema, worse even than the amendments Washington was trying to force on them.

Lieutenant Governor Dunn strongly supported Pinchback's bill. He had not forgiven Warmoth for pushing through legislation allowing the governor to run for a second term. He knew that this civil rights bill put Warmoth in a box: veto it and lose the support of the Black community, or sign it and lose support among both Democratic and even some Republican white voters.

Initially Warmoth relied on a pocket veto, letting the bill sit unsigned on his desk until the legislative term ended. But when the legislature passed it a second time he had little choice but to respond. In early February 1869, the same day President Grant told reporters that Black citizens would not be invited to his inaugural ball, Warmoth was forced to explain to Black legislators why he had vetoed their bill, telling them, "We cannot hope by legislation to control questions of personal association; much less can we hope to force on those who differ from our views of what is humane, or courteous or Christianlike..."

It was a marvel of political rhetoric, criticizing Democratic party values while serving their interests. But it did little to soften the blow.

Pinchback and Dunn knew serious damage had been inflicted on Warmoth, but they accepted his veto. "I consider myself just as far above coming into company that does not want me," Pinchback said, "as they are above my coming into an elevation with them..." But, he added, while he was not going to force anyone to associate with other people, he continued to demand equal accommodation.

Besides, he noted, the ratification of the Fifteenth Amendment by the legislature legally gave Black citizens all the rights included in this bill.

Although nothing was said about enforcing those rights.

Where Warmoth was most vulnerable was corruption. Southern politicians and newspapers had successfully created the image of corrupt northerners who raced down south after the war to "steal enough to fill his carpet bag." Warmoth's opponents had begun referring to him as "the Prince of carpetbaggers." In America, politics had always been a profitable profession, and voters had always resented the fact. Almost a half century earlier Andrew Jackson had run for the presidency as the anti-corruption candidate. In 1860 the *New York Times* had described Washington, DC, as a place where "the prize of life is a grab at the contents of UNCLE SAM's till." While many Louisianians begrudgingly accepted corruption as a by-product of government, few politicians had been as open about engaging in it as Warmoth. Although officially his annual salary was $8,000, the general perception was that he had managed to collect as much as $100,000 during his first year in office. People didn't know whether to be impressed at the incredible amount or appalled by it. When a committee asked him about it, he admitted he had made that claim to a friend but refused to confirm it was true.

Bribes were common, and few bills were introduced or passed from which someone did not stand to profit. Bills that failed simply hadn't been paid for properly. For example, Warmoth claimed he had vetoed the bill to pave St. Charles Avenue out of a sense of moral rectitude because he had been offered a $50,000 bribe and a share of the construction company's profits by a man named John Walsh. Walsh disputed Warmoth's account of upright behavior, instead claiming that the real reason the governor had vetoed the bill was that he demanded $75,000. When Warmoth called him a liar, Walsh challenged him to a duel, a challenge the governor turned down.

The bribery system wasn't a secret, and Warmoth wasn't alone. Supposedly, on occasion bribes were paid in cash on the House floor. It was rumored that an office had been opened where people willing to pay for legislation would make their deals.

Testifying in front of a committee of concerned citizens

formed to investigate corruption, Warmoth said, "Do you know a proposition of bribes is a matter of almost everyday occurrence, and if I should come forward and publish the men who offered me the bribe what would be the result? The Democratic press would attack me, and instead of giving me credit, would say I have made enough money, and consequently did not care to make any more."

The people paying those bribes, he added, were "the very best people of this city." By *best* he meant the *wealthiest*. When a grand jury formed after the investigation challenged him to reveal their identity, he refused, pointing out accurately that there were no laws that prohibited offering or accepting bribes in Louisiana.

It wasn't just bribery. Politicians had discovered numerous ways of profiting from their office, many of them not even technically illegal. For example, there was no law prohibiting the governor from awarding the lucrative state printing contract to a publishing company in which he was a partner. And it was widely believed that Warmoth—just like many other legislators—profited from inside information. Knowing what legislation was proposed, they could buy shares in companies at a modest price and then sell them for a profit after passing a bill that benefited them.

Kickbacks were common and expected. People who were given state jobs, often at exorbitant salaries, were expected to pay for them out of those salaries.

By 1870 Warmoth had established himself as an experienced, clever politician. Few people doubted he would be reelected in two years. In fact, one of the state's US senators was leaving office, and there were strong whispers that after winning the gubernatorial election Warmoth, at that point old enough to take office, would resign and allow the legislature to appoint him to that seat. And after serving a Senate term...anything was possible.

Even those people who didn't like him had to admit he had stabilized the state government. When he had taken office, the entire South was still reeling from the aftermath of the war. The old ways were done. People were anxious about their future. It seemed like no one was in charge. Their lives were being dictated by northern politicians in Washington. That no longer was true. Warmoth was in charge.

Due at least partially to his policies, the state's economy was normalizing. The recovery was slow and too many people were still suffering, but at least there was a hint of optimism. One way of reinforcing that feeling was bringing back popular traditions. In New Orleans, nothing was more traditional, nothing made people happier, nothing provided more of a boost to the local economy than Mardi Gras.

Mardi Gras, a public party to welcome Lent, had been a tradition in the region since French explorers Pierre Le Moyne d'Iberville and Sieur de Bienville landed there in 1699. The first costumed parade through the streets of New Orleans had taken place in 1837 and since then had grown into a grand carnival. It was celebrated with masked balls and lavish dinners. Officially halted during the war, the parades had begun again in 1866.

By 1870, Mardi Gras's luster had returned. That year a new, all-white krewe, the Twelfth Night Revelers, introduced the Lord of Misrule, tossing trinkets to the crowd and extending the carnival back to the Christmas holidays by holding a ball in early January. "The population of the city turned out to see the procession," the *Picayune* reported. "All along the route the streets, banquettes and balconies were full of people... The young and the old, the rich and the poor came out to watch the curious array and unite in the festivities it occasioned."

No one enjoyed it more than Warmoth. Not only did it unite the people, it reinforced the feeling that the city had survived the devastation and was regaining its national prominence. Warmoth was a highly visible presence throughout the celebration, smiling broadly, enjoying the social whirl—and reminding people that he had made it all possible.

It helped restore hope. And that benefited Warmoth.

He was at the height of his power, but his political enemies were already working to stop him. First, they had to deny him reelection. In their efforts to accomplish that, they set in motion a chain of tragic events unlike anything ever seen in American history.

3

In George Washington's September 1796 Farewell Address, written with the assistance of Alexander Hamilton and James Madison, the president warned against the rise of political parties. "All combinations and associations...serve to organize faction," he cautioned, "to give it an artificial and extraordinary force, to put in the place of the delegated will of the nation the will of a party, often a small but artful and enterprising minority of the community...[They] are likely, in the course of time and things to become potent engines by which cunning, ambitious and unprincipled men will be enabled to subvert the will of the people and to usurp for themselves the range of government..."

It was an incredibly prescient speech, but while it was greatly admired, no one paid any attention to his warning.

The concept of a political party, a group of people uniting around one or more issues, was relatively recent. Before the Revolutionary War the colonies were divided into Whigs and Tories. The Tories disappeared with Washington's victory while the Whigs evolved into a political party, and a new group, the

Federalists, emerged in opposition. As the nation was being created there were intense debates about what form it would take. How tightly would the states be bound together? How much power would the states cede to the central government? What alliances would it build with the great European powers? Especially England?

Groups coalesced around issues, creating parties to represent them. Among the first great political debates was whether America should support the French Revolution. Liberty! Equality! Fraternity! were slogans that resonated with many Americans. Then, when the new French Republic declared war against Britain, Thomas Jefferson strongly favored providing support. But the Federalists wanted to stay free of foreign entanglements.

Those Federalists who agreed with Jefferson joined with the Whigs to form the Republican party.

Even as Washington published his warning against political parties, the Federalists and Republicans were already promoting very different visions of America. The Federalists, led by Treasury Secretary Alexander Hamilton, favored a stronger central government, including the creation of a Bank of the United States to fund the building of a nation.

Thomas Jefferson and James Madison's Republican party advocated a national government with limited power. They opposed the creation of a large standing army, fearing it would make the national government stronger than the individual states.

Washington had been elected as an Independent, but that was not to be repeated. In 1796 Republican Jefferson faced Federalist John Adams. Adams won by three electoral votes.

While there were two national political parties, there was a far greater abundance of opinion. The parties were neither big enough nor strong enough to encompass all the competing ideas. Those original political parties had the uniformity of mercury: they were continually evolving and splitting into smaller parts.

Splinter groups emerged from both the Federalists and Republicans. As a result, in 1824 four Republicans were on the presidential ballot, each representing a different faction of the party. Four years later another Republican offshoot, this one led by 1812 War–hero Andrew Jackson and Martin Van Buren, formed the Democratic party. Democrats supported free trade with Europe, a strict interpretation of the Constitution and state sovereignty.

This new party then generated offshoots of its own. Disaffected Democrats joined with remnants of the Republican party to create the Whig party, which advocated protectionist economic policies, a national bank and a stronger national government.

For the next few decades, the Democrats and Whigs essentially established a two-party system, both electing presidents, until 1854, when abolitionist Whigs joined with northern Democrats to form the Republican party, which was created to abolish slavery. Meanwhile, Southern Democrats wanted slavery legally recognized nationally.

In 1860 Republican Abraham Lincoln faced Democrat Stephen Douglas. But Douglas refused to campaign strongly enough against abolition, so Southern Democrats nominated their own candidate, former vice president John Breckinridge, ultimately splitting the party vote. Lincoln's victory sparked the Civil War.

By 1870 the two parties were more strongly entrenched than ever before. Everybody knew what they stood for. Republicans were the proud party of Lincoln, the party of northerners, abolitionists and Black citizens. Republicans believed in a strong central government. Democrats, which included most former Confederates, supported states' rights and limited suffrage for freed slaves.

Rather than ending the rancor between North and South, between Republicans and Democrats, the war and advances in technology and transportation may have made the friction even worse. The telegraph had brought the world closer together than ever before. The nation was connected coast-to-coast, allowing news and opinion to be shared more rapidly than had previously been possible. The completion of the transatlantic cable in 1866 put America and Europe in almost instantaneous communication. News of events on the continent, which once took weeks to be reported, now could be transmitted the same day they took place.

The increased ability to spread the news and the expanding diversity of opinion were reflected by the incredible growth in newspapers across the nation. By 1870 there were an estimated 4,500 local newspapers, with literally dozens more opening weekly. Every sizable town had at least one local paper.

The 1869 Golden Spike ceremony at Promontory, Utah, officially united the country by transcontinental railroad, and new routes were being rapidly opened in every state.

As a result of this progress more people had more access to more opinions than ever before possible in history. One consequence of that was that extreme, outlier points of view were able to attract more supporters, so while there were only two major political parties, each of them again split into factions and had to deal with internal battles over their stance on issues.

Nowhere was this truer than in Louisiana. A diverse population gave the state its unique character as well as its varied and competing interests. Although Republicans held a clear majority, due largely to newly enfranchised freedmen, the party was an unmanageable tangle. The coalition Warmoth had managed to knit together to win election had been ripped to shreds. His fight to overturn the one-term rule had done tremendous damage.

Lieutenant Governor Dunn began maneuvering to control the Black vote. In response, Warmoth tried to gain some support from disaffected white Democrats by appointing white men to state positions, which cost him more Republican voters.

Dunn, Senator William Pitt Kellogg, US Marshal Stephen B. Packard and Grant's brother-in-law James Casey, whom the president had appointed to the lucrative position of collector of the port, formed the "Custom House" wing of the party. It was named after the building in which Packard, the leader of the group, had an office where they often met. At that time the imposing Custom House was the largest building in the United States.

The fact that Packard, Kellogg and Casey were federal employees made them immune from any pressure Warmoth could apply. He couldn't attack Dunn either, who had earned a reputation as an unusually honest politician, without alienating a large number of Black voters.

The struggle for power between Warmoth and this Custom House group was not only about their positions on issues, money and power. It was personal. Politicians often have egos that overwhelm other aspects of their personality. It has been said that the phrase *shy politician* is a contradiction in terms. There are altruistic politicians, men and women who dedicate their talents to improving the lives of others. From reports, Lieutenant Governor Oscar Dunn was one of those people. But there also are many who enter politics for opportunity, attention and affection. For at least some of them, affection is a distant third. That might have defined Governor Henry Warmoth.

For people like that, winning a political fight can become more important than the satisfactory resolution of an issue. Defeating people who criticize you, who don't show the proper respect, can provide overwhelming satisfaction.

The battle for control of the party publicly erupted at the Republican convention in 1870. If it hadn't marked the beginning of years of chaos—and many hundred deaths—it probably would have been quickly forgotten. But that's not what happened.

The Custom House faction seized control of the party's central committee. That meant they would make all the decisions about the party operations. Warmoth couldn't afford to let that happen—literally. The ability to control legislation is precisely what lobbyists and campaign contributors pay for. Warmoth was an unusually clever man who believed that the best defense was an attack: he responded by creating his own committee, which then gained control of the convention.

He had become a master of the art of politics. Warmoth successfully forged a coalition between his remaining Republican supporters and Democrats to take away all state patronage from Dunn and the Custom House faction, greatly weakening that group.

The feud escalated. Dunn bitterly accused the governor of "selling out" Black voters and warned his supporters against taking any "bribes" Warmoth might offer them. Warmoth accused Dunn and the Custom House of using graft and corruption to maintain support.

It was a classic political brawl, a battle of words, threats and political deeds. But that changed in the summer of '71 when the guns came out. While Warmoth was in Mississippi, recovering from an operation to repair an injury to his right foot suffered in a boating accident, Packard hastily scheduled a state party convention. The Custom House Republicans intended to take advantage of Warmoth's absence to consolidate control of the party.

In the weeks leading up to that gathering, both sides used every possible method to ensure local political clubs sent their supporters to New Orleans. Hired thugs broke up meetings, threats were made, bribes were paid. The Democratic *Picayune* gleefully reported, "The whole Radical [Republican] party...is absorbed in this combat; public business and interest are utterly ignored and public money ruthlessly squandered to promote the fortunes of the one or the other faction. Every species of fraud, deceit, violence and trickery is employed to the same end."

It was too good an opportunity for a politician as skilled as Warmoth to miss. The day before the convention opened, completely unexpectedly, he hobbled into New Orleans on crutches. The image was political gold: the wounded warrior returning to defend his city. Great crowds of his supporters greeted his triumphant arrival with a rally and cheers.

Packard panicked. The convention had been scheduled to take place in the State House. Somehow, Warmoth had to be kept out. As head of the central committee, Packard announced that the location had been changed. The state convention would now be held…in the Custom House. Only those delegates with official tickets would be permitted to enter.

And he issued the official tickets.

To make sure Warmoth and his followers were kept out, Packard deputized dozens of new US Marshals and called for military support. "To preserve the peace," the *Picayune* noted with irony, the Custom House was surrounded by three infantry regiments, armed with two Gatling guns. They were supplemented by eighty police officers. Inside the massive building the newly sworn deputies guarded every door. There was no possible way Warmoth was going to get inside.

Warmoth didn't care. Getting inside was never part of his plan. Far more important, reporters would be there to cover the confrontation. Warmoth never saw a reporter's notebook he didn't like. Praise him, criticize him, he didn't seem to care, as long as they wrote about him. So he was going to hand them a great story.

His carriage arrived at the Custom House midmorning and was met there by more than a hundred loyal delegates. He managed to talk his way into the public building, but marshals prevented him from entering the courtroom. That was perfect. He called for a chair and struggled dramatically to stand on it—supported by his crutches. After silencing the crowd, he said, "We are called upon today to witness a sight which has never before been seen since the foundation of this government. We stand here today in the presence of three companies of the United States Army, who have been brought here to intimidate the free Republican voters of Louisiana."

The commander of the troops told Warmoth to end the spectacle. The governor stood tall and told the crowd his Republican convention would be held at a building called Turner Hall and urged them to follow him there.

As he began hobbling slowly down the stairs, Custom House supporters crowded into the building. One of them attempted to kick away the governor's crutches. The two sides started shouting threats. Pistols were drawn. A deputy marshal aimed his weapon at Warmoth. Instantly, a Warmoth man grabbed the gun.

The governor's supporters crowded in to protect him. By the time they got him outside, several thousand people had gathered. He stood on his carriage and repeated his speech to deafening cheers. When he concluded his remarks, the incredibly enthusiastic crowd picked up the chant *To Turner Hall!*

As Warmoth's carriage moved slowly up Canal Street his supporters stopped it. The two horses were unhitched, and several men picked up the shafts, pulling it themselves at a fireman's run. They shouted loudly and gleefully as they led the crowd to the hall, "limited only by the supply of oxygen in their lungs."

The opposition papers described the scene quite differently, writing, "Governor Warmoth attempted to force his way into the Customhouse without credentials or a ticket of admission. He was met at the front of the stairs by two officers of the convention, who put him out without ceremony or hesitation. He then attempted to address the crowd, but was driven from this position by an officer who would not permit him to open his mouth. The bolting governor then took to his carriage and incontinently fled, dragging behind him a crowd of officeholders and paid emissaries, who could find nothing else to do but take the place of the horses and drag their master in his carriage through the streets, like so many braying asses."

Four thousand Black and white men, Republicans as well as many Democrats, jammed into Turner Hall. That convention began by the entire crowd singing the rousing song "John Brown," then symbolically hanging an American flag from a window, which was marked by three cheers.

When Warmoth spoke, he railed against the presence of soldiers at the Custom House, telling an anecdote about a conversation between a friend of his and a Spaniard concerning the struggle for power between the Whigs and Democrats. "Said the Spaniard to him, 'Sir, on which side of the contest is the army? In Spain, as the army goes, so goes the election.' It has been our boast, up to this time, that the army of the United States has nothing to do with the election of candidates...." The crowd rose and cheered when he continued, "This is the first instance in our great republic when it has been otherwise." He paused, then added softly, "May it be the last."

He was just warming up. He played to the emotions of the aroused crowd, which punctuated every sentence with an ovation. "We want in this State and in this broad country, liberty of the people!" They cheered. "We want liberty for the white man and liberty for the Black man." They cheered. "We want no Black man to have any right not accorded to every white man, and no white man to have any right not accorded to every Black man.

"That is the great landmark of the Republican party; that is the great beacon light by which we have steered through many years of war, bloodshed and unhappiness." He looked out at the assembly and asked, "Shall we turn back now?"

They roared, "No! No! We will not turn back."

Meanwhile, at the Custom House Warmoth was denounced as a thief, a man who took bribes and "the greatest living practical liar." Serious conversations took place about beginning impeachment hearings. The convention then endorsed President Grant for a second term and said that there was no longer a place for Warmoth—whose followers did not support Grant—in the Republican party. Finally, they declared that the *New Orleans Republican* would no longer be the official organ of the Republican party, threatening its publishing contract.

By the end of the day the rift was complete. The Republican party was in tatters. Warmoth no longer was assured of being the Republican nominee for governor in the next election. There was already speculation the Custom House faction would nominate the popular Lieutenant Governor Dunn, who would be an extremely formidable opponent.

A substantial number of the Black voters who had carried Warmoth to victory in '68 were lost to him. So he began building a new coalition.

Everything had changed. And then everything changed again. On November 22, Oscar Dunn died.

It was a stunning turn. He had died of "congestion of the brain," his doctor announced. Apparently, he had been ailing for several weeks but rather than consulting a physician had been taking Dr. Ayer's Cherry Pectoral, a cold medicine that contained opium or morphine and other common remedies. All the while he had met visitors in his home, among them Warmoth, and while they were distressed by his condition, no one believed it to be fatal.

By the time his family called the doctor it was too late. "Pneumonia had taken such a hold of the system that medical skill could not avail," the doctor explained. He had lapsed into a coma and then, waking to utter the final words, "Come, Jesus. Jesus, come," he had closed his eyes at last.

But even that detailed report did not stop the suspicions from spreading. Dunn's death seemed far too convenient. Rumors began circulating, the lieutenant governor had been poisoned by one of Warmoth's henchmen. There was no evidence of any kind, but the circumstances were enough for people who already believed Warmoth was capable of such an act to be certain he was guilty.

The city of New Orleans turned out for Dunn's funeral. "Perhaps no public event in years has produced a demonstration so large in every respect," the *Picayune* reported. "It was not only

participated in by people of his own race, but by a large part of
the white population, who have felt for the deceased a genuine
respect... The sorrow of his death was widespread and general,
confined to no class or condition of society."

Five hundred police officers marched. Several bands played
mournful tunes. The state militia, the local Masons, religious
societies and political clubs joined the melancholy procession.
And Henry Warmoth?

The governor was properly and publicly somber. He provided
his private carriage to Dunn's family and walked through New
Orleans with the other pallbearers to the cemetery. Undoubtedly his mind was churning. The lieutenant governor was next
in line to the governor. The State Senate would elect Dunn's
successor. If the position wasn't filled, the speaker of the house,
a Custom House leader, would be next in line.

The decision on which candidate to support was made even
more pressing by the fact his political enemies were actively dis-
cussing impeachment. If Warmoth was impeached before Dunn's
replacement was in office, the speaker of the house would become governor.

Some politicians are instinctive: they make decisions based on
what they feel at the moment. That wasn't Warmoth. He was
deliberative. He carefully calibrated every move to determine
the potential pluses and minuses before moving forward. This
time, though, he had to act quickly. It was believed his enemies
would initiate impeachment hearings when the legislature convened as scheduled in early January. But if one of Warmoth's
men was next in line, there would be no political benefit in replacing him. The day after Dunn's funeral he called the State
Senate into special session.

The best choice for him was State Senator P. B. S. Pinchback.
Not necessarily a good choice, as Pinchback was independent
and ambitious and at times had voted against Warmoth, but he
was Warmoth's best choice. He was not in league with the Cus-

tom House. The opposition nominated its own candidate. The first vote was tied. Warmoth went to the floor of the Senate "to stiffen the members," he said, by conversation, good manners, but most important, to make deals. Both sides offered bribes for support. "The chances are that the vote will be tied," read a note received by one senator from Custom House leaders. "I can hold $5,000 ready to place in your hands if you change your vote to our man."

It turned out that would have been a bargain. It supposedly cost Warmoth $15,000 to induce a senator to change his vote. Pinchback was elected.

This was all happening in smoke-filled back rooms and dark, quiet corners. Publicly, the honest men of the state legislature were busy doing the people's business. But no one anticipated the turmoil that erupted when the official legislative session opened in early January.

The new legislative session started with the election of a speaker, expected to be Custom House leader George W. Carter. Carter and Warmoth had once been friends. Carter was the attorney who had successfully defended the governor against the embezzlement charges in Texas, and in response Warmoth had literally created a new parish in southwest Louisiana and arranged for Carter to be elected as its representative. But in the pursuit of power—and in this case, revenue from printing contracts—the two men had fallen out and become bitter enemies.

In response to Pinchback's election in the special session, Custom House Republicans had negotiated a deal with Democrats to reject that vote and impeach the governor. That would make Carter the governor. But getting it done was extremely complicated. It required successfully manipulating a lot of parts—procedural and human—and there was doubt Carter could pull it off.

The impeachment process begins when the House brings charges against an elected official, who is then tried in the Senate. Once that official is impeached they are suspended from office until the Senate reaches a verdict. So Carter devised a different, perfectly legal strategy. He intended to impeach Warmoth, elevating himself to governor, then keep Warmoth in limbo by keeping friendly senators out of the chamber, denying the Senate the quorum it needed to conduct business. He arranged for fourteen senators to take a leisurely cruise on the federally owned revenue ship *Wilderness*; while the lower House debated, these men spent a week living mostly belowdecks and then were set ashore in Bay St. Louis, Mississippi, out of legal reach of Louisiana law.

It was a clever plan, but Carter had made one huge mistake: he had underestimated his opponent. The South was still healing from Union General Sherman's ruthless March to the Sea, in which his army burned everything in its path. It was an apt metaphor for the way in which Warmoth approached politics. He never played defense. He attacked.

He went after Carter, attempting to replace him as speaker. A complex battle of procedural motions basically ended in a stalemate. Marshal Packard raised the ante, bringing in federal troops, supposedly to preserve the peace—and then ordered the arrest of Warmoth, Pinchback, eighteen representatives and four senators for conspiring "by violence to eject the Speaker of the House, and (engaging) in bribery and corruption of divers members of said House of Representatives...and to incite riot."

To incite riot. It was an extraordinary charge. The federal government was arresting the leaders of a state government. Warmoth was enraged, but he and the others surrendered peacefully. They were marched through a boisterous crowd to the federal courtroom inside the Custom House where they were made to wait several hours—supposedly because the proper forms were misplaced—then arraigned and released on bail.

Charges and countercharges were being hurled so rapidly it was impossible for citizens to keep pace. Warmoth called upon his Metropolitan Police to protect his members inside the Mechanics Institute where the legislature was meeting. Carter issued an order prohibiting police in the building. The next day several hundred neatly dressed "civilians" showed up, badges concealed under their coats, and took positions around the building.

Inside, Carter attempted to bring some kind of order to the House. Instead, one of the most bizarre spectacles ever seen in an American legislature unfolded. As soon as he gaveled the session to order, a motion was made by Warmoth's representatives to declare the speaker's chair vacant, and supposedly was approved by acclamation. But as the governor's people moved forward to enforce that act, Carter leaned back in his chair and pointed at the door behind the speaker's platform.

The door instantly swung open and thirty men, "thugs and Ku-Klux," according to the *New Orleans Republican*, "swarmed around their leader and with hands upon their weapons showed a ready desire to shed blood...

"There was an instant of almost breathless anxiety. The Republican members realized that assassination stared them in the face, but determined if they must die to fall at their posts and awaited the attack... Had they exhibited the least panic at this astounding demonstration there is every reason to believe they would have been slaughtered like sheep..."

Later reports claimed the armed men included Deputy US Marshals and "three conspicuous long-haired Texans."

Even as that session ended in chaos, several police officers took positions around Warmoth's office after threats on his life were made. A large crowd of Carter's supporters gathered outside the building, chanting, "Hang Warmoth! Hang Warmoth!"

Warmoth very publicly dismissed the danger. But the next day he again ordered a large number of armed Metropolitan Police officers to surround the Mechanics Institute. When they refused to admit Custom House representatives, Carter convened his legislature in a hall above a Royal Street saloon. Lacking sufficient members to conduct business he sent out the sergeant at arms to arrest and, by force if necessary, drag members to the groghouse. That night, as some members remained in hiding, armed "deputies" broke into private homes and brought them back under guard. Representative Walter Wheyland resisted, and in the melee two sergeants at arms shot and killed him. They were arrested and a coroner's jury indicted Carter as an accessory to the murder.

The following day a once-again fittingly solemn Warmoth, accompanied by aides and reporters, attended Wheyland's funeral. He made a point to pay tribute in time to make the evening's editions.

The January 6 front page of the *Picayune* declared, "The Lord of Misrule appeared upon our streets last night." While the paper was actually reporting about the beginning of Mardi Gras— "Revelers on the Streets!"—it was an apt description of the situation. Two legislatures were convening daily, but neither one could raise a quorum. Several members moved back and forth as it seemed like one side might be gaining an advantage. Democrats stayed quietly on the sidelines, resisting offers—Warmoth supposedly promised the speakership to a Democrat if that party supported him—knowing that a broken, dispirited Republican party was the best possible outcome for them. As the Democratic paper *Bee* reported, "It is evident that we no longer have any government—and are in a state of complete anarchy."

When the Custom House finally accepted the reality that its legislature would never have a quorum, it made several forcible attempts to take control of the State House. On January 13, Carter issued a proclamation calling on citizens to take arms to help him overthrow the government. Warmoth appealed to Grant for federal troops, but the president refused to declare martial law or commit troops.

The next morning an estimated six thousand Custom House supporters filled the streets outside the Mechanics Institute. Several speeches were made—and once again, after each disparaging remark about Warmoth, the crowd chanted, "Hang him! Hang him!"

A final attempt to take over the legislature happened on the twenty-second. Two days before, Carter distributed handbills urging "TO ARMS! TO ARMS! TO ARMS!" The time and place to gather was announced, and people were urged to "let those who have dared to trample on your rights as freemen and citizens tremble until the marrow of their bones shakes. Let the cry be: DOWN WITH WARMOTH AND HIS THIEVING CREW... LIBERTY OR DEATH."

Carter also issued a proclamation informing supporters that they would be sworn in as assistant sergeants at arms, giving them legal protection in "protecting their way."

That night, perhaps in preparation, intruders broke into a militia armory and stole numerous rifles.

The city prepared for the showdown. Newspapers urged readers to stay away from the area. Shopkeepers locked their doors and lowered their shutters. Bankers and financial dealers shipped money boxes to Mobile, fearing an out-of-control mob would rampage through the city.

The showdown was scheduled for eleven o'clock The next morning four thousand men, carrying rifles, muskets, shotguns, revolvers and clubs, met by the ten-year-old statue of Henry Clay at the intersection of Canal and Royal Streets. More than two thousand members of the state militia and the Metropolitan Police department, armed with rifles and a battery of artillery, were waiting for them at the State House. A bloodbath seemed inevitable.

Carter addressed his "army," exhorting them to get rid of "that creature who by fraud occupies the Chair of State." He was a fine speaker and built the crowd to an emotional pitch. And while he warned this heavily armed mob against resorting to violence to oust Warmoth, they understood his real meaning had little to do with peace.

Incredibly, as he reached the crescendo of his remarks, his arms waving, his voice rising to a peak, he was handed a note from General William Emory, commander of the US Army in Louisiana, informing him that he had just received a telegram from the secretary of war in Washington: "The President directs you to hold your troops in readiness to suppress a conflict of armed bodies of men, should such occur, and to guard public property from pillage or destruction."

Carter knew these supporters could not stand against regular army troops. Moving against this warning would invite loss of life. He paused, waited, then read the message out loud. It was greeted with unhappy murmurs. He quickly changed course and began calming the crowd. "It's no use, gentlemen, we can't fight against the United States government... As it stands now, you are not required to perform any further duty...you must deport yourselves every way as good citizens should...

"I command you now, that you do hereafter abstain from all violence; that you do nothing to bring on a collision with minions of usurped authority. Gentleman, I have done. For the present the question is settled. General Emory has whipped this fight."

The crowd lingered for a time, unsure how to respond, then gradually drifted into the afternoon.

Perhaps desperate to surrender gracefully and preserve his honor, Carter ended up dueling with Metropolitan Police Superintendent General A. S. Badger. Each fired a single shot wide and announced they were satisfied.

The battle wasn't quite done. President Grant had decided to support his brother-in-law James Casey, one of Warmoth's political enemies, whom he had appointed to the lucrative position of running the ports. Republicans in Washington sent a House committee to Louisiana to try to settle the situation. The five-man committee interviewed numerous witnesses, who were permitted to testify to rumors, innuendo and newspaper stories. One witness, asked if he was testifying to facts, responded,

"I am reciting facts which are generally believed... Of course, I cannot have any personal knowledge of many of the charges set forth..."

Looking back years later, Warmoth complained, "Every personal and political enemy of mine was given a chance at me... If one percent of the charges had been true I should still be in the State Penitentiary."

The governor testified for several hours. At its conclusion one Republican member summed up the general feeling about Warmoth: "We cannot determine whether you are an angel from Heaven, or a Devil from Hell."

The final report castigated Warmoth, although by the time it was issued the Custom House effort to take control had been defeated. But great damage had been done.

For Warmoth, there was no returning to the Republican party. But he was still very much an ambitious man, still held power as governor, and for someone as clever as he was there were other political paths he might forge. And so he set out in a different direction.

The prelude was over.

4

More than two millennia ago Plato praised democracy in the *Republic*, calling it "a charming form of government, full of variety and disorder, and dispensing a sort of equality to equals and unequals alike." But then he added the warning, "Democracy passes into despotism."

For thousands of years civilizations had been struggling to find a sustainable political system which provided the most benefit for the most people, at least most of the time. The results have been, at best, mixed.

By the beginning of the 1870s, historic monarchies and dictatorships were evolving into various forms of popular rule as governments, under pressure from within, searched for a structure that offered security and opportunity to its citizens. Borders and rulers were in flux. In England, while the benevolent Queen Victoria sat upon the throne, industrial working men had gotten the right to vote for an increasingly powerful Parliament. France's Napoleon III, who had been elected that nation's first president but declared himself emperor after being constitutionally barred from reelection, had been deposed in 1870. With Prussia's victory in the Franco-Prussian War of 1871, hundreds of smaller German states were consolidated into a single nation with an elected representative government, and the German empire was created. After winning its independence in 1821, Mexico had tried more than fifty different governments and was trying desperately to sustain its fragile elected government. China still was ruled by an emperor, the Son of Heaven, who maintained total control over the state.

In the United States the search for an acceptable balance of powers between the individual states and the federal government continued, even after the Civil War had failed to finally settle the issue. The unique political system devised by the Founding Fathers had been tested numerous times, often in unanticipated ways, but it had proved surprisingly resilient. Somehow, it had endured. At least so far.

But in Louisiana all the flaws of that system were about to be exposed.

The battle between Warmoth and the Custom House faction had destroyed the two-party system in the state. To convince reluctant legislators to return to work, the governor agreed to allow them to repeal his controversial election and registration laws. When one of his supporters questioned that decision, Warmoth replied confidently, "Never mind, Charley, we'll pass new ones. And worse."

The legislature repealed the bills, and while publicly the governor supported the action, behind the scenes he took all the necessary steps to keep a strong version of those laws in place. In some ways he even managed to strengthen them. His defense was simple: the reforms had worked. Republicans had a huge majority of voters, but in the election before those laws were passed, Democrats carried the state by 88,000 votes. In response to that, other elected officials—not him, of course—had written and passed bills to ensure a fair vote. He had signed it, and Republicans had won the 1870 election by 20,000 votes.

Like *Humpty Dumpty*, the old English nursery rhyme, which only recently had enjoyed a successful run on New York's Broadway as a musical pantomime, the Louisiana Republican party was shattered and could not be put back together. It had been split into three major factions: Packard's Custom House, Warmoth's remaining backers under the banner of Liberal Republicans and Black voters who had rallied behind Lieutenant Governor Pinchback. With presidential and gubernatorial elections scheduled for November, potential candidates began maneuvering for support. There were deals to be made, alliances to be formed, for anyone who hoped to grab a slice of power.

After refusing to sign the civil rights bill, Warmoth had lost most of his power in the Black community. His problem, wrote the *Picayune*, was that by this "systematic violation of good faith…he had lost his hold on them and now must make terms with the whites whom he had so long and so systematically oppressed."

In the grand political tradition, Warmoth's political rivals now jumped at the chance to attack the wounded leader. Republican newspapers called him "a traitor to the state." Democrats railed he had "stabbed public virtue to the heart and trampled it under his feet." His enemies referred to him as a vulture, a highwayman, a political leper, a liar, a thief and a pest.

Although he continued to command support from both Black and white voters, he was a man without a party. But for the next few months he was still governor, so he controlled a tremendous amount of power and patronage. That made him an enticing figure to dealmakers. Several Democrats floated the idea of joining with him to defeat the Custom House, but the state Democratic Committee blasted that proposal, calling Warmoth unworthy of respect.

The situation grew increasingly more confused. To take advantage of the void, the Reform party was formed in February to "overthrow the present putrid Government of our state." The new party hoped to bring together those people disgusted with both parties and willing to consider any alternative.

Pinchback, fearing Democrats would take advantage of the rupture, embraced the devil he knew. At a convention of his remaining Republican supporters, he made a final effort to reconcile the party, calling for unity and nominating...Henry Warmoth for governor.

The most celebrated author of the time, Charles Dickens, had written in his novel *Pickwick Papers*, "adversity brings a man acquainted with strange bedfellows." The possibility of Pinchback supporting Warmoth might have seemed impossible. But he did it—perhaps confident that Warmoth's reelection also would secure his own position as lieutenant governor.

There was no way the Republican party led by President Grant was ever going to give Warmoth the nomination. Knowing that, the governor rejected the party before it could reject him. He declined, explaining that accepting the nomination would require him to make peace with "those whom I consider the most dangerous enemies of the country and the state, with the arrogant dictatorial and corrupt administration of General Grant."

Instead, he continued, "I have resolved to devote all my energies to the service of the Liberal Republican party..." to save the country "from Grantism with its attendant tyranny and corruption."

Warmoth had grown to despise the president, who he believed had publicly "outraged and humiliated me" by siding with Casey. One reason for that, it was suggested darkly, was that as director of one of the nation's busiest ports, Casey could funnel more money to Grant than Warmoth.

The Liberal Republican party had been created in Missouri with the objective of defeating Grant. It had a very small, mostly

German following in Louisiana, but for Warmoth it had the same appeal an empty shell has for a hermit crab. It had a functioning apparatus, a national media presence and, in Louisiana, no leadership. He certainly knew the party was too small by itself to serve his purpose, but it provided a base he could use to broker a deal with a more potent party. It was estimated by his enemies that he was still capable of delivering as many as 20,000 votes, a huge number in the state.

The Liberal Republicans' national convention was held in Cincinnati in early May to select its nominee for the presidency. Basically, that would be anybody but Grant. The convention lacked the numbers or the excitement of the traditional party gatherings, but it was still taken seriously and covered by the national media. Among the observers were a large number of prominent Democrats, including several members of Congress. The Democrats had no obvious nominee, and they were not strong enough to beat Grant on their own. But if they could agree on a candidate with the Liberals they just might have a chance. So while they had no formal role in the selection of a candidate, they had a lot of influence.

Warmoth controlled the convention with the hundred and twenty-five delegates he had brought with him, by far the largest delegation. At the beginning of the convention Charles Francis Adams Sr., the son and grandson of former presidents, was favored for the nomination. But after six ballots the Liberal Republicans nominated *New York Tribune* publisher Horace Greeley to oppose Grant. Horace Greeley was considered odd, eccentric, erratic, brusque, opinionated and brilliant. He was known, and enjoyed, for being blunt and outspoken: "I never said all Democrats are saloonkeepers," he once wrote—*saloonkeepers* meaning *uneducated people*—"what I said was all saloonkeepers were Democrats." He practically invented the modern newspaper, believed in spiritualism and strongly advocated westward expansion, continually urging young Americans to "Go west, young man, and grow up with the country."

Greeley had used his newspaper to promote progressive policies. He had been among the founders of the modern Republican party and had served a term in Congress. After Lincoln refused to commit to ending slavery early in the Civil War, Greeley opposed his second nomination. He didn't like Andrew Johnson or Grant too much either, believing their Reconstruction policies were too harsh on the South—and he thought Grant was a crook. He had even chipped in to post bail after Confederate President Jefferson Davis had been arrested.

But he was among the most widely known and respected Americans—and his newspaper had the largest circulation in the county—and that convinced the Liberal Republicans to back him. Two months later Democrats met in Baltimore. The convention lasted six hours, long enough to endorse Greeley and the Liberal Republican platform. For the first time in American history a major party would not run its own candidate, instead choosing to back another party's nominee. The hope was that the combination of Liberal Republicans and Democrats could defeat Grant. It was unlikely, but not impossible.

Adding to the political mayhem, at the same time Greeley was being nominated in Cincinnati, the fledgling Equal Rights party meeting in New York nominated suffrage leader Victoria Woodhull for president and famed author and former slave Frederick Douglass for vice president. That convention also called for a new constitution, deciding the existing document was "behind the present age of civilization."

The Louisiana Liberal Republicans convened in August to nominate its slate for state offices. State politics were in such disarray it made the national elections look normal. Like Greeley, Warmoth couldn't win the election without the support of a second, larger party. During the previous few months, he had tried to make an alliance with one of the other state parties but had

failed. He had offered deals, he had threatened, cajoled, pulled
out all the tricks in his bag—it was rumored he had approached
both President Grant and the so-called Custom House Republican party and offered to compromise—but he was rebuffed.
Half the Republicans and most of the Democrats hated him. He
finally accepted the reality that he would not be renominated
by a major party.

The possibility that this might be the beginning of the end of
his political career probably never occurred to him. His mind
didn't work that way. Warmoth was a survivor, always had been,
a man who had been able to turn each defeat in his life into a
greater victory. During the war he'd been cashiered, supposedly
for leaving his post, although in fact he had been injured and
left to recuperate. Instead of accepting that decision, he'd cajoled his way right into President Lincoln's office in the White
House, got his commission back and later received a political
appointment directly from the president.

He still held a politically strong hand. He would be in office, with all the power that came with it, through the end of
the year. He had thousands of loyal supporters who would follow his direction, whichever way he pointed. He wasn't going
to be the next governor.

But senator?

According to the Constitution, each state legislature elected
two senators. If Warmoth used his power smartly, if he helped
put people to office, if a Senate seat became open...

As the Liberal Republican convention opened, Chairman
W. W. Pugh declared, "A great revolution is at hand. The sci-
entist who prophesied the coming of a great tidal wave which
was to engulf and destroy our planet was mistaken as to the
element which was to work such great changes among us.
This element is the revolution in the opinions and politics of
the masses of our countrymen, a tidal wave which affects the
minds of men..."

D. B. PENN.

THE HISTORIC NEW ORLEANS COLLECTION, 1974.25.9.312

Throughout the convention party leaders attempted to create a fusion ticket, with a committee meeting regularly with Democrats and Reformers. When that failed, the party pretty much abandoned any effort to attract Black support by nominating former Confederate General Davidson Bradfute Penn for governor. Penn, who came from a wealthy, distinguished Louisiana family, had fought at Chancellorsville and Gettysburg, then been captured and imprisoned for more than a year. After being released at the end of the war he came home and made a fortune in the sugar industry.

Like many rich businessmen, Penn had maintained strong political relationships. Among them Governor Warmoth.

Rather than suffering a public defeat Warmoth told the convention what it already knew, he would not be any party's candidate for governor. He made an odd and unusually moving speech: reflective, poignant, defensive and, for a politician, remarkably honest. "All I ask of the Democrats," he told a rapt, absolutely silent audience, "is that they will do me simple justice and charge me of that of which I am guilty. I am responsible for enough, God knows. I do not start out with the proposition that I am one of the saints, nor do I admit that they are to be named in that category either. Since our starting out we have all done wrong and made many mistakes. Let us take our lessons to heart and do so no more."

He withdrew his name from consideration, promising, "I had no ambitions or aspirations which shall be in the way of this movement... I now declare to you that you have no honors to confer upon me which I could give my consent to receive..."

The eloquence of his closing remarks reminded delegates why he had achieved so much at such a young age. He asked the party to nominate a ticket "as will form such a band of union in its constitution, between the white men and the [B]lack men as to be like the rainbow set in the heavens, a covenant that the [B]lack people shall never be deprived of their civil and political rights, that will show that you look not at the color of the man, but that in the future you will look only to his character and capabilities..."

D. B. Penn was the convention's nominee, but Warmoth was its hero. The love, the acclaim the convention bestowed on him was astonishing. These were his people, Warmothites, people who had followed him out of the Custom House Republican party. They supported him unconditionally, oblivious to his faults; they adored him, and this was their opportunity to show it.

After Penn was officially nominated, according to the *Republican*, "the Governor appeared advancing through the parquette. He had scarcely ascended the first step to reach the stage when he was welcomed by a gale of cheers which endured for several minutes and was echoed and re-echoed from the arches that touched the floor to the glister of lights in the dome. Amid this whirlwind of excitement, while men wildly waved their hats and handkerchiefs, tossed aloft their canes and threw their arms wildly about, Governor Warmoth said, 'Let me not interrupt the proceedings, you have made the best nomination.' The storm of cheering rose again…"

Minutes later the doors of the hall opened, and delegates burst out to parade through the streets. To the distress of his opponents, Warmoth was not going away quietly; in fact, he had no intention of going away at all. He was still a young man with the potential for an amazing career. There were more deals to be made, more elections to win.

First, he was going to play a crucial role in the coming elections. The extraordinary response of the convention was proof, decided the *New Orleans Times*, "that the public are anxious to have the assistance of Governor Warmoth in the great contest… and will prove grateful for such services." And undoubtedly, he was equally pleased to provide them.

His political transformation had been astonishing. He had won election four years earlier as a champion of racial justice. "He had received from [a Black majority] a degree of power never dreamed of by any chief executive…but by a systematic violation of good faith with these people he had lost his hold upon them and now must make terms with the [voters] he had so long and so systematically oppressed."

JOHN F. M'ENERY.

By the end of summer five parties had nominated candidates. The Democrats had nominated thirty-nine-year-old
Colonel John McEnery, a popular Confederate war hero and
self-educated lawyer who eventually would become a judge.
Custom House Republicans supported Senator William Pitt
Kellogg, a Union army colonel whom Lincoln had appointed
a justice and then collector of customs in New Orleans before
winning election to the Senate in 1868. Lieutenant Governor
Pinckney Benton Stewart Pinchback was the candidate of the
so-called Pinchback wing of the Republican party. D. B. Penn
led the Liberal Republican ticket, and the Reform party named
George Williamson.

The horse trading began almost immediately as the various
parties looked to partner for power. Bargains were struck. Deals
were made. Warmoth didn't have sufficient support to win an
election, but combined with another party's voters, he could
swing an election. Under his direction the Liberal Republicans
allied with the Democrats to form a fusion ticket supporting
McEnery for governor and Penn for lieutenant governor. It was
widely believed that the price McEnery paid for the support was
an agreement to make Warmoth a senator. Warmoth did his best
to calm those from both parties who felt betrayed, telling them
that although he "hated" Democrats, "prejudices and bicker-
ings must be laid aside... If I can forget my own, you ought to
lay aside yours." Although some Democrats refused to support
any alliance in which Warmoth was involved, the mainstream
party swallowed its pride for a chance of victory.

Detractors began referring to supporters of this union as "last
ditchers," a nickname that originally referred to Confederates
who continued fighting when hope was gone, standing and
dying in the "last ditch."

Meanwhile, Pinchback made a deal with the Custom House,
agreeing to back Kellogg for governor in return for a nomination to Congress. Williamson withdrew, saying that the only

real chance for reform of Louisiana politics lay with the election of "the honest and intelligent" Kellogg.

The nominations were set: for president, Republican U. S. Grant faced quasi-Democrat/Liberal Republican Horace Greeley. For governor of Louisiana, Democrat John McEnery ran against Republican William P. Kellogg.

It is a cliché to say that the future is always on the ballot, but in this case it was the present that was at stake. The fighting of the War Between the States was done; the chaos it left in its immediate aftermath was done. Reconstruction had been imposed and mostly failed. The Thirteenth, Fourteenth and Fifteenth Amendments had been ratified. Although the bitterness and hatred had not faded—the wounds were too deep and too raw for any real forgiveness on either side—voters were looking to their future rather than still fighting in the past.

The elections of 1868 had taken place in the ruins of the war. The makeshift political system throughout the South was fragile and dominated by newly arrived carpetbaggers. In many places Confederates had not been allowed to vote. The leader of the Union army had been rewarded with the presidency.

In Louisiana, the '68 campaign had been marked by violence and fraud. There had been acceptable excuses: there were tens of thousands of first-time voters, there were problems setting up a viable voting structure—including questions about everything from registration eligibility to casting ballots—and there had been disputes about how to count the votes, but the failures in every aspect of the system had left many people doubtful about the results.

There had been numerous changes made in each aspect of process following that election. The Fourteenth and Fifteenth Constitutional Amendments, which granted freedmen citizenship and the right to vote, were now law. Warmoth's registration bills supposedly had addressed some of the confusion created by those Amendments. Confederate veterans were required to take a loyalty oath before their voting rights were restored.

The contrast in party platforms was clear. As any incumbent, Grant was running on his record. Among his accomplishments, he had instituted Reconstruction policies to bring the country together, had successfully overseen three Amendments added to the Constitution and founded a federal Department of Justice to protect the rights of all Americans. Southerners believed Grant's Reconstruction policies had crippled their economic recovery and his Department of Justice was formed to encroach on states' rights. Greeley strongly opposed Grant's policies. He did not equivocate, saying, "All the political rights and franchises lost through our late bloody convulsion...must be promptly restored and re-established."

By extension, the question of the right of states to make their own laws versus the obligation of the federal government to protect and defend all American citizens—which had remained unresolved since the ink dried on the Constitution—was also on the ballot. All Southerners had to do was look around to see the bluecoats still stationed in the region. Once again, Greeley did not hold back: "Subject to our solemn constitutional obligations to maintain the equal rights of all citizens our policy should aim at local self-government and not at centralization."

Some newspapers even wondered why an electoral college system was used to vote for president rather than allowing people to vote directly, suggesting it heavily favored larger northern states. Southern-born presidents Andrew Jackson and Andrew Johnson had recommended dissolving the electoral college and, as the *Times-Picayune* reminded readers, only a year earlier Massachusetts senator Charles Sumner had introduced "a joint resolution proposing to establish by an amendment of the constitution a new mode of choosing the president." The direct election of the president by popular vote would put the election in the hands of the people rather than "caucuses of politicians."

The differences between Kellogg and McEnery were just as obvious. Senator Kellogg had not pursued the nomination and only reluctantly accepted it, but his sympathies were well-known. He had been among the Republican electors who voted Lincoln into the White House and then had been his last official appointment before the president's assassination. That marked him as one of the early carpetbaggers. Conversely, no white Southerner questioned Virginia-born McEnery's loyalty. As a member of the House, he had been a strong supporter of President Johnson, voting against the Fourteenth Amendment and for various laws legalizing forms of racial discrimination.

Traditionally, presidential candidates did not actively campaign on the theory that "the office picks the man." Instead, they were represented by surrogates, well-known men who appeared at rallies to urge voters to support their candidate. Greeley, though, generally considered among the country's most gifted public speakers, took to the stump. His friends and supporters worried about his habit of saying out loud sometimes controversial thoughts that seemingly just popped into his mind, while Republicans welcomed him, hopeful he would commit some irreparable indiscretion.

Gubernatorial candidates often campaigned personally, although they also used surrogates.

As the fall campaign season began, New Orleanians were focused on more immediate problems, including a serious shortage of ice. For reasons no one seemed to understand, an unusually large number of ice ships had been delayed. Smaller buyers had seen their monthly supplies cut in half. Saloons especially were suffering, and some desperate saloonkeepers were trying to bring ice supplies from Mobile.

Crime also remained a primary concern. "One murder a day and one conviction a year," the *Republican* wrote, complaining about authorities being too soft on criminals. "The reason for this unhappy state of affairs is that our juries are, under the present laws and practice, organized to acquit, not convict. If we were to infuse into our criminal practice a slight dash of the principles that rule in 'Judge Lynch's' court we should soon see a marked improvement... For efficiency lynch law is superior to statute law, but the latter can very easily be made more perfect."

As far as amusements were concerned, both the Academy of Music and the Varieties offered a full slate of shows and concerts. It also was reported that P. T. Barnum's show, with its "myriad wonders and curiosities" thus far had been unable to secure the four or five acres needed to "receive the canvas" anywhere in the city, but Barnum remained hopeful that he would find a suitable location to pitch his tents.

Politics had not yet taken hold of the public's full attention. In New Orleans, a three-year-old child was run down and seriously injured by a wagon, and unfortunately "the driver succeeded in making his escape." And Goodspeed's Empire Book House was advertising for agents to sell Mark Twain's new book, telling them, "Don't work on books no one wants, but take one people will stop you in the streets to subscribe for..."

As usual, there was trouble on the Mexican border. In Brownsville, Texas, two prominent frontier merchants had been attacked by bandits. One of the Texans had been shot to death. In response, "A strong feeling was manifested to organize a force" and pursue the killers into Mexico.

It wasn't until early October that the public began focusing on the campaigns. They were a big draw. Political rallies were major social events. Thousands of people would show up outdoors or crowd into theaters for the opportunity to see these celebrities in person. Bands played lively tunes, and everyone would join together loudly singing the popular songs, especially "Dixie." There was some drinking, of course, and rallies often were punctuated with firecrackers and rockets. As the *Picayune* described a Greeley rally, "A large platform was erected in the center of Lafayette Square, which was profusely illuminated.

Greeley's name was conspicuous on a large transparency which arched the speaker's rostrum. At each corner of the square large bonfires were lighted...

"At 8 o'clock the opening of the meeting was announced by the firing of two hundred guns by the artillery regiment." About a dozen prominent local men were seated on the platform. "A fair computation of the people assembled...would place the number at about five thousand and hundreds more visited during the evening."

At the conclusion of the rally, it was announced, the band would march to Liberal Republican headquarters to serenade Governor Warmoth. All were welcome to join the procession.

And so it went in towns and cities throughout Louisiana and the rest of America. Warmoth and his close friend George Sheridan, whom he had appointed brigadier general of the state militia, acted as surrogates for both Greeley and McEnery. In Minden, Louisiana, they were escorted into the town by six hundred men on horseback, the procession led by a band in "a chariot led by six horses."

At some of these rallies women were welcome, even seated up front as candidates implored them to make sure their men voted!

As much as people turned out to see Warmoth, Sheridan was equally popular. He was considered to be among the country's most gifted public speakers, known for his down-home common sense, his humor and his political rhetoric. At an outdoor rally in support of Colonel McEnery held in Lafayette Square, Sheridan pointed out how much had changed in the last two years. "When I started out on this campaign," he said, as spectators crowded close to the platform to hear him, "I said to Governor Warmoth, 'How do you feel about canvassing the State?' Said he, 'I think the people will be better pleased to see us than they were in seventy.' And everything drifted along pleasantly until one night we got lost in the piney woods, near Natchitoches, and it became very dark.

"I said, 'Governor Warmoth, have you reflected that we are off the great line of travel, that the people of Louisiana do not often get the newspapers and have probably not heard of your change of politics?' Said he to our driver, 'Drive a little faster, Randolph.' After a little while we ran across two regular specimens of backwoodsmen with shotguns on their shoulders. I mildly suggested to Governor Warmoth, Ku-Klux come at last. Said he, 'Sheridan, as you are the praying man of this concern, you had better begin to pray.'

"I suggested to him that as his legs were the longest, he had better do the praying and let me get a start!"

Throughout the fall the rival campaigns proceeded with the expected hoopla. The usual promises were made—the public's money would not be wasted, taxes would not be raised, the working man would be represented—platforms were defended and lots of mud was slung. Grant accused Greeley of duplicity, trying to win favor with Southerners by telling an audience in Vicksburg, Mississippi, that one day Confederate soldiers who fought with General Robert E. Lee "would occupy as proud a position in the hearts of Americans as the soldiers who fought with Grant and Sherman."

Greeley angrily denied that, responding that he actually had said he "trusted the day would come when the soldierly qualities and military genius of Lee and Jackson would be regarded as part of the heritage of the American people…"

Grant was regularly vilified: he was called just about every reprehensible name imaginable. Democratic newspapers wrote, "He has degraded that office in the estimation of the people and the eyes of the world…has used his influence to secure his own promotion, and reward his own relatives and friends…"

Greeley was attacked so intensely, he joked, that he was forced to wonder if he was running for the presidency or the penitentiary.

The state campaigns were equally nasty. Warmoth accused

Republicans of illegally "bringing [people] from other States and registering them in New Orleans and the parishes by the river."

Kellogg campaigned relentlessly, visiting more cities and towns than any candidate before him, speaking at a rally every day from late September through election day. He spoke for as long as three hours at each stop, his voice growing hoarse, telling tens of thousands of supporters that Democrats were fraudulently registering ineligible voters and had "declared publicly if he was beaten he would send all the leading Liberals in the State to the Penitentiary."

Colonel McEnery knew that to win he had to reduce Kellogg's support in the Black community, so he took every opportunity to remind Republicans that, among other transgressions, "when Mr. Kellogg was in the Senate of the United States he had not the moral courage to vote yea or nay upon the civil rights bill, which was defeated in consequences." Rumors spread that Kellogg hated Louisiana and was a racist who always wore a glove when shaking hands with a Black man.

As the election approached, the candidates tried to scare their supporters to the polls by warning what would happen if the opposition was elected. Democrats emphasized the fact that Kellogg was a carpetbagger who had never really lived in the state and claimed that after being elected he would resign and return to the Senate, making Black Lieutenant Governor C. C. Antoine the governor.

Republicans countered by warning that McEnery secretly supported the white supremacist groups and if elected would allow organizations like the Ku Klux free rein to spread terror.

Away from the torchlights and the colorful rockets, though, a different, darker campaign was being waged. Guns came out. Newspapers played a key role, further inflaming an already-tense situation. Local papers ran sensational stories about towns being burned, newspaper offices being blown up and local law enforcement officers being shot. In an early local election in Macon,

Georgia, Black men were driven away from the polls with "a shower of brickbats and bullets." In Monroe, Louisiana, it was reported a State Senate candidate was surrounded "by a mob of ruffians" who threatened, "If the Republicans are defeated, not only carpetbaggers but every man who has affiliated with the Republican party will have to leave North Louisiana or die."

The *New York Herald* summed up the entire campaign with disgust. "It has been a season of civil war among the politicians, and all the passions engendered by internal strife has been called into play to embitter and intensify the contest...

"The party organs have been reckless in their attacks and careless of the result, their apparent object being to fan the flame of discord and to increase violence and factional hate."

But the election really came down to one person. A Congressional investigation convened in Louisiana after the events to try to understand how the disaster unfolded. The conclusion they reached was unambiguous: "The organization of the election throughout the whole State originated with and was controlled by Warmoth. It is not denied that Warmoth meant fraud, and that he had the power to affect it."

5

"TO ABSENTEES," the *Times-Picayune* pleaded as the election approached, "Return to your homes promptly and prepare to vote. The most important duty before you is that of voting and inducing your fellow-citizens to vote. Business can be sacrificed to this great purpose, and the man who would weigh pleasure in the same scale with voting is guilty... Voters, come back!"

Once again, ordinary Americans were going to the polls to freely choose their representatives. Creating a government of the people, by the people and for the people, just as the Founding Fathers had envisioned. Free elections were the hallmark of democracy, the reason subjugated people around the world looked to America for hope.

It was a noble endeavor.

Except, in Louisiana in 1872, it was a myth. The entire system—from registration through counting the votes—had been corrupted. At every step in the process there existed some type of intimidation, cheating or fraud intended to change the outcome.

There had always been a modicum of dishonesty in the electoral process. It was as persistent and bothersome as mosquitoes, and it had proved equally impossible to get rid of. And like a mosquito bite, in most cases it was little more than an irritant, an itch that needed to be scratched. Except in places like Louisiana, where mosquitoes had unleashed a yellow fever epidemic that had led to widespread and controversial quarantines—although at the time the disease was believed to be transmitted by immigrants.

The *New York Times* railed that "the violation of the integrity of the ballot-box constitute offenses against the public welfare more criminal than Congressmen...who accepted bribes." But most instances of cheating in elections were overlooked, and as long as they didn't dramatically impact the outcome it was accepted as an unresolved evil.

Politicians long ago had become skilled at legally rigging state elections by creating voting districts favorable to their party. The goal of drawing election districts was to stuff as many of the opposition's supporters into as few districts as possible. The practice was as old as the Republic; when the first Congressional maps were drawn in 1788, Anti-Federalists in Virginia put Federalist James Madison in the same Anti-Federalist area as their candidate, James Monroe.

The original district boundary lines were reasonably straight, but the practice was taken to a new level in 1812 when Massachusetts governor Elbridge Gerry drew a district that bent and curved like a salamander to include as many of his Democratic-Republican voters as possible. Gerrymandering, as the process became called, was a legal method of stuffing ballot boxes. The majority party in every state created its own maps; as a result, by 1872 in New York it took 90,000 Republican votes to elect a representative while Democrats required 160,000. In Indiana three Republican votes had as much effect as two Democratic votes. While the ratios differed from state to state it was, concluded the *Times*, "nothing less than a conspiracy to cheat citizens out of their constitutional rights."

But gerrymandering was entirely legal. Following the war Louisiana's Republican legislature had redrawn its districts to give their candidates the greatest possible advantage. That was just the beginning. That gerrymander only mattered if all votes were legitimately cast and fairly counted. With tens of thousands of newly enfranchised Republican voters, Democrats couldn't afford to let that happen. Republicans were well aware of that and took their own steps to guarantee the outcome. Neither side seemed overly concerned about the law.

The result could have served as a guide to all the methods that might be used to steal an election.

Historically, many different methods of cheating had been employed. There was no secret ballot, so observers could monitor votes. Ballot stuffing and bribery were common, but so were things like "cooping," in which street gangs literally kidnapped men and locked them up, got them drunk and then forced them to vote in disguise numerous times. Many people believed author Edgar Allan Poe had been a cooping victim, having been found drunk, delirious and disheveled in a Baltimore tavern on election day without offering any explanation for how he got in that condition.

One of the most unusual methods of cheating took place in New Jersey, which for a time allowed some women to vote. Supposedly men were voting legally, then donning petticoats and wigs and voting a second time. To prevent that from continuing, the vote was taken away from women.

In Louisiana, the corruption began with the registration process. The concept of registering voters, making sure they were eligible to vote, was a relatively recent innovation. In England, an unsuccessful effort was made to introduce voter registration in 1788, and it wasn't until 1832 that Parliament finally passed a bill requiring voters prove their eligibility to be included on an approved list.

In the early 1800s several American states became concerned

that too many transient foreigners were voting in local elections. To ensure that only male citizens voted, many northern states, beginning with Massachusetts in 1800, introduced registration. It was not especially welcomed: Democrats complained the system prevented legal immigrants and others from voting. Several decades passed before other northern states introduced similar laws.

The Constitution did not include any mention of who might be eligible to vote. Each state established its own unique requirements. It was only after the Civil War that the federal government intervened to ensure all American men were permitted to vote.

Louisiana, like most of the other Southern states, had passed laws after the Civil War allowing all male voters over twenty-one years old to register and vote. Democratic politicians grumbled about it—until they discovered how easily those laws could be manipulated. It was considerably easier to prevent someone from registering than voting.

It was easy to make it hard to register: "One day the registrar is absent and the office is closed," it was reported. "Another and he is out of blank forms. Again, there is a rush of applicants and the business is conducted so slowly that many have to go away." In Caddo Parish five Black men were the first to arrive at the registrar's office early in the morning—then stood patiently until seventy-three white men who came after them had registered. In St. Mary Parish the supervisor refused to advertise the times and places people could register and would not allow his movements to be known, making it impossible to register. The supervisor in Natchitoches kept the front door locked and let in white men through a hidden back door. The Rapides Parish supervisor "would hide in his house and have [Black] men seeking registration told he was gone to the country while white men were hunted up and all registered. He systematically obstructed registration by browbeating and refusing to appear at times and places advertised...registered Democrats and unnaturalized foreigners." In another parish at least thirteen underage Democrats were registered.

The strategy worked. Tens of thousands of eligible voters were prevented from registering. In an effort to prove the election was rigged, Republicans collected affidavits from men who were denied registration. Although, as it turned out, many of those affidavits also were counterfeit or forged.

Throughout the South every possible means was used to prevent people from voting. States like Georgia required literacy tests or imposed a poll tax on otherwise legal voters.

To combat that, the federal government appropriated funds to pay the tax.

Louisiana employed its own methods to control the vote. It was up to local officials to determine how many polls would be open and where they would be located. In the cities, where the majority of Republican voters lived, that was not a problem. But in rural areas, only a limited number of polls were opened, and they were situated as far as possible from concentrations of Republican voters. In some parishes the nearest station was ten miles or more away. In Plaquemines only six polls were opened for twelve wards, and the majority of Republicans had to travel thirty-five miles to vote. At many places, the number of ballot boxes was limited, and voters were required to swear to each fact on their registration papers, resulting in them having to wait in long lines for hours—causing many frustrated voters to just walk away.

Just to make it even more difficult the actual location of the polls was not advertised, and local officials were encouraged to send anyone who asked on a wild-goose chase. The day before the election one Democratic supervisor admitted he had told his commissioners "to locate the boxes wherever they damn please—under a pine tree if necessary."

Election day was November 4. The sun was shining brightly that morning, although there was a chance of showers in the late afternoon. In New Orleans, most businesses were closed so employees could vote. Kellogg and McEnery voted early and made appearances at different polling stations throughout the day.

The biggest national news story of the day came from Rochester, New York, where warrants were issued accusing Susan B. Anthony and fifteen other women of illegally trying to vote.

While in the city voting seemed to proceed well, Republican voters in many rural towns discovered the polls had been moved from scheduled locations. In Beulah, the ballot box was hidden in an abandoned fodder shed in a field several miles from town. Republican voters tracked Democrats through the woods to find it—and even when they got there many of them were not permitted to vote. Polls were located on islands in lakes, on bayous, anyplace difficult to reach. In one parish two ballot boxes were set up—all votes from newly registered voters were dropped in one box, votes from previously registered people went in the other. Only one box was opened and its votes counted.

In some areas preprinted counterfeit tickets were handed out to voters by friendly volunteers. These ballots looked exactly like legitimate ballots, bearing the correct party symbols and colors—but at least some information on them was false. Candidates were left off the ballot or their names were spelled incorrectly or listed in the wrong district or any other small change that would make a vote invalid. Voters took the ticket without bothering to check the details and deposited it in the ballot box.

Although by law people were prohibited from carrying weapons unless specifically authorized by the governor or his officials, there were numerous reports of violence and intimidation. In Livingston two Republicans who tried to vote early in the morning were shot, discouraging others from showing up. In St. Landry as many as five hundred men were "compelled to vote the Democratic ticket on pain of a repetition of the terrible massacre of 1868." In numerous other places weapons were produced to remind Republicans how dangerous it might be for them to vote.

There was the usual ballot box stuffing. The most common method was to fold several ballots inside one legal ticket when voting. When the box was moved the ballots would separate.

None of this was unique. Both parties were aware of it, and neither of them objected. According to newly Democratic Governor Warmoth, "There never was a more peaceful, free or fair campaign and election held in the state of Louisiana. There were no riots nor disturbances of any kind anywhere in the State."

Republican Senator Kellogg agreed, describing it as "the fullest and fairest election that ever occurred in the city, so far as immunity from violence or unjust interference was concerned."

The polls were closed. The voting was finished. Election officials opened the boxes and started counting the votes. Tallies slowly trickled in from every district. And over the next few days and weeks, the magnitude of the fraud became clear.

It turned out both parties had laid plans to rig the election long before the first vote. Starting months earlier, Republican carpetbagger Congressman J. Hale Sypher had told election supervisors to register as many names as possible, no matter where the names came from, so that "the votes cast [in this election] should not exceed registration." They were careful to make certain there were a sufficient number of registered voters to account for every vote counted.

Democrats had their own scheme: in the registration books a letter *D* was written next to numerous Black voters. It was later discovered that this was a secret instruction to Democratic supervisors, alerting them that a duplicate ballot had been issued to a white Democrat so when the Black man showed up at the poll he should not be allowed to vote.

It worked: in Cotile, for example, on election day almost two thousand legally registered Black voters were turned away from the poll.

When it came to counting votes, the result was in the hands of the ballot box holder. In theory it was simple: after the polls closed, the commissioners in each district unlocked the box and counted the ballots by hand. The results were recorded and submitted to the supervisor. In reality, it didn't work that way: in district after district the returns were incomplete, inaccurate or just impossible to believe. Ballot boxes disappeared, or were stolen, but mostly were stuffed with fraudulent votes. One New Orleans resident appeared to have voted seventeen times. Thousands of men were deprived of the right to vote, while thousands of fraudulent ballots were deposited.

A state investigation weeks after the election concluded that in only three or four of the fifty-eight parishes in the state was the reported count based directly on the votes in the locked box—although even in those cases there was no evidence how those ballots got into the box. The Democratic supervisor of Madison Parish admitted he had taken the box with him to New Orleans. There were too many Republicans in the parish, he told investigators, so he had hidden in an apartment in the city where his friends protected him, destroyed the votes and replaced them with Democratic votes. In the town of Mooringsport, three hundred and ten registered Republicans voted, but when the box was opened there were only eighteen Republican votes. In Pointe Coupee, "460 Republican and 63 Democratic votes were cast. But after sleeping one night with the Democratic supervisor the Republican votes melted to 20."

In some areas where ballot boxes were not sufficiently stuffed, they were taken from supervisors—who were supposed to retain possession—sometimes at gunpoint, and delivered unlocked hours later to headquarters. At least four hundred Republican votes were cast in Jefferson Parish, but the supervisor was not allowed to ride in a carriage transporting the box—and when it was opened there wasn't a single vote for Grant or Kellogg.

In some cases, boxes did not get to the proper place for several days, and no one knew where they had been in the interim.

"The Fifteenth Amendment means more than this," the *New Orleans Republican* complained several days after the election. "A vote is of no use to a man unless it is honestly counted, and to give him the right to put it in a ballot box, and at the same time [give] another the right to withdraw it, or refuse to count it is to vex his ear with vain promise."

According to the final count, Grant won the presidential election in Louisiana. But the results were so obviously corrupt that Congress wouldn't allow the state's delegates to participate in the electoral college vote.

Who won the gubernatorial election? It depended entirely on which ballots were accepted and counted. It was up to the Returning Board to determine whether Kellogg or McEnery would be the next governor.

And who controlled the Returning Board? Henry Warmoth.

He had given himself that power two years earlier and zealously protected it. He had the right to appoint a five-man Returning Board with complete authority to examine election returns and reject the results from any polling station, district or parish if—in their opinion—the vote had been influenced by violence or fraud. Warmoth understood how vital this law was if he was to continue controlling the political process and had beaten back several attempts to rescind it. The greatest threat had come only a month earlier and resulted in one of the most unusual events in American political history.

The reasonably good working relationship between Warmoth and Lieutenant Governor Pinchback had ended with the split of the Republican party. Whatever trust that once existed between them was gone.

The previous January the state legislature had passed modified registration and election bills curtailing the governor's power to name his own Returning Board. Rather than vetoing it, Warmoth did nothing, knowing he had until his term ended in January 1873 to act on it. So the laws remained in limbo.

In October, the National Republican Committee invited Pinchback to speak in New York. The lieutenant governor had become one of the most respected Black politicians in the country, he'd gotten a lot of attention in the national media, and people wanted to see him in person. And Pinchback wanted to meet the party leaders. Who knew what opportunities lay ahead?

That trip attracted Warmoth's curiosity. He invented his own reasons to go to New York and see for himself what was going on. His first day there he just *happened* to meet Pinchback walking on the avenue with a state senator and invited him to meet later that night at the Fifth Avenue Hotel. Perhaps they might find a common ground, he suggested. Pinchback readily accepted.

But he didn't show up. Warmoth assumed he had "fallen to the allurements of New York" and simply forgotten their meeting. The next morning, he asked the senator what had happened to the lieutenant governor. The man shrugged; he hadn't seen him since the previous afternoon. It turned out no one had seen him. Pinchback seemingly had disappeared. A spokesman for Grant's reelection committee hastily announced Pinchback was en route to Pittsburgh to deliver an address.

That was a lie. Warmoth got a message from a knowledgeable "friend" in the Custom House camp that something far more devious was in action. The chairman of the Custom House Republicans, US Marshal Stephen Packard, had initiated a plan to overthrow the governor while he was out of the state.

With Warmoth and Pinchback out of the state the speaker of the house would become the acting governor. Packard planned to convene the legislature, have the speaker sign the amended registration and election bills, which instantly would become law, direct the legislature to impeach the governor and other officials—especially the registrars of voters—and reorganize the Metropolitan Police force. Custom House members of the legislature had been informed of the plan and were ready to carry it out.

Pinchback had not been part of it at first. He didn't even know about it. The speaker had agreed to it. But when he reneged at the last minute Packard contacted Pinchback, who was already in New York. Rather than meeting Warmoth as he had intended, Pinchback had secretly taken a train back to New Orleans.

A proclamation setting the whole plan in motion by convening the legislature had been printed and was awaiting Pinchback's arrival in Amity City. It was to be telegraphed to New Orleans. It would take no more than fifteen minutes once the legislature was in session to run the bills through both houses. Several militias also were prepared to protect the coup's participants and, if necessary, maintain the new government by force.

There also was some discussion about staging a riot, which would allow President Grant to declare martial law, guaranteeing he would carry the state in the upcoming election. It was not known how much, if any, advance notice Grant had about this attempt to overthrow the governor, but newspapers noted that his brother-in-law Casey was sent out of the state before the coup began.

Warmoth had only one hope: somehow, he had to get back to New Orleans before Pinchback got there. That seemed impossible. The lieutenant governor had a half-day head start.

But what Pinchback didn't have were Warmoth's contacts or his cunning. The race for control of Louisiana was on.

The chairman of the McEnery campaign committee was Major E. A. Burke, who conveniently also was the manager of the Illinois Central Railroad in New Orleans. Warmoth and Burke had a good working relationship. He sent Burke a long, detailed telegram laying out the situation. Do not let Pinchback get over the state border before me, he wired; do whatever you have to do to stop him. He then asked Burke to arrange a special car and engine to help him beat the lieutenant governor to the city.

Edward Austin Burke and Warmoth made a fine pair. Burke had arrived in New Orleans only a few years earlier, emerging from a somewhat shadowy background. He had served in the Confederate army, but there were questions about his rank; on occasion he claimed to have been a colonel. It was rumored he had added the *e* to his last name after arriving in New Orleans to confuse creditors he'd left in Texas. Once settled, he quickly became involved in Louisiana politics, New Orleans society and white supremacist militias. Like Warmoth, he was crafty. He weighed the consequences and picked his side: there would be great benefits for him if he saved Warmoth.

Burke ordered a locomotive and one car for the governor. He ordered all train traffic off hundreds of miles of Mississippi and Jackson track. But even at the amazing speed of forty miles an hour Warmoth wouldn't be able to catch Pinchback. Somehow, Pinchback had to be slowed.

In desperation, the two men devised a clever plan. Burke found out what train Pinchback was on. That train had to stop briefly in Canton, Mississippi, for coal and water in the middle of the night. When the train arrived the stationmaster boarded and told the lieutenant governor there was an important dispatch waiting for him in the office. Whatever it was, it had to be handed to him in person. Pinchback left the train and went into the station. He was handed the message and without reading it, turned to rush back to the train.

The station door was locked. He couldn't get out. No one seemed able to open it. In desperation, he climbed out the window onto the platform. Too late. The train had left without him.

He still was standing on the platform, forlorn and defeated, when Warmoth arrived the next morning. "I shall never forget the triumphant expression on his face," Pinchback recalled. "He was standing on the front platform of his special train as it came lumbering into town. 'Well, Governor,' I said, 'your lucky star is still in the ascendant.'"

"Hello, old fellow," Warmoth greeted him, smiling broadly, "what are you doing here?" The governor then graciously asked the lieutenant governor to join him for the remainder of the trip. Pinchback accepted. It is not known what the men discussed on the ride home.

Warmoth had put together an incredible operation in only a few hours. Men were stationed all along the train route to telegraph reports of Pinchback's progress. Had the ploy failed at that train station or if the lieutenant governor had taken a different route, an "impassible barrier" awaited him when he reached Mobile.

With Pinchback on board, the race home continued. The "meteoric flight of Governor Warmoth," as it was reported, took only sixty-two hours to cover the seventeen hundred miles from New York to New Orleans, the fastest recorded railroad trip in history!

A master mechanic who examined the engine at the end of the journey found that the bands which held springs together had burst, and in another ten miles would have caused a "first class accident," possibly resulting in serious injuries.

The Custom House coup had failed. Warmoth had kept control of the Returning Board. And in any other election that would have made all the difference.

Not this time, though; not in this election. The reported vote totals couldn't be trusted and didn't include the thousands of eligible voters who had been kept away from the polls. Both parties could make a strong argument that the other party had cheated; it was impossible to determine the actual winner.

The American electoral system hadn't been designed to deal with this type of problem. It had been cobbled together out of tested parts from various countries, then tempered with compromise. There were elements from ancient Rome and Athens, from the methods used to select Holy Roman emperors and popes.

The Fifteenth Amendment to the Constitution had resulted in the largest number of people in American history being eligible to vote. Hundreds of thousands of new voters had been added to the rolls. The election of 1872 was a test of the resiliency of the system. No one had considered the possibility that the system could collapse.

When there had been unanticipated problems in the past, reasonable men had figured out how to deal with them. The presidential election of 1800 had resulted in an electoral tie and had taken six days and thirty-six votes in the House of Representatives before deals were struck and Thomas Jefferson became the president. To make sure that didn't happen again, the Twelfth Amendment was passed to make the necessary changes in the system. When no candidate received a majority of the electoral votes in 1824, the House finally elected John Quincy Adams—after Henry Clay, who finished fourth, gave his support to Adams in return for being named secretary of state. This election exposed the inherent dangers of having more than two competing parties in the electoral college system. There had been anecdotal stories of close or tied local elections being settled by the flip of a coin, picking a name out of a hat, bribery or even an agreement to share or rotate the office. But an acceptable solution always had been found.

Americans had gotten used to dealing with the complaints and claims that arose after every election. Louisianians expected this would be no different. One of the first lawsuits arising from this one was filed within days by Colonel Charles Lowell, postmaster of Jefferson Parish, who accused commissioners, supervisors "and all other parties on whom responsibility can be laid" of stealing his vote. At some point the poll box at the former Confederate fort of Camp Parapet had been changed, making it appear Lowell had voted against Grant, Kellogg...and himself.

According to the returns, four hundred other registered Republicans in the precinct also had voted a straight Democratic ticket.

About this action, the *Republican* wrote, "There is serious discomfort for some people brewing."

More than a week after the election, returns were still being delivered. In numerous cases they were far different than had been expected. Strong Republican parishes had gone for Greeley and McEnery, while marginally Democratic areas had delivered unexpectedly large majorities. It was reported, "Developments of illegal and fraudulent proceedings are being brought to light." Republican officials remained confident, claiming they had carried the state by 30,000 votes. Democratic committee leaders were equally confident, setting their winning margin at 20,000 votes.

As the counting continued, people were relying on observers to ensure the totals were honest. It was hard to cheat with people watching. But in some cases, those observers were denied the right to watch the proceedings. A group of armed Black citizens had followed a ballot box from their polling station to the State House. Legally, they had every right to go inside to monitor the counting. But the sheriff refused to admit them, so they stood at the window outside watching the box. They stood throughout the day and night. Every few hours new, fresh watchers replaced them.

By the second week reporters also were routinely being denied access to the Mechanics Institute.

The mechanics of an election were obscure. Until Warmoth had made his fight to control it, most people were not aware there was such a body as a Returning Board. In many cases being a member of the Returning Board was considered an honorary commission. Theoretically, it had the ultimate power in an election, as the Board declared the winner; but in reality there wasn't much to do other than confirm the reported numbers.

Two weeks after the election, the Returning Board met in Governor Warmoth's office to examine the reported results and declare the winners. The governor had fought the legislature and set a railroad speed record to maintain control of the Board. But he had lost confidence in some of its members, so even before the Board officially convened he tried to replace them with people he believed were more loyal to him.

The consequences of that would become a life-and-death matter and eventually be settled with machine guns in the streets of New Orleans.

6

As the counting proceeded with agonizing slowness and debate had begun over the makeup of the Returning Board, national problems diverted attention away from the State House. There were serious problems on the Mexican border: it was wide-open, and bandits and other immigrants were crossing it with impunity. Grant, who had been reelected, talked tough about sealing the border, but there was little he could actually do to close it or protect Americans. According to newspapers, reports "leaked" from government sources "in anticipation of official documents [claimed] that the President, in conference with Mexican border commissioners elicited the opinion that $100,000,000 would not more than cover the injury to American interests on the southeastern frontier...for which Mexico is directly or indirectly responsible...

"Nor less idle would it be to think of a complete military guard for the thousand or more miles of American frontier contiguous to wild stretches of Mexican territory... That public opinion in this country would sanction such a measure is by no means probable... It certainly would not pacify the border or give the desired encouragement to American commerce and industry."

Complicating the situation, the story continued, was the weakness of the Mexican government, which was "liable to fly to pieces like the fabled jointed snakes."

Ironically, only a few days later the *Rapides Gazette* for the first time raised the possibility that Louisiana's government might collapse. There were no provisions in the state or the federal constitution that would help to deal with this situation. What happens to a state when it is impossible to determine the winner of its gubernatorial election? What happens when a sizable segment of the populace doesn't recognize the legitimacy of a government? What happens when half of the voters refuse to accept the results of an election? Anarchy? Chaos? Government by force and fiat? The *Gazette* asked a question to which no one had an answer: "Can two separate governments be erected and the question of legitimacy decided by the recognition and support of one of them by the federal government?"

While it would be several decades before good losers began offering a public concession speech, many defeated politicians showed proper manners by congratulating the winner and offering no protest about the results. Not this time, though. Given the bitterness between the parties, a concession from either side seemed unlikely.

The only hope was that the Returning Board could make some sense out of the jumble of fraudulent votes and people kept away from the polls and arrive at a fair conclusion. Complicating matters, Republicans had submitted thousands of affidavits from people claiming they had been denied the right to vote and demanded those be counted as Republican votes, while Democrats contended many of those affidavits were fraudulent.

Somehow the Returning Board had to sort it all out. But the Board was a political creation, and its members had no expertise in electoral matters. They were politicians. They knew how to please voters, not count their votes.

Governor Warmoth cared little about the legal niceties. He had one objective: make sure his man, McEnery, became governor. He didn't seem to care how. As soon as the Board assembled, the governor challenged its makeup. It was comprised of the governor, the lieutenant governor, the secretary of state and two state senators. But a law prohibited anyone running for elective office from serving on that board. Lieutenant Governor Pinchback had run for a Congressional seat, and State Senator General Thomas C. Anderson had run for reelection. Therefore, they were ineligible. But there was no legal guidance on how to replace them. The men chosen to fill those two seats would control the Board—and therefore the election. Warmoth claimed the power to select them.

As he later explained, "If the Kellogg–Grant party could have captured the Returning Board they hoped to be able to throw out enough Fusion votes, on one excuse or another, to change the result and give them victory."

And if that happened any possibility of him being appointed to the Senate seat would disappear. So he had to make sure his men got those seats. Years later he claimed that Republicans offered that prize to him as a bribe if he dropped McEnery and supported Kellogg. They "dangled before my eyes the seat in the United States Senate which would be made vacant by the election of Senator Kellogg to the Governorship." Naturally, he would claim, he was far too ethical to use "the power of the Returning Board...to wipe out the Greeley–McEnery majority."

Instead, when the Board met he announced he was removing the acting secretary of state, war hero and US Marshal Francis J. Herron. He immediately appointed Colonel Jack Wharton, a loyal supporter, to that seat. Fortunately, Wharton happened to be waiting in a room nearby. He also named Colonel Frank Hatch and Durant da Ponte to the vacant seats left by Pinchback and Anderson. Both men were sworn in. That gave him total control of the Board.

Herron objected, claiming Warmoth had no right to replace him, and nominated General James Longstreet and Jacob Hawkins to fill the two open spots. The other remaining member of the Board, John Lynch, supported those nominations. Both men were sworn in. That gave Herron a majority of the five-member Board and total control of it.

Nonsense, Warmoth countered. Less than two months earlier, after a battle with the legislature, he had quietly replaced then secretary of state George Bovee with Herron. Bovee learned he had been replaced when he went to his office and found Herron—and four police officers—waiting there. The two men started brawling, and Bovee was arrested for assault and battery.

Warmoth pointed out that Herron had recognized the governor's power to replace the secretary of state in that instance, and nothing had changed that in the previous few weeks. Now he was replacing him.

Herron responded that his appointment was legal, and he had the commission to prove it.

Not quite legal, Warmoth said. While working as a collector of taxes Herron had been accused of misappropriating $1,000, a charge that had to be resolved before he could legally become a state officer. In fact, Warmoth said, he'd loaned the man $1,400 to settle that charge before appointing him and had only recently discovered that no payment had been made. Therefore, Herron's appointment as secretary of state was illegal. The position was vacant, allowing him to fill it with Jack Wharton.

Neither side would back down; suddenly, there were two Returning Boards.

Each side sued the other, hoping the court might be able to restore some semblance of order. Only six years earlier in Philadelphia, an enterprising man had created the first baseball scorecard, a tool that enabled observers to identify all the participants—among them Brooklyn's first baseman, Bob "Death to Flying Things" Ferguson—and track the progress of the game. Unfortunately, there was no similar way to make sense of everything that was going on in Louisiana. Each day brought a new tactic, making the already-complex situation far more difficult to understand. It was like tying knots in knots. Events were moving so quickly that even the already-partisan newspapers couldn't keep their readers informed. The only thing that everybody knew was obvious: nobody had the slightest idea who had won the election or, more important, which Board would determine who the next governor of Louisiana was going to be.

As this was going on, Henry Warmoth sat in the governor's office, directing events with the skill of a seasoned railroad dispatcher, bringing lawsuits and defending against other lawsuits, trying to maintain control of the legislature, calling in favors and making promises, doing whatever was necessary for his own political survival. "The utterly unscrupulous political character of Warmoth," wrote a *New York Herald* reporter, "has been shown in the fact that he flies from principle to principle and from party to party, animated by no other disposition than to retain his supremacy. At the present time he is playing the desperate game of fighting the courts of his own state, the courts of the United States, the administration at Washington and risking the possibility of a terrible riot in order to make one step further and descend from his reckless enjoyment of power to be a dignified Senator."

Senator? Warmoth was ready for this battle. He had been seeding the system since taking office. Before he'd entered the governor's office, the state constitution established seven district courts in New Orleans and its environs. The judges of those seven district courts were elected. The courts basically had equal powers and at times issued conflicting or contradictory rulings. The governor had little control over the judicial system. That had to change.

Warmoth couldn't fill the benches with loyalists, so he came up with another idea. In 1870 he pushed the legislature to create a new and powerful eighth district court, one that was superior to the other seven in areas that concerned him. Within this court's jurisdiction was the right "to entertain all proceedings... in which the right to any office...is in any way involved."

The governor appointed his close friend Henry Dibble the first judge of the Eighth District Court.

Dibble was a fellow carpetbagger. After arriving in Louisiana, he had aligned himself with Warmoth, serving as a member of his 1868 campaign committee. He proved to be an important ally. An excellent lawyer, he successfully represented Warmoth in a series of cases that extended the governor's control of the state's fiscal policies. The association between the two men grew stronger as Dibble played key roles in both the administration and the reelection campaign.

It turned out, though, that Dibble had a fatal flaw, as far as Warmoth was concerned: he was honest.

For Warmoth, that meant he couldn't be trusted.

The question of which Returning Board was legal went to Dibble's Eighth District Court. Judge Dibble actually had been defeated in the recent election, but because no Board had been recognized to certify the returns, his replacement had not yet been allowed to replace him.

His courtroom was mobbed for the hearing. Spectators who didn't get in "surged in great volume up and down the stairways and along the sidewalk to the post office corner." The night before the hearing Warmoth apparently offered Dibble a lucrative position. The judge responded with a nasty note rejecting the offer.

After listening to the arguments, Dibble granted the Herron Board's injunction against Warmoth, deciding "there was not another person besides the Governor in the state who did not believe Herron to be the Secretary of State... I hold that

Herron is still secretary of state." As there was no evidence that his successor, Wharton, had been sworn into office before the meeting began, Herron remained secretary, making the original Board the legal Board.

But Dibble went further in his decision, writing bitterly about his now former ally, "his acts have been so frequently designated as a brilliant *coup d'etat*, that I feel called upon to say that *coup d'etat* is not an American institution, it belongs to another country, where they have barricades, and where they meet to organize governments at midnight."

On that same day, Kellogg made the impasse a federal case. He filed a suit against the Warmoth Board in Judge Edward H. Durell's United States Circuit Court for the Eastern District of Louisiana. Judge Durell had been the Republican mayor of New Orleans during the Union occupation, and then had been appointed to the bench by Lincoln.

Warmoth's lawyers challenged the right of the federal court to even hear the case. This is about states' rights, they contended, and belongs in state court. Kellogg's lawyers protested that this was really about the Fifteenth Amendment, telling Judge Durell that ten thousand Black men had been denied the right to vote. "The court should have jurisdiction for the preservation of peace and order…the constitutional guarantees and the enforcement acts passed under them require the court to take it."

A great deal of legal bluster echoed through the courtroom, but the outcome seemed reasonably certain. Days earlier Kellogg, US Marshal Packard and Grant's brother-in-law Casey had raced to Washington and met with the president and the attorney general. They warned that this was an attempt by Warmoth to destroy the Republican party in the state. While officially Grant stayed out of it, several private notes passed back and forth from Washington to New Orleans. Kellogg continued to plead with the president and attorney general to intervene, telling them, "This is a systematic and organized attempt...to outrage every principle of justice, to override all constitutional and legal restraints..." Fearing violence, he concluded by asking for federal troops to maintain order.

All the uncounted returns, meanwhile, sat stored in the State House. Both Kellogg and McEnery continued to insist they had won and would not be cheated out of their victory. The two men each held rallies where supporters cheered their victories and jeered their opponent. This fight isn't for me, both candidates insisted, it's for you. It's you who is being cheated. Keeping supporters emotionally involved was vital.

That message was being heard. People felt it. They believed it. The differences between the two men were as wide as the gap between North and South. Louisianians' future would be very different depending on who was declared the winner. The Republicans knew with certainty that Democrats had cheated in the election, and the Democrats knew with equal certainty that Republicans had cheated to win the election.

If men of Louisiana had once believed in the integrity of the electoral process, that was gone. The only thing that mattered was winning. Thus far it had been a battle of words, fought in courtrooms and in public speeches, but it was only a matter of time before it escalated into violence.

Minor issues that previously would have attracted little attention suddenly were magnified. A statue of Benjamin Franklin was to be erected in Lafayette Square. But to McEnery supporters Franklin was no longer a man who signed the Constitution and helped create the nation; he was simply a northerner. A carpetbagger. Unworthy of being honored in New Orleans.

Judge Dibble's injunction had stopped Warmoth, at least temporarily, from claiming a victory. Whatever influence Warmoth once had over the judge clearly was gone. But he did not give up; all men had a price, he believed. So he tried again, sweetening his offer. He would remain governor for several more months and still had enormous resources. If Dibble stepped down immediately, he suggested, his future could be made considerably brighter. Dibble responded even more forcefully, replying, "It would be treason for me to act as you suggest."

Warmoth had played this hand as long as he was able, but the decision of the court ended it. So while Kellogg's supporters were celebrating their victory he played a brand-new card: *voilà!* The election bill passed months earlier by the legislature had sat unsigned on his desk. He took out his pen and signed it. One of the provisions of the bill abolished all previously existing Returning Boards, leaving it to the legislature to appoint a new one. By law, the Returning Board had to begin its work within ten days following the election. As the legislature was not in session, to comply with that timeline he was legally required to name the members of the new Board.

And so, he created a third Returning Board, which became known as the De Feriet Board, named after one of its members, G. De Feriet, a leading businessman.

At that moment there was a wonderful variety of available amusements in New Orleans. The St. Charles Theatre was offering *The Merry Wives of Windsor*, which displayed "Mr. DeBar's rare talent as a comedian." Three comedies, *Les Domestiques*, the farce *Un Caprice* and *La Grève des Forgerons*, were playing at the Opera House. And the Academy of Music was presenting the Irish comedy *Shin Fance*. But nothing was more entertaining—or less predictable—than the unfolding political and legal dramas taking place in the city.

Since Judge Dibble wouldn't accept a bribe, Warmoth decided he too had to be replaced. To accomplish that, he later explained, he examined all the returns (even though they officially had not been opened), declared that Dibble had been defeated and signed an order removing him from the Eighth District Court. To replace him, he appointed judge-elect William A. Elmore.

He did so, he said, to settle the confusion. If he didn't act swiftly the "returns would be tied up six to twelve months, perhaps."

At the same time, he also appointed the newly elected judges from the other seven courts.

The next morning, Thursday, November 21, it was reported that in the Second District Court Judge Duvigneaud had retired from the bench "with grace and politeness." In the Third District "the same quiet manner prevailed." In fact, the gavel was handed over peacefully in every courtroom—except in the Eighth District.

Word spread throughout the building, and people raced to the already-crowded courtroom to see the show. As soon as he assumed the bench, Judge Elmore had appointed a new sheriff, W. P. Harper, new deputy and new court clerk. Just as he finished swearing them in, Judge Dibble arrived, accompanied by the now "former" sheriff, C. S. Sauvinet.

It was a scene worthy of Molière. Judge Dibble ascended the bench, stood next to Judge Elmore and ordered the previous clerk to open the court. Then, according to observers, "Mr. Sauvinet began to cry it open but had not much got beyond 'Oyez, oyez' when [newly appointed] Deputy Sheriff Dick seized hold of him by his clothes and told him to stop."

"Open the court!" Judge Dibble shouted to Sauvinet, who couldn't do anything because Deputy Dick refused to let go of him.

Until that moment Judge Elmore had been silent. Looking directly at the new sheriff he pointed to Judge Dibble and ordered, "Come forward and arrest this man!" Deputy Dick released Sauvinet, climbed onto the bench and took hold of Judge Dibble.

More spectators pushed into the courtroom. The crowd outside the room continued to grow.

The two judges then turned on each other, threatening each other with legal actions. The decorum of the court disappeared.

Finally, Judge Dibble stepped down, warning Judge Elmore that he was going directly to the State Supreme Court, where his position would be supported—and the first thing he was going to do was have Judge Elmore arrested and "committed to the Parish prison for contempt of court."

Judge Elmore countered that he would have Judge Dibble arrested for disturbing the court.

Judge Dibble stormed out of the room, trailed by Sheriff Sauvinet, spectators clearing an aisle for the men as they left. Judge Elmore took a deep breath, gaveled the courtroom quiet and began the proceedings.

He was only minutes into the session when Judge Dibble and Sauvinet returned, pushing their way through the crowd. The State Supreme Court had issued a writ confirming Sheriff Sauvinet retained his office, Judge Dibble announced. Once again, he stepped onto the bench, then he ordered Sauvinet to adjourn the court until the situation could be unraveled.

Undeterred, Judge Elmore ordered Sheriff Harper to arrest Judge Dibble. Harper took hold of Judge Dibble and forcibly pushed and pulled him from the courtroom. Judge Dibble's shouted threats could be heard as he was ejected. When the courtroom settled down again, Judge Elmore called a case involving an unpaid promissory note. The spectators, realizing that "the law had got back to its original drone, gradually thinned." This day's amusement was done. At least in this courtroom.

Similar dramas were taking place in other offices throughout the city. No one knew who was in charge. Inside City Hall, according to the *Republican*, "various administrators are expecting an attempt on their official positions." That afternoon Sheriff Harper walked into Sheriff Sauvinet's office with his new commission and told Sauvinet to leave. Sauvinet refused. If they wanted him out, he said, they would have to force him out. Before a fight erupted Algernon Badger, superintendent of Warmoth's Metropolitan Police department, showed up and defused the situation. Sauvinet left peacefully.

The two secretaries of state had also argued over that office, but Herron held it.

So much was happening so quickly in so many different places that it was impossible to keep track of events. The two gubernatorial candidates were both claiming victory. Lawsuits and countersuits had been filed in state and federal courts. In the Eighth District, where several of those lawsuits would be heard, two judges were fighting over who belonged on the bench. Three Returning Boards had been formed, and all were claiming the right to count the votes. Two sheriffs and deputy sheriffs demanded their opponent surrender the office. Numerous clerks and secretaries had no idea who was in charge or if they even still had their jobs.

None of this seemed to concern Warmoth. He continued attacking. For each legal setback he found an answer. His fight to get Judge Elmore on the bench proved worthwhile. Elmore threw out the previous verdict, ruling that the new election law dissolved previous boards. He dismissed all the legal challenges. It was a victory for Warmoth. To consolidate his power, he called the newly elected legislature into a special session on December 9. But without official returns there was no way of determining who had been elected. As in other areas of government and the judiciary, often two men claimed the same seat.

While the election was being fought in courtrooms, the competing Returning Boards began counting votes. Or at least presenting tallies to justify their preferred results. Those numbers were bogus, that was well-known. That didn't seem to make any difference. Warmoth's Board appointed secretaries and clerks and "proceeded to tabulate the returns honestly." The Lynch Board created its tally from numerous sources, which allowed them to add thousands to the total that might have been cast for Kellogg if his supporters had been allowed to vote.

Warmoth's Board announced that McEnery had been elected by 10,000 votes—65,579 to Kellogg's 55,973. The Lynch Board countered by reporting that if registered voters had been permitted to vote, Kellogg would have won by 18,861 votes.

Those vote totals had no real meaning. It had become obvious the election was going to be decided in Judge Durell's federal courtroom. In anticipation of Durell's decision, the attorney general had put on alert "four thousand troops comprising artillery, cavalry and the good old reliable infantry, all dressed in blue...so that law-abiding people may calm all fears that blood will be spilled... The government does not intend...any faction shall murder American citizens..."

A worried officer told a reporter, "If we are ordered to fire upon a crowd, and that order should be illegal at law, we are liable to be tried for murder, and if we do not fire we may be court martialed for disobedience for disobeying orders."

People began lining up outside Judge Durell's courtroom the day before the trial. To prove that Black citizens had been denied the right to vote, Kellogg had collected five thousand affidavits and was prepared to present witnesses to tell their stories. These men "roosted on window ledges, lay about the floors, stow themselves away in the embrasures and let their heads fall negligently on their knees and squat in the niches of the edifice, all of them satisfied that if allowed to testify they can show such a state of affairs...which would lead whole communities to sympathize with them."

Perhaps even more important, this was no longer a local matter. It had become a huge national story. Did the federal government have jurisdiction? The decision would help define the reach of the new Amendments and the balance between states' rights and the federal government. "The Threatened Conflict Between State and Federal Power," warned a *New York Herald* headline. Numerous subheads outlined the stakes: "The Issue of Reconstruction," "Warmoth the Prince of Carpetbaggers,"

"No Public Spirit or Honesty Anywhere," "A Terrible Story of Robbery, Outrage and Wrong" and, finally, "Fears of Riot and Bloodshed in New Orleans and a Coup d'Etat."

Warmoth relentlessly attacked Judge Durell's character, telling people the judge was too old, kept his "closet stocked with choice wines and liquors" and claimed a close male friend was his "nightly companion; they were inseparable and were often together until late hours of the night."

His supporters were provoked, just as he intended. The *New York Times* reported the judge "has received several letters threatening his life, that he will be assassinated if he decides in favor [of Kellogg]." Kellogg and several other government officials connected to the case also were warned about ruling against Warmoth.

Judge Durell was not deterred.

7

An estimated three thousand people gathered outside the heavily guarded Mechanics Institute on Monday morning as the state legislature convened for the special session. It was a raucous crowd, and many were there more out of curiosity than to support either faction. No one had the slightest idea what was going to take place inside—all kinds of rumors had been spreading throughout the weekend—but even their wildest guesses could not possibly have anticipated what was about to unfold.

Governor Warmoth had a plan he was ready to spring. There was a reason he had called this special session. He knew that the first few seconds would make all the difference. In his plan, the senators who held office in the previous session would use their legislative experience to seize control of the chamber before their newly elected replacements could be sworn in. With his senate in place, Warmoth could make a fight for McEnery.

Lieutenant Governor Pinchback, presiding over the Senate, also was ready. He certainly had not forgotten the embarrassment of the great train race back from New York. This was his opportunity to get even—and if things fell into place, it could lead to an even greater victory. He had taken his seat at the front of the room long before noon, perhaps because, as the *Times-Picayune* speculated, "he feared if he waited it might become occupied by someone else."

At noon, he called the Senate to order. He asked the secretary of the Senate to call the roll. Instantly, Senator William McMillen stood and proposed a motion. Warmoth's strategy had begun.

The foundations of parliamentary procedure, the rules of order by which a legislative body conducts its business, were first written down by the clerk of England's House of Commons in 1547. These rules are intended to ensure decorum, give all members the right to be heard and guarantee majority rule. They also provide historic continuity and confidence that laws and regulations passed by all legislative assemblies followed a known and respected process. Most American lawmaking bodies followed Thomas Jefferson's *A Manual of Parliamentary Practice*, which he had based on the British rules.

But those rules are extremely complicated, at times contradictory and always subject to interpretation. They can be molded by the presiding official to assure a desired outcome. Pinchback looked at Senator McMillen. It was possible he smiled. "The roll is being called," he responded. "No motion can be entertained."

McMillen was furious. "I desire to enter my protest to this arbitrary ruling."

Pinchback ignored him as the secretary continued calling the roll. Other Democratic senators began objecting, standing, demanding to be heard.

When the secretary was done the entire body of the newly elected senators replacing the former members were sworn into office. Several Democrats refused to be sworn in or left the room, hoping to deny Pinchback the quorum required to conduct business. But there were not enough of them to stop the proceedings. By adding men supposedly elected by both Returning Boards, a legally sufficient number of senators were seated—even if there was no electoral basis for seating them.

Warmoth had been defeated.

Or so it seemed to everyone other than Warmoth.

After the chaplain had read the opening prayer Warmoth's men tried one last time, shouting that the proceedings were a sham. What was going on was not legal! It couldn't be allowed. The Senate had been organized contrary to law. It wouldn't stand! They demanded to be heard.

It was probable there had been some technical violations of the rules of order. But rather than recognizing the protestors, Pinchback stood and began speaking, stunning senators and spectators into silence with his shocking claims. The night before, he began, Governor Warmoth had launched a conspiracy to overthrow the laws of the Senate. His voice rising in anger, Pinchback continued. At midnight the previous evening Governor Warmoth and his friend Mr. C. E. Weed, the owner of the *New Orleans Evening Times*, had come to his door, where they "aroused me from my slumber, and made a proposition to me. They offered me $50,000 and said that I could name, and the appointment would be made...of any officers if I would enter into the conspiracy."

Pinchback continued, "I told them then and there that I would consider it." And he did, he said. Early the next morning he received an urgent note from Warmoth asking to meet, whatever his decision, as soon as possible. He ignored that request, instead responding with a note. "I have slept on the proposition you made last night," he wrote, "and have resolved to do my duty to my state, party and race, and I therefore respectfully decline your proposition.

"I am truly sorry for you, but I cannot help you."

It was an astonishing moment: he was accusing the most powerful politician in the state of committing a serious crime. And, for at least some people, equally astonishing was his claim that he had rejected the offer. When the hubbub finally subsided, he addressed the Warmoth senators directly and told them he knew what they were trying to do and added, "Had your conspiracy succeeded the Constitution and the laws would have again been trampled underfoot."

Senator McMillen was not at all satisfied. Once again, he began protesting that these decisions were arbitrary, they were unconstitutional. Pinchback had no right to make these rulings because he was not the legal and lawfully elected lieutenant governor. He had been a member of the State Senate when elected, and the Constitution specifically prohibits anyone holding two elective offices.

When Pinchback tried to gavel him quiet, McMillen simply raised his voice. I will not be silenced, he yelled, pounding his fist on his desk—until finally, he was silenced by the lieutenant governor.

The House of Representatives, also meeting in special session, voted overwhelmingly to impeach the governor for high crimes and misdemeanors in office and crimes committed against the Constitution and the laws of the state. The seven articles of impeachment included "unconstitutional and unlawful" commissions of judges and government officials, conspiring to restrict the right to vote and offering a $50,000 bribe and the dispensation of patronage to Pinchback.

The resolution was presented to the Senate by a House committee. The Senate took the appropriate parliamentary actions. By law, Warmoth was removed from office. According to the state constitution, that vacancy was filled by the lieutenant governor. Thirty-five-year-old Pinckney Benton Stewart Pinchback became the first Black governor in American history. And he would serve until newly elected Governor Kellogg was inaugurated in January.

In that evening's *Times* Weed admitted to being at the meeting with Pinchback but denied hearing Warmoth make any such offer. Later Pinchback issued a minor clarification in front of the Senate. "I owe it to Mr. Weed to state that he was not present at the meeting, as in my heat I first suggested." Mr. Weed had made the initial approach, he explained, asking him to meet with Warmoth at the St. Charles Hotel. Pinchback instead suggested a meeting in his parlor. The governor was nearby and arrived minutes later. "When the Governor came in," Pinchback continued, "he was careful to have the folding doors closed, leaving Mr. Weed alone in one room... The Governor was too wily to have any witnesses, doubtless thinking that in a question of veracity he could outswear me."

In the ensuing days Warmoth barely responded to the accusations. When he did finally speak, he objected to Pinchback being allowed to make claims without him having the opportunity to "disprove the statements." And he could refute them, he claimed, at least partially because "I think we will show that Mr. Pinchback is not in the habit of resisting such temptations."

Pinchback previously had been accused of wheeling and dealing. Stories had circulated that he had bought and sold public property while serving as parks commissioner. But nothing had ever been proved. That was not at all surprising.

Acting Governor Pinchback was himself an astute politician. Tall, bearded and handsomely fit, he was the child of racially mixed parents, his father being a Mississippi planter, his mother a slave he had freed. After leaving school to support his family he had served in the military and worked as a political organizer and aboard riverboats, where gamblers had befriended him and taught him their tricks. But more than anything else, he was smart, clever, personable and perhaps as ambitious and ethically adaptable as Henry Warmoth.

For some men, a moment like this might have proved too much: Pinchback embraced it. He had been preparing for the limelight his whole life. "It is said he is vain of his good looks and he certainly is possessed of very comely features," wrote the

Times-Picayune. "He is scrupulously neat in his dress, the only display indulged in being three large and very brilliant diamond studs and a massive gold watch chain.

"He was very fond of displaying his person on the avenues. If he could see a half dozen opera glasses leveled at him…he would be supremely happy…but he has a treacherous look about the eyes and is naturally very suspicious, but can easily be thrown off guard by a little flattery."

A perfect match for Henry Warmoth.

Impeaching a man as popular as Warmoth and elevating Pinchback to the office just required sufficient votes from the legislature. But enforcing that ruling was far more difficult. That might require federal intervention. Senator Kellogg telegraphed the attorney general, warning that "a conflict may ensue."

Grant hesitated.

While the Kellogg legislature was meeting at the Mechanics Institute, Warmoth assembled McEnery's supporters at Lyceum Hall, a large theater that had been founded to host intellectual gatherings but after the end of the war had been given over to theater and performances. Inside the crowded hall, plans were laid to organize a political rebellion—to form a rival legislature consisting mostly of Democrats who claimed to have been legally elected.

Two governments were being formed.

The next day, thousands of McEnery Democrats rallied outside City Hall. McEnery spoke first, telling an already-boisterous crowd that there were no laws by which "we are prohibited from assembling and petitioning the…government for relief from the oppressions…imposed on us.…

"We want law and order maintained and the candidates fairly elected put in their places."

When he concluded his remarks Warmoth stepped forward and told the outraged people what they had come to hear. There was no question that McEnery had won the election! They were being cheated out of a great victory! He still had the returns in his possession, he told them: "How can they decide whether or not this or that officer is elected?"

Warmoth presented impressive figures to prove his point, although those figures were subject to interpretation. "The total number of votes polled was 128,402 of which number John McEnery had received 68,169 and William Pitt Kellogg 60,233... the Returns likewise showed the election to the House of Representatives of about seventy-five Fusion members and about thirty-five Republican members." But "without even adopting or following any rational theory of computation [Republicans] added the enormous number of 12,657 to Senator Kellogg's vote...and to further insult the intelligence of the public had deliberately struck off 14,140 from the votes cast for Senator McEnery!"

No one could doubt these numbers, he said. No one! They were "proved by the returns sworn to by the Commissioner of Elections and the Supervisors of Registration... These returns are in existence. They are unmutilated and unfalsified. They constitute the only evidence of the late election any law recognizes or that any honest judicial tribunal would accept!... The Judge of the United States Court became a confederate of the conspirators..."

The crowd roared in support of each claim. Cheating! Fraud! Lies! Their opponents would use any tactic to defeat him. Warmoth was the most honest man in the history of the great state and his rivals were afraid of him—and afraid of the people who were fighting for the truth.

The crowd loved him. They adored him. They would follow him wherever he led.

That same afternoon a so-called people's government organized at Lyceum Hall. Reporting this, the *New York Times* warned, "Warmoth, in every way, is endeavoring to incite his followers to revolution and to overthrow the legitimate state government." In his effort he had the assistance of Weed's *Times*, which "by the incendiary appeals...is exciting the populace and violence is, by some, apprehended."

The situation was becoming increasingly dangerous. About three hundred and fifty members of the state militia, reinforced by an additional hundred volunteers, took over the Carondelet Street armory, where they had ready access to weapons and ammunition. They would not recognize the Pinchback government, they announced, and would not obey his orders.

What could not be settled by ballots might now be settled by bullets. Warmoth's militia locked all the entrances. They settled in, vowing not to leave until Governor Warmoth's government was restored. And if Pinchback's people tried to get them out... well, they would resist. Violently if necessary.

While negotiations to prevent a confrontation were ongoing, the real circus came to town. P. T. Barnum's ten tents comprised "a museum, menagerie, caravan, hippodrome, polytechnic institute, zoological, cavalcade of chariots and circus for one admission fee." If two legislatures competing for legitimacy and hundreds of soldiers holed up in an armory threatening an insurrection weren't enough of a show, Barnum brought with him thousands of "novel and interesting attractions never before seen!" Among them, he boasted, were three Wild Fuji Cannibals ransomed from King Thokamban at a cost of $16,000, a snake charmer, a rhinoceros, a drove of camels and performing elephants and one hundred performing equestrians, acrobats and "Ladies in Mediaeval Costumes." Those who purchased a copy of Barnum's 960-page autobiography at the reduced price of $2.25 would receive free admission to the show!

As the standoff at the armory went into a second day Warmoth was trying to set up his own state government under the direction of McEnery. Tremendous pressure was put on senators and representatives to defect. Each man had to figure out which legislature to support. Careers were at stake. Several members finally crossed the street to join Warmoth, enough of them to allow the Lyceum assembly to claim it had a quorum. It elected a speaker and went to work.

Meanwhile, Democrats formed the Committee of One Hundred Citizens, among them the leading businessmen in New Orleans, to go to Washington to present their case to President Grant and Congress. They brought with them a petition signed by thousands of people supporting Warmoth and McEnery, stating, "This is the greatest outrage ever attempted to be carried out in our country... It is the universal belief that the case had been misrepresented and the facts greatly distorted."

Not to be outdone, Kellogg and James Casey appealed to President Grant to "quiet matters" by recognizing "Governor Pinchback's legislature." Kellogg asked the president to send federal troops "for the protection of the legislature and the gubernatorial office."

Warmoth and McEnery also sent telegrams, but theirs implored Grant to stay out of it. "I ask that no violent action be taken," Warmoth wrote, "and no force be used by the government." McEnery begged the president to make no decision until he had met with the delegation and they could "lay before you all the facts."

It seemed like there was a new development every minute. Extra editions of newspapers were "flying around the city like leaves in autumn." Even Barnum's doubled-humped Bactrian camel, reputed to be the only such animal in the country, couldn't distract people from this confusing, dangerous situation.

Pinchback finally decided he would wait no longer. He ordered the Metropolitan Police department to take the armory. At about seven o'clock that night two hundred police officers, carrying Winchester rifles, "plentifully supplied with ball cartridges," made a line across Carondelet Street to await the order to attack. Spectators rushed to the site to see the confrontation.

The chief of police was escorted into the building to meet with the militia commander. He was told that the garrison had orders from Governor Warmoth to hold the arsenal against "all authority except that of the United States." And they intended to follow those orders.

Their allegiance to Warmoth defied description. It appeared they were willing to die, or kill, for him. The question was why? They knew he was corrupt; no one seriously doubted Pinchback's story about the $50,000 bribe offer, they knew he had profited greatly during his time in office, and he was known to like a drink and dally with women. He was a carpetbagger, a Lincoln man. But none of that seemed to make much difference to them. They forgave him all of that. He understood them; he had touched a part of them that only a few others had reached. He was fighting for them, for the way of life they once had lived.

He was fighting against the powers who had beaten them. So they gave him their loyalty.

When he attacked Pinchback, claiming he had stolen the office, slurring and insulting him, they reacted. Pinchback's life was threatened. An unsigned note warned, "If you do not resign the office of the acting Governor within three days beware, for on the fourth from this date you will be dead, stabbed in the heart."

From then on, Metropolitan Police officers began guarding the acting governor.

Over the next few hours, the situation at the garrison escalated slowly. As soon as the Metropolitan Police chief left, the militia sent out men to guard the entrance. When they appeared the Metro officers cocked their Winchesters—and took aim. No one was getting in or out. Rations were passed in through a window at the rear of the building.

Two hours later the police were ordered back to a nearby station house. Rumors spread that they were preparing to assault the building at three o'clock in the morning.

President Grant had been reluctant to interfere in a state matter. But he finally relented now that lives were at stake. Attorney General Williams sent a telegraph to Kellogg confirming it. "You are recognized by the President as the lawful executive of Louisiana, and the body assembled at Mechanics Institute is the lawful legislature of the State…all necessary assistance will be given to you…to protect the state from disorder and violence."

He sent a similar telegraph to McEnery, telling him bluntly not to bother sending the delegation. The president's decision is made, he wrote, "and will not be changed."

That was devastating to their cause. Warmoth was irate, comparing Grant to the king of Great Britain, who had imposed his will on the colonies. These messages were proof that the conspiracy to overthrow the State government was rooted in Washington. A reporter described Warmoth as "somewhat despairing. 'There was never a more wicked outrage consummated,' said he, with much feeling. 'I saw men, strong men, weep tonight at their helplessness to avert the awful future open to them. Louisiana is irredeemably ruined unless relieved…'"

Grant's action was debated across the nation. The *Chicago Times* reported, "The quarrel now seems to be whether the people of the State have the right to govern themselves, or whether the troops of the United States can step in and elect who shall legislate for the State… The military power seems to be the stronger of the two."

With the debate seemingly decided, the Metropolitan Police stood down. The city breathed.

Most members of the Democrats' committee had decided to go to Washington even after Grant's telegram had arrived; if they couldn't change the president's mind they would try to find support in the Congress. As one delegate remembered, "Thousands and thousands of people assembled around the [railroad] cars when we left, to bid us 'God speed.' It was the most mournful assemblage I ever saw."

At almost the same moment the train was picking up steam

Union Brigadier General W. H. Smith went to the arsenal. He was there to demand the militia's surrender, he announced, and if necessary would use troops to enforce that order. The president had authorized him to "use all necessary force to preserve the peace." The militia commander replied that to prevent bloodshed, his men would leave the building.

Soon afterward, to great cheers from supporters, the militia marched proudly out of the armory.

While it would be several decades before superstitious Americans would consider Friday the 13th a risky day, it proved to be bad luck for Warmoth. In Washington, the Supreme Court threw out his lawyers' request for a writ prohibiting Pinchback from accepting the returns from the Lynch Board. The Court ruled it simply did not have the legal right to interfere in state politics.

Anticipating legal action, newly appointed Governor Pinchback had nominated a new slate of judges and government officials. That turned out to be crucial once Eighth District Court Judge Elmore found Pinchback guilty of "repeated and continued contempt" for ignoring his injunction and ordered that he be arrested and imprisoned for ten days and fined fifty dollars. He ignored that ruling and, when a sheriff's deputy tried to serve the writ, informed him that a day earlier the legislature had abolished the Eighth Court. The court ceased to exist, Elmore was no longer a judge and his injunction was worthless. As the *New York Times* informed its readers on its front page, "The presence of the United States soldiers rather dampened the ardor of the would-be deputy and he hastily retired, considering discretion the better part of valor."

Similar scenes were taking place throughout the city and state as men declared elected by the Lynch Returning Board took their seats or offices. It was not always peaceful. A substantial number of Warmoth supporters had squeezed into Judge Monroe's Third District courtroom after he had made it known he was not going to be removed. When newly elected Judge Meunier stood to be recognized and present his commission, Monroe refused to surrender the bench. The Lynch Board returns were "untrue and illegal," he said, and it was his duty to maintain possession of that bench on behalf of the people of Louisiana who had elected him. Meunier's attorney told Judge Monroe in the politest legal language that he had no case, and if it became necessary the sheriff—the duly elected sheriff— would remove him by force.

Judge Monroe fought back. "I command the Sheriff....not to obey... If he does so he is assisting those who are subverting the Government and overthrowing the temple of liberty!" When the deputy sheriff ordered him to step down, the judge said he wanted it known he was not vacating the bench but being compelled to by force. "You have taken the courtroom, books and archives," he said bitterly, "and the responsibility is yours. The right to these things remains in me and in the people of this state."

Other people had to choose between loyalty and a job. Civil Sheriff Harper, for example, had been appointed to the position by Warmoth. Pinchback offered him a new commission in the same post—and to the disdain of the Warmoth people he accepted it. That made him a Pinchback man. He had to switch sides to keep the same job.

The confusion was almost impossible to sort out in the two legislatures. Warmoth was a realist. He knew the Lyceum legislature could not pass or execute any laws, but believed it was vital to keep it intact until all legal and political avenues were exhausted. Perhaps more important, and far more dangerous, was the fact that at least half or maybe even more of the population supported Warmoth's legislature. Whether its actions were legally codified, they would obey those decisions. They believed strongly they had been cheated out of victory, and they were not going to concede.

The makeup of the two bodies changed daily. Sometimes hourly. Both sides had difficulty raising a quorum. Secret inducements were offered and sometimes accepted, resulting in a continuous flow of senators and representatives moving back and forth across the street.

After a couple of weeks, Warmoth's so-called people's legislature concluded its "special session," announcing it would meet in the regular session scheduled for January. When it closed, several senators went across the street and joined the so-called Bayonet legislature—identified by that name because it was meeting with the protection of armed soldiers—so they actually were listed as members of both groups.

The Bayonet legislature stayed in session, fearful if they left the State House at the Mechanics Institute vacant, Warmoth's people would take possession. Much of its work consisted of approving nominees for government positions or dealing with budgetary issues, among them an appropriation to reimburse members for travel to and from the special session. They also met to consider the ongoing impeachment effort but, at the request of Warmoth's counsel, agreed to postpone the trial till early January.

But the assembly suddenly took an unexpected turn, passing extremely controversial laws restricting the constitutional rights of people to bear arms and to assemble in protest.

These were breathtaking pieces of legislation. These rights were bedrock principles on which the country was founded. The "Act to suppress riotous and unlawful assemblies" was passed primarily to prevent the people's legislature from meeting, but it had far greater consequences. The first part of the bill prohibited "three or more people being armed with clubs or other dangerous weapons...with intent to disturb the public peace" from acting together. The second clause made it illegal for "ten or more persons to unlawfully assemble...for an unlawful purpose."

Intent was not defined, leaving it to local law enforcement to make that determination. As a reporter pointed out, the definition might include three men with walking sticks standing peacefully in conversation on a corner, leaving it up to law enforcement to decide if they constituted a danger.

Another bill granted the governor the right to disband the militia and seize its weapons if its officers refuse to obey his orders. This was done to prevent a repeat of the embarrassing siege of the armory. The legislature handed enormous power to the state executive.

The Warmoth media was irate. "No *intents* are cognizable by law," the *Times-Picayune* wrote. "The constitution not only guarantees 'the right of the people to keep and bear arms shall not be infringed,' but makes it the duty of the Government of the United States to provide for 'arming' them as militia 'necessary to secure the security of a free state.'… Their appeal to arms may, however, show not only their consciousness of wrong, but the fears wrong always engenders…"

These bills would be tested on January 6, when Warmoth's legislature was scheduled to convene. No one knew if Pinchback would attempt to prevent that from happening. The city prepared for what seemed like an unavoidable, violent confrontation. McEnery issued a statement asking his supporters to act with prudence, dignity, firmness and moderation. Be calm, he pleaded. "In the midst of…an attempted overthrow of your liberties by an organized conspiracy, show to the people of the United States a dignity of bearing…for the maintenance of your liberties and constitutional rights… The government of the United States will not exert its great power to put down and suppress peaceable assemblies…"

But in case fighting did erupt, more than a thousand infantry troops and one cavalry company stationed in Baton Rouge quickly moved into the city "to preserve peace."

Early on the morning of the sixth "there was considerable stir throughout the city." At nine thirty a cavalry regiment made a public show, marching up Royal Street to the barracks on Magazine Street. A rumor that troops had occupied Lafayette Square proved unfounded. By ten thirty an estimated fifteen thousand people filled all the streets around the squares to protect the McEnery legislature. No one was even sure where they would meet; the city council had refused to allow them to continue using Lyceum Hall. Several other large spaces also had turned them down. Finally, at noon, fourteen senators and forty-seven representatives took possession of Odd Fellows Hall. The first thing that body did was hang an American flag out the window.

The soldiers stayed in their barracks. A token police force mostly stayed away from the area. There were no incidents. Within minutes the legislature adjourned as it did not have a quorum. But the point had been made. Warmoth still had fight left.

The breakdown of the electoral process and its impact on democracy had become major news in every city and town in the country and had even spread to Europe. The whole glorious American experiment in self-government was being tested— and seemed to be failing. No one had anticipated the collapse of the electoral system, so no one knew how to proceed. Newspapers as far away as the *London Morning Post* reported the story as it developed.

"There is no city in the United States so unique and interesting as is New Orleans," the *Morning Post* wrote as it attempted to explain this complicated situation to British readers. "No city in America has so great a variety of inhabitants as this, with such striking contrasts as manners, language and complexion…a population remarkable for personal beauty, for gaiety of disposition, and for hotness of temper…

"The elections were held and the two sets of returns in due time arrived at the capital. Those sent to the supervisors to the Governor gave to M'Enery a majority of about 10,000; but those forwarded to the marshal by his deputies not only were accompanied by affidavits from 4,000 Negro voters setting forth that they had been unlawfully prevented from voting, but showed a majority for Kellogg of 14,000 or, including the extended votes, 18,000. It was evident that one, if not both of the two parties was engaged in 'a big fraud'..."

The governor was legally stopped from counting the votes, the story continued, but he violated that injunction and declared his candidate, McEnery, and McEnery's entire ticket the winner. In response, the other side got from a judge an order for the seizure and occupation of the State House. "But now the blood of Warmoth was up, and he summoned an extraordinary meeting of the Legislature… Warmoth delivered to them a flaming message…then issued a proclamation warning all good citizens to disregard the 'revolutionary and unlawful body' assembled at the State House. The reply to this was the passage by this body of a resolution impeaching Warmoth and removing him from office.

"Warmoth retorted by ordering the State officers to obey only him and calling out the state militia to enforce his orders. And Pinchback followed suit by issuing a similar proclamation, accompanied by the very plain hint that military forces of the United States were at his back. Another day would have seen an armed collision between the rival Governors and the rival legislatures. But President Grant interfered and prevented bloodshed if he did not secure justice…

"But if this be Republicanism, what is Imperialism?"

That was as neat a summation of events as had been published. But it stopped there, not daring to predict what might come next. As it turned out, that would have been impossible.

8

On January 14, 1873, the *New York Times* reported that New York City was troubled by "a large number [of] destitute Italian immigrants...who have recently arrived." Apparently, they had congregated on Fourteenth Street "and presented a most miserable spectacle." There was great debate in the city about how to deal with this serious problem; apparently there were many suggestions but few answers.

In Illinois that day the governor Richard Oglesby was inaugurated. This was his second term in office. Among the problems the state was facing, he told the crowd, was the "unprofitableness of farming...due primarily to railroad charges," and recent changes in the criminal justice system which disqualified potential jurors in criminal cases "who were readers of the news of the day...

"The law should go further," he said, "and declare every person competent as a juror who may state in open court that he has an opinion based on rumor or representations of the facts made by those he knows, provided that any bias or opinion will not prevent him from rendering a verdict according to the evidence given in the case."

And in New Orleans "a more beautiful day could not have been imagined...the weather was clear and mild and the sun's bright rays had a most cheering effect on all." It was a day that would long be remembered in Louisiana history. Unlike Illinois, they were inaugurating two governors!

Both political parties proceeded with their celebrations without any acknowledgment of the other. Both ceremonies began around noon. In the center of Lafayette Square Democrats had erected a large platform, raised five feet off the ground and decorated with red, white and blue bunting. An American flag hung above its front. Just below the flag was a large wreath bearing one word: *Hope.*

Thousands of people had begun gathering hours before, wilting in the morning heat to secure a place close to the platform. A brass band entertained them with lively tunes, the bright sun glinting off the gold horns. A photographer had set up his four-wheeled shop in front of City Hall. Thirty or more invited dignitaries sat waiting patiently on the platform. Just after noon, impeached Governor Warmoth and Democratic candidate John McEnery emerged from Odd Fellows Hall and climbed the broad stairway as thousands of supporters welcomed them.

If McEnery's inauguration was a raucous celebration, Kellogg's was a somber ceremony. Republicans gathered inside the State House to inaugurate the governor-elect. Sunlight squeezed through clouded windows. Soldiers guarded all entrances and patrolled the corridors, extra rifles stacked in the halls. A thousand spectators, the majority of them Black men, had come for the ceremony. Among them Judge Durell, who sat with the women. One by one invited guests were stopped at the entrance and identified before being allowed to enter. When the guests were seated, as the band played "Not for Joseph," Acting Governor Pinchback escorted Kellogg into the chamber to loud but respectful applause.

The next day the *Times-Picayune* would report snidely that the band actually had played the British anthem, "God Save the Queen."

Both men were sworn into office. Kellogg spoke at great length, but rather than the array of promises typical of such an address he painted a somewhat dismal portrait of the state. "No effective means have been adopted to supply the greatest needs of the people," he said, reciting a litany of unresolved problems. Eventually, though, he addressed the current situation. He won, he said. He won by actual votes, and he won even after the Democrats had prevented people from voting and stuffed ballot boxes. "I would not hold an office to which I did not believe myself elected," he said, and he welcomed "the fullest investigation" so that "the action taken by the courts and the national administration may be vindicated."

As he left the platform the band played a jaunty version of "The Star-Spangled Banner."

Outside, in the bright sunshine, Governor Warmoth spoke first. He began by citing his accomplishments: he had built or strengthened 468 levees, stretching almost 200 miles; 300 miles of new railroad track had been laid, and soon New Orleans would be connected by rail to Shreveport and Houston. But then he turned dark and angry, using this opportunity to attack his detractors and defend his record. His words oozed bitterness as he referred to his impeachment, reminding the massive crowd that despite all of the charges pending against him not one "human being dared to raise his hand in the presence of God and deliver a jot of testimony against my official honor."

Several hundred Metropolitan policemen stayed ready inside the Lafayette Square station and by the Carondelet armory. Mostly they were bored, and the day passed remarkably peacefully. A reporter noted that the officers passed the time playing seven-up, euchre and draw poker.

GOVERNOR KELLOGG.

Both inaugurations ended at roughly the same time, but not a single confrontation between departing spectators was reported. Governor McEnery held his inauguration gala at the Exposition Hotel that night. It was a grand affair; according to the *Times-Picayune*, one that "probably exceeds anything of the kind ever held in this city, both as regards to the number and respectability of the attendance."

Governor Kellogg did not hold a reception, but the next day Republican Senator J. Henri Burch poured a strong dose of reality on the Democrats. He was confronted by a smug McEnery supporter, who chided, "Well, Senator, what do you think of our grand inauguration?" He replied, "I think that it was all out of doors, where you and your governor are sure to remain." And then he walked off.

As the media pointed out, it had been a glorious day for McEnery, but it was a show lacking any substance. People might address him as governor, they might treat him as governor, but he had no more power to perform a single legal act than the corner smithy.

Both legislatures convened the next day. If the system wasn't paralyzed, it certainly was crippled. Kellogg's assembly was able to cobble together a quorum, so legally it could debate and pass bills, but that had no real meaning. Any legislation that was passed would be ignored by McEnery's supporters.

The first order of business in both the State House and in Odd Fellows Hall was electing a senator to fill Kellogg's seat in Washington—even though it was unlikely the Senate would admit any man from Louisiana until the mess was sorted out. The Senate is the sole judge of the qualifications of its members and can admit or reject any candidate. Senate leaders instructed its Committee of Privileges and Elections to determine if the state even had a legal government—and, if it found one existed, to decide "of whom it was constituted."

An amendment to that resolution suggested that if the committee found there was no government, it should inquire when it ceased to exist and if any federal officer had anything to do with its overthrow. The committee chairman, Republican Oliver Perry Morton, summoned the rival Returning Boards to Washington for a hearing.

Meanwhile, Republicans elected P. B. S. Pinchback, making him the second Black senator in American history—if he was seated. The party celebrated this nomination, exclaiming, "We proudly point to a man of color, self-made, self-taught, filling every position in this state with remarkable ability and honor..." deserving a position "on a par with Clay, Webster and Adams." With misguided optimism they claimed "a mountain of prejudice and ill-feeling...has been swept away to eternal perdition."

The Democrats struggled to pick their nominee—even if there was little chance he would ever take office. The potential selection of Henry Warmoth threatened to rip the party apart. Traditional Democrats and reform elements of the party despised him and refused to support him, warning that if he was forced on them they would break up the legislature. His supporters, meanwhile, accused those people of bad faith and warned that if Warmoth did not get the seat they would bolt.

To try to resolve the impasse a committee of mainliners met with him and essentially begged him to withdraw his name from consideration. Withdrawing from a fight was not something Henry Warmoth did. While complaining that this candidacy "is of the smallest importance" to him and would involve great expense, he was firm that "a majority of people of this state do not believe what has been said about me, and if the legislature is permitted to express its wishes independent of threats and promises, they will give me their voice."

One newspaper compared him to the notorious Englishman Colonel Francis Charteris, who once said he would pay ten thousand pounds for a good reputation—because he then could use that to make fifty thousand pounds.

Warmoth received the most votes but not the necessary majority. Because the newly elected Senate's session would not begin for several weeks, Democrats bought some time by nominating William McMillen to fill Kellogg's seat for the remainder of the term.

The contest between Pinchback and Warmoth was reported nationally, although the *New York Herald* concluded, "It will be a humiliating spectacle to see either of them admitted to the Senate of the United States."

Given the confusion, the Senate decided not to allow the seat to be filled until there was a resolution.

For a man without an office Warmoth remained the focus of attention. His actions and words sold newspapers. He also was busy preparing to defend himself against impeachment, even though his term had expired and he was no longer in office. There was no logic to moving forward with it, of course, but where Warmoth was concerned, logic had long since been abandoned. He still engendered intense emotions in both supporters and detractors, and his enemies were loath to let him off the hook. Their fear was that, somehow, Warmoth would emerge again, perhaps as a Democratic senator, and thus he had to be convicted and stopped.

Before it went much further the chief justice of the State Supreme Court, John Ludeling—who had been appointed to the court by Warmoth—ruled that an impeachment proceeding should be confined to people currently holding office. The expense, he decided, just wasn't worth it. The Senate dismissed the charges.

Normally after an election, the losing side becomes the opposition. Sometimes loyal, often loud, they use the time to position themselves for the next election. But in this election there was no obvious losing side, and neither Republicans nor Democrats were willing to take that position. The two legislatures continued meeting daily, although Democrats were finding it increasingly difficult to raise a quorum as several members had become bored and had gone home or, in a few cases, had joined the minority inside the State House. The McEnery people denied his supporters were defecting, instead boasting about their legislature. "Those gentlemen have been pledged seventy-five dollars a week for as long as they are in session, and it is the most profitable line they ever struck…you couldn't drive them home with a club."

The Republican majority tried to move forward with the business of governing. On most days, what takes place in a state legislative body lacks drama. People are appointed to positions, financial matters are debated and voted upon, rules and regulations are promulgated, pet projects are pushed forward. It's a mishmash of the bits and pieces necessary to keep the government running as smoothly as possible. While Kellogg's legislature mostly followed that path, occasionally it pushed hard to consolidate its political power.

Only days after going to work, it passed a bill entitled "An act to regulate proceedings in contestations between persons claiming judicial office." As with almost every other elective position, both the Republican and Democratic candidates for judges were claiming victory. As Judge Durell and Judge Dibble had demonstrated, control of the judicial system is the foundation of political control. This bill passed through both houses and was signed by the governor in one day, literally giving incumbent judges twenty-four hours to vacate their bench and limiting any legal appeal.

The bill was passed specifically to put Judge Philip H. Morgan on the State Supreme Court. The previous November Warmoth had appointed Judge John Kennard to a vacant seat on the court. After taking office, Pinchback named Philip Morgan to the same seat. Kennard refused to give it up, instead suing. When the state courts ruled against him, Kennard took his case to the US Supreme Court, which placed it on the docket.

With that, all three branches of the federal government, including both Houses of Congress, had become involved in trying to figure out how to deal with the Louisiana situation.

In late December President Grant had finally agreed to meet with the Democratic Committee of One Hundred Concerned Citizens. As a Republican, it obviously was to his advantage for the Kellogg Republicans to maintain control of Louisiana's state government. The committee was "courteously received and patiently listened to." After hearing their request for an investigation, the president reiterated his belief that he had no power in the situation. But he did open a window just barely, telling them he had no objection to the Supreme Court, or even Congress for that matter, conducting an investigation. Unfortunately, he told them, he had no right to either authorize or pay for an investigation into a state election.

That would not be a problem, the committee assured him, as several patriotic men surely could be found to volunteer to do that work. The president also agreed, "with great pleasure," to submit their petition to Congress. Just by meeting with them Grant had given them hope, and by agreeing not to block anything, he had, in fact, sent a message to Congress that he did not object to an investigation.

Congress was already involved. In mid-December, the House passed a resolution authorizing the Judiciary Committee to determine what might be done "to guard against the dangers threatening the liberties of the people of Louisiana" and several other Southern states. It also asked President Grant for guidance, which came on January 13 when he submitted to the House the petition and supporting evidence given to him by the Committee.

The process proceeded legally, which meant much too slowly for Louisiana Democrats. The problem was handed to the House Judiciary Committee, with orders to sort out the situation and suggest...something. Anything. It wasn't clear that the House had the power to take action, even if it wanted to, which obviously it did not, so it followed the proven path: it gave it to a committee where it might disappear.

The Senate was doing the same thing. It would not seat a senator while the Committee on Privileges tried to figure out if Louisiana even had a state government. After refusing to allow any delegates from Louisiana to cast its electoral votes in the presidential election between Grant and the late Horace Greeley, the Senate also asked that committee to "inquire into the defects of the present electoral system and the best means of remedying them." In supporting that resolution, Illinois senator Lyman Trumball, chairman of the Judiciary Committee, argued that the country was founded as a republic, not a pure democracy. "It was not intended that the majority should have all the power," he said. "To put the government on that basis would prepare the way to a despotism."

And the Supreme Court was preparing to hear arguments about which judges could be seated.

In Louisiana, both legislatures continued to meet regularly, although no one could be certain from day-to-day if a quorum would be present. John McEnery continued to play the role of governor, appointing local tax collectors and assessors. Republicans ignored him. The *Weekly Louisianian* suggested, "as far as the validity of this...he might as well appoint a few for Mississippi, Maine or California or China," and reminded people "not to regard the attempts of these tax assessors and tax collectors [to collect taxes] as they are utterly without authorization to enforce their assessments."

What the newspapers missed completely, and what Republicans had not realized, was that these appointments were part of a broad plan "suggested" by Warmoth to resist the Kellogg government. One of Warmoth's last actions in office had been to form "an association of concerned citizens to resist unconstitutional taxes."

Unconstitutional in this case meaning any attempt by Pinchback or Kellogg to collect regular taxes.

If Republicans had expected McEnery to grow bored of this standoff and fade away, they could not have been more wrong. McEnery was a Warmoth disciple. He wasn't going anywhere. He believed that he had been robbed in the election. Republicans had stolen it from him.

He was going to fight for it. No matter how long it took, no matter how many people got hurt.

Two weeks earlier the Odd Fellows legislature had voted to prohibit payment of taxes to Kellogg's appointed collectors. It signaled the beginning of a Democratic plan to stage a tax strike, which would deprive the Kellogg government of the revenue it needed to govern. McEnery eventually issued an order warning all tax and license payers in New Orleans "to refuse and resist... any notice or demand" from "certain persons pretending to be tax collectors and threatening penalties or violence," promising that his government guaranteed full protection.

Which it could not provide. Any power McEnery had to influence events came solely from the loyalty of his followers. Not a shred of it was legal or constitutional. But if enough people followed his directions, he remained a real threat to the Kellogg government.

This proclamation was a test of his power. How far did their loyalty extend? For the first time his followers would have to break the law. They would transition from spectator to participant. Refusing to pay state taxes or a license fee was an act of civil disobedience—with potentially serious penalties. They could be fined or, in extreme instances, imprisoned.

Each man had to decide how much he would risk.

The various investigations slowly ground forward. The situation was deteriorating, anger was growing. It was obvious no decision would satisfy everyone, so legislators were trying to agree on a solution that might prevent violence. On January 24, the State Supreme Court ruled that the Lynch Returning Board was the legal one and Kellogg was therefore governor.

That same day representatives of the Lynch and Warmoth Returning Boards arrived in Washington to appear before the Senate Committee on Privileges and Elections. They brought with them four large trunkloads of returns and affidavits, as well as additional documents that would help them make their case. While the hearing had been convened specifically to determine which senator had been elected, it was in effect an attempt to settle the election.

All of the significant players journeyed to the Capitol for the hearing. Warmoth and Pinchback, McEnery and Kellogg, judges and generals, all of them sat in the same room and answered questions for more than a week.

It didn't take long for the proceedings to heat up. Soon after the hearing began, a Republican attorney asked permission to present evidence that Warmoth had offered Pinchback a bribe to allow him to take control of the legislature. Warmoth replied that he had no objection to that—*but* he had to summon witnesses from New Orleans to prove it was not true. Then he added, almost as an aside, that it was well-known "Pinchback was not in the habit of resisting temptation of that kind."

Pinchback glared at him. "If you can establish anything of that kind, Governor," he challenged, "I think you ought to do it."

Warmoth shrugged. "Well, if the committee wants to take that latitude, I have no objection."

For the first of several times during the next few days spectators and reporters were asked to leave while senators decided exactly how deeply they were willing to explore the situation. It was safest to stay on the well-trod path. The story of the attempted bribe was not relevant, they decided.

Witness by witness, each side made its case. Warmoth claimed that members of the Lynch Board admitted "that they demanded of me the official returns and...without having received them they made up the composition of the legislature." They had relied on everything except actual votes, from affidavits to their own opinion.

Republicans countered that thousands of registered, legal voters had been denied the right to cast their ballots. For residents of the mostly Black Plaquemines Parish, for example, the nearest poll had been opened thirty-five miles away.

Democrats did not dispute that—instead, they claimed that affidavits supposedly signed by people who had been denied their right to vote had been forged. A witness was asked, "Under whose administration did that take place?"

Governor Warmoth.

Governor Warmoth perked up when that accusation was made. "Was I present?" he asked.

"No," the witness replied, "you were not."

"What was said about it?" Warmoth asked.

The witness admitted sheepishly, "Mr. Sypher [his superior] told me not to let you know anything about it." The room burst into laughter.

For days, the testimony bounced back and forth; for every claim there was a counterclaim, for every accusation there was a more serious charge. It was a mix of fact and fiction, although it was impossible to determine which was which. After listening to this for several days the frustrated New York attorney Charles F. Southmayd told a witness it was enough to make a man's hair stand on end to see the manipulations which the returns had undergone.

When the investigation concluded, the participants returned to Louisiana to await the report. But time was running out for a peaceful solution.

On February 20, the Senate Committee issued its report. It had compiled more than a thousand pages of testimony. The report accomplished an almost impossible feat: it actually made the situation worse, further muddying the already-murky waters, giving just enough credence to both sides to allow them both to claim some sort of victory.

"The utmost that can be claimed for this decision," the decision read, "is that the court recognizes the Kellogg government as the government *de facto*, which may be conceded...whether it has been published by regular election or set up and published by the usurpation of the individuals composing it, sustained by the military forces of the United States..."

The election result was not a judicial question, it continued, so no court could answer it. It was a political question, "to be determined by the political department of the Government." But this political body refused to answer it.

Politicians didn't have the right to determine the outcome either, reported the politicians. "The constitution expressly gives to each state the organization of its own legislature," meaning Federal Judge Durell had no right to become involved, and therefore his decision supporting the Lynch Returning Board had no validity. Meaning the decision putting Kellogg in office was not legal. In fact, it continued, "the committee fails to find words with which to express their abhorrence of the action of Durell."

Had the election been conducted fairly, based on the returns the McEnery ticket should be recognized as the legal government. But further testimony proved the election had not been conducted fairly; therefore, the result couldn't be determined by the returns.

The majority of the committee concluded "There is no State Government at present existing in the State of Louisiana," which meant there was no legal legislature and so neither senator could be seated. To resolve the problem the Committee offered a bill it had written declaring the November election "null and void" and setting up an entirely new election the following May.

That bill included another astonishing suggestion: Governor Warmoth and all his appointed officials should be reinstated with full authority and remain in office until the next election.

Three minority opinions also were published. One of them stated that the frauds were not extensive enough to overturn the election, as Durell had done, and that McEnery should be recognized as Louisiana's governor. A second opinion stated that just as Federal Judge Durell had no right to interfere in a state election, the United States Senate had no right to involve itself in Louisiana's affairs, and Kellogg should stay in office until that state's legislature acted. The third dissent imagined a creative solution: rather than annulling the entire election, those members of the state legislature who both sides agreed had been fairly elected should meet, wherever possible determine which representatives and senators had won, and then that entire body should settle on the governor and lieutenant governor.

In what later proved to be a massive misjudgment, the *New York Times* speculated, "there is a feeling that if matters are left alone, time will heal the trouble and obviate Congressional interference."

The paper could not have been any more wrong. Democrats felt the Senate had confirmed what they already knew: the McEnery ticket had been cheated out of its victory. But politicians and judges had refused to rectify that outrage. The months of nominations and relentless campaigning, the contested vote, the fight over the Returning Boards, the myriad legal challenges and the endless political debates were done. The Democrats had pursued every path—and every attempt had been rebuffed.

No one really knew how far Warmoth would go in pursuit of power. Soon they would discover he had few boundaries.

The next morning the *Republican* boldly declared on its front page, "Warmoth Wants Blood: A Violent Revolution the Sole Hope." The story read, "A leading Fusionist declares that H. C. Warmoth had telegraphed Mr. McEnery that violence must be resorted to if necessary to establish his so-called government...

"So 'let chaos come.' He has nothing to lose and may do harm to his enemies; possibly from the wreck of others' political fortunes may mend his own."

Let chaos come.

Warmoth once again had seized the opportunity to place himself at the center of events. In other accounts, the telegram he sent to McEnery actually urged, "If you are a government, do something to show it now. Action! Action! Action!"

Incendiary rumors began spreading. Supposedly Judge Elmore was to be reinstalled in the Eighth District Court, by force if necessary, and if the sheriff objected he, too, would be replaced. Once that was done, all the members of the legislature named to their seats by the Lynch Board were to be arrested and removed from the Mechanics Institute. Newspapers reported that the head of the state Artillery Battalion had met secretly in the night with the commanders of McEnery's militia and "pledged his allegiance for any enterprise that might be ordered." The officer denied that, but that story included too many details for it to be complete fiction.

In the middle of that same night several of New Orleans's most prominent and wealthy citizens went to Governor Kellogg's home to assure him of their continued support. He also received a reassuring telegram from the Grant administration, telling him, "Do not change your position in any respect. You will be fully sustained." An acceptable way of promising that should there be an uprising, the United States Army was prepared to put it down.

McEnery also got the message; he had to make a stand. His whole public posture toughened; his words became belligerent. He asked New Orleans mayor Louis Wiltz to pay his militia to protect the city rather than rely on the regular police force. The city council turned him down by a single vote.

Asked by a reporter the next day if he would lead the threatened tax strike, he was adamant. "The moment they dare to attempt this [the collection of taxes] I shall protect the citizens to the best of my power." Then he added ominously, "I shall not stop at bloodshed to protect them." The presence of federal troops would not deter him, he continued. "They would not dare meddle with us. There are not enough of them to take part in the struggle. No sir, there are not enough regulars in the state to whip us."

The city was alive with possibilities. The whispers grew in intensity. Something was coming. Keep your weapons close by.

"Recruiting for the attack on the government is uphill work," the *Republican* reported. "We do not think...there will be any blood spilled. The forces of the government are well in hand, well-armed and their esprit is all that could be desired... It is difficult in this practical age to get men to engage in a violation of the law wherein there is a reasonable certainty of getting killed or wounded."

In Washington, President Grant was trying desperately to stave off the rebellion. He called for an extra session of Congress. His hope was that the two parties might still find a compromise that would avoid federal interference. But admittedly there was "little prospect of heroic treatment."

Grant had few options. When it became clear Congress was not going to intercede, he finally had to take a stand. The president had proved his toughness during the war, so no one doubted his words. After noting that the existing situation—the two governors and two legislatures claiming to have been elected— had created confusion and uncertainty that had paralyzed the state, he said, "Having no opportunity or power to canvass the votes, and exigencies of the case demanding an immediate decision, I conceived it to be my duty to recognize those persons as elected, who received and held their credentials to office... from the legal returning board...

"I shall feel obligated, as far as I can by the exercise of legitimate authority, to put an end to the unhappy controversy which disturbs the peace...by the recognition and support of that government which is recognized and upheld by the courts of the States."

Kellogg.

It was a neat bit of political legerdemain. While acknowledging that the federal government had no right to interfere with state elections, he did exactly that by threatening to use federal troops to uphold the state court decision.

McEnery responded within hours, issuing an "official" proclamation calling upon "all citizens of the parish of Orleans, between the age of eighteen and forty-five, subject to and capable of militia duty, to report forthwith to the headquarters...for the purpose of enrollment and assignment to the several militia commands now in the process of organization."

The "people's legislature" supported him, passing a resolution calling on Governor McEnery "to use the civil and, if necessary, the military power of the State to reinstate the Judges...and sustain them in the exercise of their judicial powers."

The Civil War had ended eight years before. The war to end Reconstruction was just beginning.

9

The use of violence to achieve political aims was firmly ingrained in American history. Patrick Henry's legendary declaration "Give me liberty or give me death" had been a rallying cry of the Revolution. Decades later the nation had fought the Civil War over the failure to forge a political compromise about slavery.

The orderly and transparent electoral process created by the Constitution had been an attempt to prevent violence, not initiate it. The peaceful transition of political power on every level from town mayors to the presidency had been the foundation of democracy. The world noticed. Although there had been isolated incidents as well as complaints and challenges, with few exceptions it had worked amazingly well.

But there was no precedent for the events unfolding in Louisiana.

Depending on your point of view, Louisiana had two governments, or no government, or one legal government and one usurper. The only certain thing it had was a population that was divided and growing increasingly angry.

All legal options gone, McEnery began taking action. His supporters were meeting regularly to plot their strategy. On the night of February 9, as the Exposition Roller Skating Association scheduled its forthcoming tournament, and the Church of Sts. Peter and Paul was hosting its annual fair, Democrats were finalizing a plan to overthrow the Kellogg government. The leader of the attack would be Confederate Colonel Fred Ogden, a well-spoken man who sold cotton machinery by day and commanded the white militia at night. They would begin by seizing the main police stations, then attack the Cabildo—the former courthouse in which the Metropolitan Police armory was currently located. After capturing the weapons stored there they would then take control of the State House and install the people's legislature.

But spies leaked Ogden's plan to Kellogg, who responded by doubling the guards and bolstering security at the armory. The attack was postponed.

Warmoth remained at the heart of it, pushing, pushing, pushing. The *New York Herald* reported that he had left Washington the previous Saturday evening "on very important business. That business was to incite the supporters of the McEnery government to acts of violence."

Governor Kellogg, aware of the imminent danger, told the media, "Governor Warmoth telegraphs, urging a collision. I don't think the opposition can get strength enough; they are fast losing the confidence of the community…"

Although Warmoth's people denied he had taken this stance or sent such telegrams, it seemed likely to be true. The media was thrilled to be in the middle of it, circulating extra editions as fast as their presses could churn them out. Even the usually sympathetic *Picayune* warned "…the so-called McEnery Government, without a shadow of title under the law, was now endeavoring to stir up resistance to the actual Government—resistance which must lead to strife and bloodshed."

McEnery probed for weaknesses. The day after commanding all men from eighteen to forty-five to report for militia duty, he issued a notice to top police department officials ordering them to report to the Odd Fellows legislature to be relieved of their position. While no officers took this seriously, and not a single man obeyed it, McEnery's regular release of official-sounding notices, commands, documents and orders had the effect of keeping his shadow government on the front pages, giving it at least a semblance of quasiofficial existence.

McEnery and the media enjoyed a symbiotic relationship; he needed the newspapers to inform and inflame his supporters, and the more his supporters were inflamed the more newspapers were sold.

Colonel Ogden's plan was quietly put into action on the night of March 4. More than two hundred of McEnery's militiamen, many of them Ku Kluxers, overwhelmed the officers inside the two-story Seventh District station in Jefferson Parish. It was only lightly guarded as most of the men stationed there had been transferred days earlier to other posts, leaving only five patrolmen on duty.

The attackers, armed mostly with double-barreled shotguns and pistols, shot out the doors and windows, and announced they had been ordered to take control of the station by the McEnery Board of Police Commissioners. No one was hurt. The five Metropolitans inside offered no resistance; they were chased into the street and ran for their lives. The Western Union operator working in the building was forced to stay in his office.

Then the invaders began preparing for an expected counterassault. They took positions at the windows, watching for the police to try to recover the building. About midnight, General

GENERAL BADGER.

Ogden and several of his officers arrived to congratulate them. They were in great spirits, as the opening salvo of the plan had been successful. "You are the leading fist in the coup," Ogden told the men occupying the building, "the knife that tests the flesh." You must hold the precinct, he said, reminding them that tomorrow he would lead three hundred men in an attack on the Cabildo.

Finally, after shaking every man's hand, he left to prepare for the next day.

The Western Union telegrapher was ordered to wire the news to the North. Within hours the *New York Times* reported "A Riot in New Orleans." The *New York Herald* was far more dramatic: "Blood Runs in the Streets of New Orleans."

McEnery's men waited at the windows, guns cocked. Throughout the night reinforcements straggled in. But there was no sign of the police.

The next morning Metropolitan Police Superintendent Algernon Badger told reporters he had no intention of taking action to reclaim the Seventh Precinct, as he had no use for it even if he should recapture it. In fact, he told the *Times-Democrat*, "He regarded the 'bold capture' as rather farcical, and not worthy of receiving serious attention."

In reality, he was not going to split his forces. The rumors that had been circulating for weeks had suddenly gotten more specific: Tonight is the night. Kellogg is to be overthrown tonight. Supposedly during the afternoon one of the large political clubs told McEnery they would put four thousand men in the streets. Badger took it all seriously. The seizure of the Seventh Precinct was a diversion, nothing more, and it would be dealt with on his timetable.

Throughout the day he moved his men into positions. Weapons were checked and loaded. A sizable force guarded the armory.

At dusk McEnery's men began gathering in small groups on the streets near police stations throughout the city. Most of them carried arms. Shotguns. Pistols. Rifles. Breechloaders. Swords. Bayonets. And, as the *Picayune* reported, "...other warlike instruments." They were loosely organized, united only by their anger. Although some of these men had fought in the war, many of them were not soldiers. These were ordinary citizens, some of them aroused by injustice, others members of white supremacist organizations looking for retribution.

They had been driven to violence by a feeling of extraordinary unfairness. They believed they had been cheated, that the election had been rigged against them. That McEnery's ticket had won, and Grant had imposed Kellogg on them.

But it was Henry Warmoth who had given a voice to their resentments and brought them to the streets.

One squad assembled at the base of Camp Street, another gathered at Poydras and Magazine, still others waited near the Sugar Sheds. Runners kept them in good contact with each other.

In the night McEnery's men formed several large groups. The gaslights on Chartres Street had been turned off for several

The Parish Police Station was overwhelmed.

blocks, darkening the streets. At nine o'clock two detachments, somewhere between fifty and seventy-five men, advanced on the Third Precinct police station, located in the French Quarter. They marched past the station, then split into smaller groups and took positions behind shrubbery and a fence. Within minutes they caught five officers trying to reach the station and seized their revolvers.

The militia remained in that position for several minutes. Then they opened fire.

The first shots of the long night smashed through the windows of the police station. The hundred and twenty heavily armed police officers inside the well-barricaded building returned fire. They had to hold off the attackers until reinforcements arrived. No one knew how long that might take. After the first few salvos the attackers fell back to better protected places behind the St. Louis Cathedral.

General Ogden, the leader of the assault, stepped into the open. The firing stopped. "You are surrounded," he screamed. "Surrender the station!"

While his words were still echoing through the square a single shot rang out. He was grazed in the shoulder.

News that the first shots of the insurrection had been fired reverberated throughout the city; men raced from surrounding neighborhoods to the Quarter to reinforce the militia. A large group ransacked the two gun shops on Chartres Street, Guilfoux's and P. Baum's, taking every pistol, every long gun and all the ammunition.

Governor Kellogg was in his office at the Mechanics Institute with General Longstreet when the firing began. A flow of telegraphs kept him aware of the movements. A crowd of armed men at Poydras Street. Moving downtown. About fifty of them. Armed men roaming throughout the city.

The police had been preparing for this night for weeks. The station had been reinforced by an additional hundred men, who would wait in the shadows until the attackers had crossed Canal Street, then follow rapidly in their rear. Kellogg and Longstreet waited. The militia crossed Canal Street. Longstreet told the governor, "I shall give the order to open on them."

Kellogg was aware of the possible consequences. "Why, General," he replied, "would you fire on that crowd of people at the risk of sacrificing many lives before there has been any bloodshed?"

Longstreet had been through terrible events in the war. He

GENERAL LONGSTREET.

recognized the danger of hesitation. A coup was in progress. Should it succeed, far more force would be required to save the legal government. "Yes," he said, according to the *Republican*. "That's the only way to deal with these people. The mistake Warmoth always made was in not being willing to open fire on the mob. We mustn't fall into the same error."

Badger was in his headquarters, receiving reports, calmly assessing the situation. At about nine thirty, he received a telegram from General Longstreet asking *Are your forces moving? They have opened fire at the Third Precinct.* Badger led three companies, about two hundred and fifty men, to the armory. They loaded a twelve-pound Napoleon onto a carriage, and rushed toward the stationhouse to relieve the besieged officers.

The officers carried lever-action repeating Winchesters, capable of rapid fire. The horse-drawn twelve-pounder was a lethal artillery piece. It had proved its deadly accuracy, especially at close range, during the Civil War when both Union and Confederate troops relied on it.

McEnery's men were ready for them, hidden in several of the buildings along Chartres Street. As the officers moved steadily forward, snipers began shooting at them from second- and third-story windows, as well as from inside Guilfoux's gun store. Badger's men returned fire but kept heading toward the station.

One mounted officer was separated from his unit. As he turned the corner at Chartres and Toulouse, he was ordered to stop. Instead, he tried to push forward. Guns came out. "Shoot him," people shouted, caught up in the excitement of the moment, "shoot him." Several brave men took positions between the officer and the rioters. They backed him out of the confrontation, saving his life, then took his weapon and placed him under guard.

By ten o'clock Badger's troops were approaching the Third Precinct. They marched in ranks of four, staying mostly in the shadows on the raised wooden sidewalks lining both sides of the streets. McEnery's men were pinched between the officers firing from inside the stationhouse and Badger's Metropolitan Police coming from behind. When the first Metropolitans appeared the warning was passed: "Here they come. Here they come!"

And they had a twelve-pounder with them.

As the troops moved into position on Toulouse Street, Badger gave the militia one warning, ordering them to disperse. They responded with gunfire. The Napoleon was rolled into position. Within minutes its first shot boomed through the city, the thunder echoing off buildings, shattering glass all along the street.

Too many of the men had heard that thunder too often several years earlier. They knew the carnage that gun could produce.

Incredibly, no one was hurt. Badger had fired a warning shot, a blank cartridge. But that was sufficient for many of McEnery's people, who scattered in great disorder. Others, though, continued firing.

Badger had given them fair warning. He ordered the gun loaded with deadly grapeshot, a bag of small projectiles rather than a single twelve-pound shell. It was fired into the crowd. A dozen men went down. One man was struck in the head and fell dead on the spot.

Newspapers across the country would report every detail. A contested election had led to bodies in the streets of a major American city: the Metropolitans advanced in a skirmish line, firing as they moved forward. The McEnery men were pushed back into St. Peter Street. Their commanders screamed at them, trying to hold their line, "Keep shooting, keep shooting."

They responded helplessly, "Give us ammunition! How can we fight without ammunition?"

A militia commander moved bravely into the middle of the street, his back to the Metros, screaming madly, "My God! Can't I get anyone to support me?" In response, several men moved forward and continued firing.

The Napoleon boomed again. Several more men fell. Others had seen enough; they were done. They retreated.

Union infantry troops got there just before midnight. They had been ordered there by General William T. Sherman, who had telegraphed from Washington, "The President directs you to prevent any violent interference with the State Government of Louisiana."

When the bluecoats arrived, Union Lieutenant King demanded to see "the commander of the mob."

He was corrected. This is not a mob, he was told, but rather "the real citizens of New Orleans."

General Ogden finally responded and told the young lieutenant his men would not engage federal troops. Sporadic firing continued for several minutes, but the battle at the Third Precinct was done.

The toll was far less than anyone could have assumed. In the furious exchange only two attackers had been killed and less than twenty of them had been wounded. Two police officers had suffered minor injuries.

The Metropolitan Police swept into Jackson Square and began making arrests. Scores of men were detained, charged and locked up.

That settled, Badger turned his attention to the Seventh Precinct. Eighty men marched the three miles toward the station on Magazine Street. They brought the Napoleon with them.

Just in case.

It had been a long day inside the building. McEnery's men had passed the time talking, boosting each other's confidence. The street had remained mostly quiet. Occasionally a trolley had trundled by. The only business opened on Magazine was a barrelhouse, which poured beer to a few stragglers.

At two in the morning, the Metropolitans surrounded the Seventh Precinct. Badger sent a plainclothes officer, W. H. Murphy, with several men to ask for a peaceful surrender. In response the militiamen fired on the small party. Given no choice, Badger gave the order to commence firing. The police fired into the windows. After a barrage they smashed through the bolted door. Several defenders were shot, the rest quickly dropped their weapons. One of them, Kendrick Chandler, put the stock of his weapon to the floor, its barrel pointed at the ceiling. A police officer fired wildly, his bullet ricocheting off the muzzle of the gun and into Chandler's chest.

He was the single fatality. Most of McEnery's men fled through back windows and a door. But thirteen men stood fast and were arrested and dragged outside.

The coup had been defeated.

The next morning armed soldiers and police officers maintained a visible presence throughout the city, just in case. Hundreds of people strolled quietly through the area around Jackson Square to look at the damage. To most of them, it seemed impossible so few men had been killed or wounded. A battle had taken place in the middle of the city. Buildings and trees were riddled with hundreds of bullet holes. Tree limbs littered the streets. Windows in the shops in the square had been shot out. Railings were broken. Shutters were gone. A hollow iron column supporting a balcony had been knocked down, presumably hit by grape, and lay splintered in the street. The balcony now hanging above it, one length missing, seemed oddly incomplete as if it had lost its balance. Inside the police station, logbooks had been hit by bullets, a stair railing was perforated and every window was gone.

Both the Bayonet legislature and the people's legislature convened in competing efforts to impose a semblance of normalcy on the shaken city. Kellogg was ready to fight back.

Just after eleven o'clock, an estimated three hundred police officers closed the square, while an additional one hundred "picked sharpshooters" descended on Odd Fellows Hall and took possession of the building. Following orders from General Longstreet, they proceeded to arrest all the members of the McEnery legislature. Supposedly, McEnery himself was in his office there but escaped through a rear entrance. The legislators were marched to the First Precinct station, where they were locked into the drunkard cells. Those cells, according to the irate speaker of McEnery's House, John Conway Moncure, were a "dirty, loathsome, lousy, felon's dungeon, the stench of which made us all sick."

Seemingly spontaneously, a crowd materialized in front of the station. In the face of the heavily armed soldiers, the mob remained subdued. The legislators were held there for a bit more than an hour before Governor Kellogg ordered them released.

They gathered again, this time in the expansive lobby of the St. James Hotel. Although no count was given, a quorum was declared. The legislature passed a resolution asking General Emory exactly who had ordered their arrest. Their question was a disguised accusation: Did federal troops illegally follow an order from a state government official? Following that, the legislature adjourned with the understanding they would reconvene when summoned by Governor McEnery, an event, local papers reported cheekily, not likely to take place anytime soon.

The people's legislature was done. It would never meet again.

It was rumored that McEnery also had been arrested and was being held at the central police station, but that proved untrue. In fact, he had spent the day in private, at the office of a friend. A New York reporter who found him there described him as "very much depressed at the turn affairs had taken." McEnery was in a melancholy mood, reflective rather than animated, his energy drained. Yes, he had approved the attacks, he admitted to the reporter, explaining he had no options left. At least a portion of his objective had been successful, he said; he wanted to force President Grant to take a stand, to make it clear to the American people that the federal government would use military force to impose its will on the States.

Oh yes, he said, he was terribly upset that good men had been killed and wounded, but he was not responsible for any of that.

Their blood was on the hands of the opposite faction, meaning Grant and Kellogg.

He had hoped for a better outcome, he continued, but he was not done fighting "to maintain and establish his authority." As for the future, "he contemplated only passive resistance, and acknowledged that the only success possible was to be found in the determined resistance of people to the payment of taxes or recognizing in any other manner the Kellogg authority."

The violence was finished, he emphasized. And when he said it, undoubtedly he meant it. But he had let loose a monster that was already out of his control. He had approved violence as an acceptable means to resolve political disputes. That message reverberated throughout the state. The price paid by his supporters was small, two dead and less than twenty wounded, considering the message that had been sent.

Two dead? A small price to pay for what had been achieved: the city, the state, the entire nation had been galvanized by reports of the insurrection. They had gotten attention, they had fueled the existing debate about states' rights, they had sent a warning. And they had no intention of stopping there.

His point made by bullets, McEnery used the attention to immediately form a central committee, with members from every parish, to resist and delay the payment of taxes. If Kellogg forces couldn't be beaten, they would be starved of revenue.

Former Governor Warmoth was in a far more ebullient mood when the same reporter found him surrounded by friends and politicians in the office of his private secretary. With his "usual gallantry and geniality," he said that the battle had been lost long before the previous day's fighting, when Congress failed to act. The only remaining hope for the people of Louisiana lay with "Kellogg's inherent treachery, which will show itself in immediate plans to sell out his present friends and allies."

No one pointed out that was exactly what he had done, when

he left the Republican party and aligned himself with elements of the Democratic party.

As for the attacks, well, in retrospect, he thought, it wasn't a very good idea. But only because it had failed. There was an elementary political lesson to be learned: "Without the assurance of success it should not have been made."

In case anyone doubted President Grant's position, the White House released a statement. The president had authorized General Emory to use whatever force necessary to preserve the peace—but only after McEnery's militia committed an overt act. Let them start it, then finish it. The official statement was unequivocal. "If the people of New Orleans are not convinced by this time that [the president] is in earnest and resolved to the discountenance all further efforts of the McEnery government to remain in power, whether *de facto* or *de jure*, it will not be his fault. The issue having been made, the administration adheres to its original position, and, right or wrong, Kellogg will be protected, if it is necessary to hedge his office with federal bayonets."

Lost in the hullabaloo created by the attack, few people were even aware that the Kellogg legislature had taken a significant step to better defend his administration. For a politician that was not unusual. Elected officials have always used the powers of their office to strengthen their hold on it. Warmoth, for example, in his first months in office, had gotten legislation passed allowing him to run for a second term. So it was not the fact that Kellogg took action, it was what he did that was so unusual. This was literally a power grab.

On March 5, while McEnery's militia was gathering on corners for its attack, the legislature quietly approved several acts that transformed the Metropolitan Police into the governor's personal army. It gave him military control of the state. It was astonishing, audacious and arguably unconstitutional. And at least partially done in response to McEnery's attempt to raise his own militia.

Act #37 made the Metropolitan Police a part of the state militia, transformed into the Metropolitan Brigade. It also allowed the force to be greatly increased in size, calling for as many as three brigades comprising as many as three thousand men. Most importantly, it put the governor in complete command, allowing him to, "whenever in his opinion there is a public exigency, order the Metropolitan Police force to be mustered as the Metropolitan Brigade…and may order the Metropolitan Brigade to perform military duty in any part of the state."

Democratic newspapers railed against the creation of "the Standing Army of Louisiana." It clearly was unconstitutional, the *Picayune* claimed, citing Article I Section 10 of the Constitution, which reads, "No state shall, without the consent of Congress…keep troops or ships of war in time of peace."

The paper speculated this army had been formed in response to the threatened tax strike. "This is the first instance in the history of the country that a standing military force has been authorized by law to support any State government," it continued, explaining, "It is designed…to enforce the collection of money out of the people." The message was blunt. Should anyone dare resist Kellogg's tax collectors, the governor could call on this "standing army of three thousand soldiers to assist in overawing—to shoot, slay and murder the People of Louisiana, who shall dare to resist his despotism."

Tax revenue is the blood of politics. Government on every level depends on it. By depriving an administration of the funds needed to operate, a party out of power can influence and control policy.

The concept of starving Kellogg's administration for money had come from Henry Warmoth, who admitted it would be much less effective in the cities than in rural areas, where tax collectors were more isolated and therefore vulnerable. It had been embraced by McEnery, who began organizing the strike in late March. In a letter he circulated throughout the state, "Gov-

ernor" McEnery wrote that he "respectfully suggests that, with
as little delay as possible, there be called in your parish a mass
meeting of citizens to perfect a complete and thorough organization, with a view to the resistance of collection of taxes by
the Kellogg government."

The justification for refusing to pay taxes supposed that the
Kellogg government was illegal, put in power by the federal
government, which had no right to do so, and therefore Kellogg
had no legal right to appoint tax collectors, and since the tax
collectors had not been legally appointed, people did not have
to pay them. It was a flimsy argument with little legal basis, but
the idea of protesting by holding on to your money was, not
surprisingly, very popular.

"Withholding money supplies is not a new method of con-
fronting tyranny," the *Picayune* told its readers. It went further,
though, claiming the action was legal, the federal government
could do nothing to stop it and "it may in a few months starve
out the Kellogg government. And force it to surrender."

It was an ancient tactic. Almost two thousand years earlier Ju-
daeans refused to pay a Roman poll tax, and the Gospel of Luke
suggests that Jesus was accused of promoting tax resistance by refusing to pay tribute to Caesar. When Florentines refused to pay
a war tax in 1289, the government canceled it. Normans rioted
against taxes in the mid-fourteenth century, burning the houses
of tax collectors and destroying their equipment. In 1525, England's Henry VIII was forced to abandon his dream of invading
France when the nation's wealthiest men resisted the collectors.
And only twenty-five years earlier, when German aristocrats
refused to allow the first popularly elected parliament to meet,
Karl Marx wrote, "It is high treason to pay taxes. Refusal to
pay taxes is the primary duty of the citizen."

America had a long history of refusing to pay taxes as a means
of political protest. In 1637 the indigenous Algonquins had refused a demand from Dutch settlers to pay for improved secu-

rity. New Englanders declared fifty years later "it was not the town's duty" to assist the British in collecting a new tax. Several other colonies, among them New Jersey, Connecticut and North Carolina, used the nonpayment of taxes to protest political decisions. In 1794, when farmers and distillers refused to pay a new federal tax on all distilled spirits, President George Washington had led an army of thirteen thousand militiamen into western Pennsylvania to put down the Whiskey Rebellion (or Whiskey Insurrection). Most recently, the author of *Civil Disobedience*, Henry David Thoreau, had gone to prison for failing to pay taxes to protest the Fugitive Slave Act and the Mexican–American War.

The *Picayune* wrote that *not* paying taxes was literally the foundation of democracy, writing, "The preservation of English liberty for so long a time has been due to the same resistance to the payment of taxes illegally imposed." It was the duty of citizens not to pay taxes to Kellogg, adding, "The English people knew that as long as they held the purse they could hold the King... the enemies to their State cannot live without the money of the people; but with the money of the people, their oppression can and will be perpetuated."

Ironically, this tactic had been introduced to Louisiana politics a year earlier—in opposition to Governor Warmoth. The Tax Resisting Association had been formed by "the most intelligent and wealthiest citizens of New Orleans" to resist high assessments. If a man could be found who enjoyed paying his taxes, said an association spokesman, "Barnum ought to get him or any other cheerful taxpayer." The association had been formed, it announced, "to resist, by legal means, the present exorbitant, illegal and unconstitutional taxes now attempted to be extorted from us..."

By the time this group was formed, most people had already paid their taxes, so it had little effect, and the Warmoth legislature was done by the time taxes again became due. So the strategy remained the same, but in those few months it had been embraced by an entirely different body of people.

While the goal of Democrats was to financially starve the Kellogg administration into oblivion, the argument it made was that the tax rate was unfair, benefiting the rich carpetbaggers. Democrats asserted, "Those whom they [Republicans] represent do not pay them... They look upon them only as spoils to be appropriated."

Republicans used the same argument, but from a different perspective. Kellogg issued a statement pointing out that "Experience shows that tax resisting associations result in the wealthier classes escaping payment of their taxes while the poorer men are not only compelled to pay their taxes, but additional penalties and costs..."

Breaking a tax strike is difficult. Washington had needed an army to do so. Reasoning with the protestors had rarely worked. The Republican media reminded readers that the people hurt most by the loss of tax revenue would be the people who needed it most. In an effort to evoke sympathy, they grouped these people as "widows and children." The city would be left in the dark, uncollected garbage would spill onto the streets and crime would soar because the courts would remain closed. Travelers would avoid the city, hurting business. Ordinary upkeep and necessary repairs to public buildings could not be done. While the wealthy would continue to prosper, the rest of the population would suffer.

Not surprisingly, the appeal to sympathy didn't work. The tax protest grew. Some Democrats voluntarily paid their taxes—but they paid them to the McEnery government. To combat this, Kellogg's legislature instituted a variety of harsh penalties and punishments to be carried out by both civil and criminal prosecutions. People had ten days after being given written or published notice to pay their taxes. If they failed to do so, their property could be seized and sold. The delinquent taxpayer had no legal recourse.

The penalties were enforced. For example, Edward Booth, supposedly a state senator in the people's legislature, was arrested when he refused to pay a hundred-dollar licensing fee for his hat shop on Magazine Street. After one day being "enjoined, sued, arrested, fined, imprisoned, seized, closed," he announced he was forced to "ransom my person from imprisonment." He paid his taxes and was released.

His resistance had emboldened Democrats, and as he left the prison he was greeted by hundreds of cheering people. Led by a band and marching four abreast, a long procession snaked through the city streets. It was a glorious celebration. Spectators cheered from the walks or leaned out of windows, waving hats and handkerchiefs until his carriage stopped in front of his store. Standing on a box he quoted Benjamin Franklin, who said about British taxation before the Revolution, "It is better and cheaper to pay nineteen shillings to defend one shilling than to surrender one shilling to save nineteen."

Following the impromptu rally, a straw figure labeled *Wm. P. Kellogg* was raised on a lamppost and hung by its neck. People threw stones at the effigy, beat it with sticks and finally set it ablaze. When it was reduced to a pile of ashes, a placard was placed in front, reading, *Here fell Wm. P. Kellogg, the usurper.*

The *New Orleans Times-Picayune*, among the leading advocates for the strike, adamantly refused to pay more than $2,150 in overdue taxes. In late April tax collector N. C. Folger published a notice that he intended to sell "at public auction...the name, good will, presses, types, material, stock in trade, right and credits" owned by the publishing company for "cash on the spot."

A day before the auction the newspaper paid its bill.

But by then the tax strike had taken hold. In early May the newspapers listed the names and tax debts of hundreds and hundreds of people, in preparation for seizing their property. Henry Warmoth's name did not appear on the lists.

The contested election had led to rancorous debate, substantial violence and now a tax strike. The bitterness, frustration and anger had continued escalating, without relief, for more than a year. And now, finally, it was about to explode.

What happened next would reverberate throughout American history for the next century.

10

There was no place in the state of Louisiana that did not suffer
from the political turmoil. No place.

The town of Colfax was three hundred and fifty miles from
New Orleans, although it barely qualified as a town. It consisted
of four or five houses, several of which offered rooms to passing
travelers, three stores, a schoolhouse and one brick building, a
stable that had been converted into the parish courthouse.

Colfax served as the seat, the administrative center, of Grant
Parish. The parish and the town had been carved out of four
adjoining parishes in 1868, as much to provide additional political patronage as for any other reason, and had been named after
President Grant and his vice president, Schuyler Colfax. Grant
Parish had an estimated forty-five hundred residents, many of
them freedmen who now worked the fields for a wage. Politically, it was split roughly evenly between the two parties.

The area had once been part of the sprawling Calhoun Plantation. In the late 1830s Meredith Calhoun purchased as many
as a thousand slaves in Huntsville, Alabama, the majority of

them teenagers, and brought them chained or yoked together in a half-mile-long caravan to Louisiana. It was believed to be the largest overland movement of slaves in cotton industry history, requiring one hundred wagons and a thousand mules.

He brought them to an unusually lush area on the banks of the Red River. It was estimated the fertile soil could produce as much as a bale and a half of cotton or forty bushels of corn per acre. Calhoun's slaves cleared an estimated twelve thousand acres, cutting trees, shrubs and bush, filling swamps, and using the timber to build magnificent homes for the masters as well as rudimentary slave quarters. They also built the second-largest sugar refinery in the country. The abundant cotton harvests and sugar revenue from his plantations made Meredith Calhoun wealthy enough to live in splendor in Europe, where he purchased a title, Count Calhoun, from France.

Calhoun had no moral qualms about slavery and was known for imposing brutal punishments to maintain control. Author Harriet Beecher Stowe supposedly said that the villainous slave master she depicted in *Uncle Tom's Cabin*, Simon Legree, was based at least partially on Meredith Calhoun.

Through the early years of the Civil War, Calhoun remained confident that England and France, in need of the South's cotton and sugar, would break the Union's naval blockade. But Lincoln's Red River campaign, with its fifty-boat flotilla, ended that belief. When the Union army arrived, almost four hundred thousand slaves declared themselves war contraband, walked off Southern plantations and surrendered to the Union Army. Nearly half of them enlisted to fight for their freedom.

Meredith died in 1869 and by the beginning of Reconstruction, what remained of the once-vast plantations were being run by his son William. "Willie" Calhoun was a hunchback who committed the most grievous act possible by a Southern gentleman: he fell in love with a mixed-race woman named Olivia Williams. Following the war, reported the *Shreveport Times*,

Calhoun had gone to New Orleans to purchase mules and supplies. While there he met "a handsome mulatto girl, became enamored of her and sought to win her to his soft embraces...

"The enraptured hunchback was forced to pay down to the mother five thousand dollars...and in a short time married his concubine in the most approved fashion."

Rather than hiding this socially scandalous relationship, Willie and Olivia were married in New Orleans's St. Louis Cathedral. As a result of this as well as several other civil rights programs he sponsored, Willie Calhoun gained the loyalty of the freedmen, among them many of his former slaves, and became a leader of the national Republican party. Supposedly, Grant Parish was created at his behest.

By 1872 the Calhoun plantations were in disarray, mortgaged for far greater sums than their current worth. Most of the fields were abandoned, fences were down, farm buildings were falling into disrepair, and the animal herds were gone. Willie Calhoun was rumored to be bankrupt.

Situated literally hundreds of miles from the political rancor of New Orleans, a rural place like Colfax might seem immune from the dangers created by a shattered government. But it wasn't. Like a slowly spreading poison, the mayhem reached every part of the state.

Grant Parish was racially divided; its Black and white residents settled comfortably among their own folk. Most of the freedmen lived in and around Colfax, many of them in the former slave quarters on the nearby Smithfield Plantation. White residents generally built their homesteads in the hills or farmed land along the boundaries of the parish, as much as twenty to forty miles from the village, but the small white settlement of Montgomery was only about twelve miles away. As a result, the substantial Black population was surrounded by white farmers. The races generally didn't socialize, but they mostly peacefully tolerated each other's presence.

There was no reason to suspect that a torrent of Black blood would soon flow through the parish.

The seeds of conflict were planted in 1870. Warmoth's appointed registrar of voters remained in Colfax only long enough to register every Black voter in the parish, then began moving around, making it difficult for white voters to find him to register. To ensure the election of Warmoth's "Radical" Republicans, he also supposedly added another two hundred fictitious Black voters, placed ballot boxes in places difficult for white voters to reach and finally took the unopened boxes with him to New Orleans before a count could be made.

As Louisiana prepared for the 1872 election, white voters in the parish were determined they would not be cheated again. But the Republican candidate for a seat in the state legislature was a widely respected Black leader, Captain William Ward.

Ward was a hero in Colfax. He had been among the first Black men enlisted in the Union Army. As a member of the First Colored Cavalry, he fought in the Virginia campaign, rising to become sergeant, the highest rank available to a Black soldier. Following the war, he had joined General Longstreet's Louisiana State Militia and, after obtaining weapons, organized his own eighty-five-man militia to combat the growing threat of white supremacist organizations. To avenge the murder of a popular former sheriff, Ward thrilled Colfax by turning his company into a posse comitatus, capturing the killers and handing them over to New Orleans law enforcement.

Noting his growing popularity, in 1871 Governor Warmoth named him to the five-member parish "police jury," the local governing board. But within months a small group of wealthy white supremacists led by cotton planter William Cruikshank forced him out of office, claiming he was ineligible because he had not been a resident of the parish for the required two consecutive years. Cruikshank took his place.

That action made Ward even more popular among freedmen, and more threatening to the white population.

The specter of an armed, well-trained Black militia terrified white residents of Grant Parish. Many of them had grown up hearing terrifying stories about the horrific 1791 rebellion that had ended slavery in Santo Domingo, which had served as justification for the brutal treatment of American slaves—and still was used by white politicians to scare out the vote.

William Ward was the embodiment of the fear that lived deep in the minds of many white people. During the 1872 campaign, Conservatives warned that Ward had promised freedmen that if Kellogg was elected they would be given the land on which they had once toiled as slaves. While the Republican media portrayed him as "fierce, resolute and bold...brave and determined, a good man," Democratic papers wrote he had become "an absolute dictator," overruling Calhoun, who had "sunk into utter insignificance."

In the election Ward ran against Democrat James Hadnot, a plantation owner who possibly had been behind violent efforts to prevent Black citizens from voting in '68. The difference between the two candidates could not have been starker: the white supremacist against the Black militant.

Throughout the campaign both sides ginned up fear to excite and motivate its voters.

Election day was peaceful, as it was throughout the state. The trouble began afterward. The Fusion press claimed the votes were counted in the courthouse under federal supervision, with its doors wide-open to allow interested observers to monitor the count. The Radical papers reported that white state officials had held the locked ballot box overnight—and when it was produced the next day it had a suspicious hole in its side.

Although there were about one hundred more registered Black voters than white in Grant Parish, according to the Warmoth Returning Board, Democrats had won a landslide victory. McEnery had beaten Kellogg, Hadnot had beaten Ward, Alphonse Cazabat had been elected parish judge, and Ku Kluxer Christopher Columbus Nash had been elected sheriff.

William Ward was especially angered by the decision. With more Black voters than white voters in the parish it seemed improbable he had been beaten—especially when the announced tally included several hundred fewer Black votes had been cast than in the previous election.

The *Picayune* informed readers that Ward admitted he had lost, supposedly telling Hadnot, "You have beaten me fairly, but I will represent the parish in the legislature, notwithstanding." It was highly unlikely Ward would have said anything like this, especially to a Klan leader, but the story helped plant the idea that Radical Republicans intended to take illegal—and maybe violent—steps to seize control.

Colfax may have been more than three hundred miles from New Orleans, with a population of less than a few of that city's blocks, but the potential consequences of an unsettled election there were just as grim. It was as true then and there as it had been through all recorded history: people will kill for power.

Before officially leaving the governor's office, Warmoth issued the necessary legal commissions to Fusionist candidates Cazabat and Nash, who took their oaths of office in the Colfax courthouse on January 2.

Weeks later new governor Kellogg issued commissions to the same offices to the Republican candidates, appointing Robert Register to the parish bench and naming Daniel Shaw the new sheriff. Neither man could be sworn into office though, as C. C. Nash refused to surrender the keys to the courthouse.

Kellogg tried to keep the peace, and after meeting in New Orleans with Fusionist lawyers from Grant Parish he supposedly offered a compromise: he would agree to keep several of their people in local office—but not Sheriff Nash.

Nash or no one, Judge William Rutland and attorney Wilson Richardson warned.

Kellogg refused. It couldn't be done. The lawyers stormed out of his office into perilous territory. Rutland was heard to say, "There would be hell in Grant Parish."

The Colfax Courthouse was the center of power in Grant Parish. There was nothing glamorous about it. A one-story whitewashed building facing the Red River, it was a drab, functional brick structure that held both a courtroom and several administrative offices. What had once been the hayloft was now used for storage. There was an open crawl space below and a cypress-shingled roof above.

But the courthouse was just as important to Grant Parish as the Mechanics Institute was to New Orleans. It was the symbol of government. Nash was not going to give it up. As long as Fusionists held it he would remain sheriff.

Late in the night of March 25, several Republicans, led by Robert Register, broke into the courthouse through a side window and took possession. The next morning, before the Fusionists even knew about it, Dan Shaw and several other men were sworn into office. They immediately sent copies of their signed oath to New Orleans, where the forms were legally filed.

They had staged a quiet coup, taking control of local government and law enforcement.

Nash told the story quite differently. In his far more self-serving version, a body of men "ejected the legally elected...they fired upon myself and others, compelling us to flee for our lives."

Even then, Nash said, he returned with law officers to find a peaceful solution, "but was again fired upon and threats made by the rioters who said they would anyhow drink my blood."

The Fusionists were certain of one thing: this would not stand. The freedmen, the former slaves, would not be allowed to overturn the election. They spread the word: Meet at the courthouse on April 1. Bring your guns. The attack was supposed to remain secret, but Hadnot had bragged to one of his Black laborers that he was going to lynch William Ward and all the other men who got in his way.

When Ward learned about the plot to kill him, he called for reinforcements. Sheriff Shaw swore in enough men to form a large posse to defend the courthouse. They, too, were told: bring your guns.

Newspapers fed the flames, writing that one of Ward's men had promised "he would have Hadnot's head on a pole in twenty-four hours."

Both sides had been preparing for this fight since the end of the Civil War. Reconstruction and the three new constitutional Amendments had drastically changed their worlds. The scars of history were too deep and still raw.

Once fear had been loosed, it grew. Wild rumors spread among the white population. Men would be killed. Women raped. In the days leading up to the confrontation, white residents of Colfax moved away, some of them claiming they were driven out, while hundreds of Black people from surrounding areas gathered inside the town, squeezing into the Smithfield Quarters or setting up campsites.

As armed men raced into the parish to reinforce both sides, several incidents took place to further inflame the situation. Among those who left town was Judge Rutland, who sent his family to safety across the river and then was given safe passage by Ward's men. After he was gone they broke into his house; readers were told that the men "took from there a coffin in which his child was embalmed, thinking that it contained money...broke it open but finding out what it was, left the dead body of the child on the road."

After escaping, Rutland filed a criminal complaint against the men who had ransacked his house. He included Ward, Register and Calhoun in his papers, obtaining a warrant for their arrest— which provided legal protection for a posse to carry it out.

Weeks later Rutland corrected the story, explaining the coffin actually contained the embalmed body of a young girl who had died six years earlier in Lake Charles, which he intended to reinter in Red River. He also said he had been told that the coffin had been burned.

Additional stories recounted in detail Ward's posse ransacking other houses, shooting at people, stealing jewelry, "which the scoundrels sold for two bottles of whisky," and boarding a steamer that landed there "armed with cutlasses, sabers, guns and pistols…and declaring there was going to be 'hell to pay here tonight.'"

But Nash's militia was equally violent. In the first days of April former slave Jesse McKinney was repairing a fence in front of his house about three miles out of town. A dozen riders suddenly appeared; their horses leaped the fence and without warning, in front of his wife and child, they shot him in the head. McKinney died several hours later—and any doubt in the Black community that it was under attack died with him. Hundreds more people took shelter in the town.

Ward's men began constructing a defensive perimeter. Men were stationed on all the roads within twenty miles of Colfax to provide early warning. Shallow trenches were dug and earthen works no higher than three feet stretched in a rough semicircle around the front of the courthouse. The defenders had mostly shotguns and not nearly enough for all the men. They began stockpiling ammunition, a good portion of it homemade. They cut lengths of cast-iron stovepipe into makeshift cannons and positioned them above the main road.

Then they waited.

The Fusionists were also preparing, drilling the volunteers in units, scouting the preparations being made in town, stealing horses and mules from Black homesteads, and taking the four-inch deck cannon from a steamship and mounting it on a wagon.

There were some minor encounters. On April 1, nineteen

men, led by Hadnot, made a display of force, racing through
the town carrying rifles. A day later, a patrol led by Register
encountered a scouting party near Smithfield Quarters. After
a harmless exchange of fire, the scouts retreated. On April 5,
Ward and several of his men encountered several white riders.
They killed one of the horses and shot the thumb off a rider.
The men fled, one of them later saying, "it seemed to me to be
4000 more coming our way."

Meanwhile, outside of Grant Parish, few people knew what
was brewing there. Or even if they had heard the stories, they
dismissed them. A small article in the *Republican* warned that the
Black "majority" in Grant Parish was prepared to "clean out"
the white "minority...in twenty-four hours if not prevented."

Another story, this one in the *Picayune*, about the ransacking
of Judge Rutland's house, claimed "Fearful Atrocities" had taken
place, with "No Respect Shown to the Dead." The *Republican*
refuted it, writing there was no evidence anything other than
the ousting of "McEnery pretenders to office" had taken place.

Too much was happening around the world for people to be
concerned about rumblings from a small town. Instead, headlines
focused on the wreck of the steamship *Atlantic*, which had run
aground and tipped over less than one hundred yards off the coast
of Nova Scotia. The *Atlantic* was the pride of England's White Star
company and was considered one of the most modern ships afloat.
According to *Associated Press* reports, the ship was well off course
and traveling at full speed when it smashed into shoals in the middle of the night. As many as seven hundred people drowned in
their berths or were swept overboard in waves reaching as high
as fifty feet, including every woman on board and every child
but one, making it the largest passenger-ship disaster in history.

In Opelousas people were reading about anti-Semitism spreading in Texas. One legislator there objected to an effort to in-
corporate the Hebrew Association, admitting, "I do not much

like Jews." In response, B. R. Plumly stood and said, "I *do* like
Jews... It is a foolish and cruel custom to deride the Jews...

"We do nearly everything that Christ condemned," he pointed
out, "and we leave undone almost everything that He required
to be done." His stirring defense of Hebrews continued, paying
"tribute to the Jewish race, the tenacity of its life, the courage
and endurance with which it met and mastered all conditions;
its existence as a great people at a period so remote that what
we call history is lost in tradition...having laws which have become the laws of the world, and permeated its civilization, gifts
and activities felt even now in commerce, finance, musical and
dramatic art, statesmanship, literature and eloquence...

"...I realize the feeling of Disraeli when, in the British Parliament, taunted with being a Jew, he is said to have replied, 'I
am a Jew. When the gentleman's ancestors were naked savages
on these islands, mine were princes of the temple...'"

In Evansville, Indiana, the *Journal* cautioned readers about the
dangers of carrying concealed weapons, relating the sad tale of a
young man whose revolver, hidden in his hip pocket, discharged
accidently when he was visiting his beloved. The accidental
shot set his pants on fire, which caused both his intended and
her mother to faint. Her father, hearing the shot and seeing his
wife and daughter on the floor, attacked the man, who crashed
through a window to escape, pursued by the family dog. As the
man ran for safety he fired at the dog, killing it, and ending forever his relationship.

But no one in Grant Parish had time to be concerned about
the shipwreck, anti-Semitism in Texas or the tragic end of a
comical encounter: each hour brought them closer to open warfare. Both sides sent word to New Orleans requesting assistance.
If their messages ever reached Kellogg, he did not respond.

Several cursory attempts were made to reach a compromise.
On April 5 leaders of both sides met in an open field to exchange
peace proposals. But those negotiations ended when riders in-

terrupted to tell Ward that Jesse McKinney had been murdered. Days later Willie Calhoun delivered letters suggesting a compromise to both sides, in an effort, he said, "to prevent bloodshed."

Just before Easter, William Ward boarded a steamer headed downriver toward New Orleans, where he planned to do whatever was necessary to meet with Governor Kellogg to plead for federal intervention. Ward was a sick man, weakened by tuberculosis and rheumatism, but he knew that Kellogg was the only one who could stop Nash. Kellogg was already aware that violence was stirring in Grant Parish. But rather than riling things up by sending troops, he dispatched General Longstreet to go there and investigate. Longstreet had difficulty finding transportation; most of the boatmen refused to take him there, fearing the loss of business if they cooperated with the Republicans.

On April 13, Easter morning, Nash—in his role as the Fusion Sheriff—set out for Colfax with an estimated hundred and sixty-five well-armed men. He carried with him arrest warrants for the men who had destroyed Rutland's home. Grant Parish's representative in the people's legislature, forty-nine-year-old James Hadnot, rode with him, the bright red sergeant's sash and rosette medallion he had worn while serving in a Confederate reserve unit draped across his chest and carrying his war sword.

The posse crossed a stream and paused yards from the now-deserted Smithfield Quarters. Holding aloft a white flag, Nash and three men came forward. Lev Allen, leading the defense with Ward in New Orleans, rode out to meet them. Men on both sides readied their weapons. Their conversation was brief. "We want the courthouse," Nash said, meaning he would take his place as the elected sheriff. If Allen's men put down their arms they would be allowed to leave in peace.

Nash could not be trusted. Too many Black men had been attacked in the past months. McKinney had been fixing his fence when he was killed. If they put down their guns, Allen knew, they would be helpless. His people would stay right where they were, he replied—but boldly suggested that Nash's men should leave their guns and take off before people got hurt.

Nash gave one final warning: You have thirty minutes to move your women and children to safety, he said.

After parting embraces, the women and children walked down the road, out of the line of fire, heading for a nearby plantation. Three white men had remained at the courthouse, among them Republican Sheriff Shaw, and they left the town with them, leaving only the Black freedmen.

As the Fusion forces took strategic positions around the courthouse, the defenders dug in behind the breastworks. An hour passed. The noon sun beat down hard on all of them. Two hours. Some men traded insults and threats. A sniper on the courthouse roof took several potshots at men playing seven-up for one dollar a hand; when one bullet missed by only a few feet, the cardplayers finally quit their game.

The shooting began at two o'clock. Nineteen marksmen with Spencer and Sharps rifles, Smith and Wesson pistols and one Colt revolving rifle opened fire on the defenders. Those outgunned men crouched behind the breastworks, sporadically returning fire, trying to conserve ammunition. The attackers set up the wagon-mounted deck cannon in Willie Calhoun's front yard, loaded it with trace chains, brickbats, rocks, canisters, milk cans filled with small deadly pellets known as "blue whistlers"— whatever they had—and began firing.

Shrapnel sliced open the abdomen of freedman Adam Kimball. As his intestines dripped out he was carried into the courthouse. The first man was dead. There would be so many more.

The thunder of the cannon, the shots flying, the tufts of dirt kicked up, the occasional screams of pain brought many of the men back a decade to the battlefields of the war.

The shooting continued through the afternoon. Several Black

men were killed, but the defenders managed to hold out. Unable to make progress, Nash sent a few men down to the river to see if it was possible to outflank the men in front of the courthouse. His scouts moved quietly under the cover of the riverbank. Within minutes they came upon a gap in the unprotected levee behind the breastworks. It was a stunning discovery. It left the entire line of defense vulnerable.

Nash organized the attack. Thirty men crept into position. As the men in front of the defense began an assault, the river detachment raced through the gap and opened fire.

Outgunned, outflanked, outnumbered and outsmarted, the defenders left their dead and wounded in the trenches and abandoned their position. Dozens of them ran for the woods, many of them gunned down before they could get there. Some of them were captured, held briefly, then shot.

Lev Allen was among the few who managed to get into the woods and hide there. Other men made it to the river or a nearby pond—where they spent hours in the water, submerging themselves when the attackers came near.

Between thirty and forty men were taken prisoner.

About one hundred men, maybe more, reached the safety of the brick courthouse. They opened fire from the ten large windows. Nash's three-man cannon crew moved their gun into position about eighty yards in front of the building. A shot from inside the courthouse nicked one of the crew, Stephen Decatur Parrish, in his leg, severing his femoral artery. The *Picayune* described his death thus: "The din of the battle were the last earthly sounds that fell upon the ear of as gallant a hero as ever glanced over a field of strife."

What happened afterward was open to dispute, as the media reported events in a manner most favorable, and sympathetic, to their readers.

According to the *Shreveport Times*, at about three o'clock the gunfire from the courthouse slackened. Pieces of torn white cloth, signaling ceasefire, or perhaps surrender, popped out of several windows on the ends of rifles. The firing ended. After a few moments, a small group of white men, including James Hadnot and Sidney Harris, approached the courthouse.

"Mr. Harris and two other men were in front of Hadnot, and as the door was thrown open...they walked in," the story continued. "Instantly a volley was fired upon Hadnot, and a door was closed upon Harris and his two companions and opened fire on them; that they were not literally torn to pieces is simply a miracle. They drew their six-shooters...and began firing. As Harris neared the door he was shot from the side, the ball entering his shoulder, and he fell against the door...the door swung open against his weight and he rolled out, and his companions jumped out...

"Mr. Hadnot received eleven buckshot in his leg and a ball through his stomach, from which he subsequently died... There was no possible way of dislodging the besieged..."

In fact, there was one way that would work: all reports agreed that the courthouse roof was set afire, though they disagreed about exactly how that was done. One version claimed a flaming arrow had started the blaze. An unnamed witness said a combustible material shot from the cannon caused the shingles to burst into flame. The *Picayune* would even write that the building had been set on fire by the men inside. The most detailed explanation was that Nash gave a captured elderly Black man, Pinckney Chambers, a choice: either set the courthouse on fire with a torch or be killed where he stood.

In that version a combustible material, either straw or cloth, was affixed to a long bamboo fishing pole, dipped in kerosene and lit. While sharpshooters kept the defenders away from the windows, "Pink" crept up to the courthouse and touched the makeshift torch to the eaves. The shingled roof caught instantly.

The order in which those two events took place, the shooting of Hadnot and the courthouse being set on fire, were disputed. Several survivors claimed that Harris and Hadnot were shot in the melee after the courthouse was burning, or that after being allowed to flee the fire Ward's men produced guns and shot them. But no one denied what happened next.

As the now-unarmed defenders rushed out of the building the slaughter began. Nash's men, irate at the shooting of Hadnot, opened fire from close range. They shot them down in the doorway or as they climbed through the windows. Wounded men were shot, stabbed with bowie knives or "pinned to the ground by bayonets." Most of those who somehow got out of the courthouse were tracked down and shot. Bodies were found miles away. The *New York Times*, calling this "wholesale murder," reported "one hundred of their number were shot as they fled."

Several men, rather than being shot or burning to death, tore out floorboards and tried to take refuge in the crawl space or beneath a nearby warehouse. They died there.

That night forty or more prisoners were taken into the woods. Once again, the details are murky, but not the outcome. They were shot or hanged. Supposedly some of them were shot on the riverbank and fell into river. Others were lined up back-to-back, or three or four together, and shot in a quest to determine how many men could be killed with a single rifle bullet. Bill Cruikshank shot two men that way but Jim Hadnot's son Luke lined up five men and killed them, although it required two shots.

No one was able to make an accurate count of the number of Black men killed that day, with estimates ranging from a hundred and fifty up to several hundred. It was agreed, though, that what was already beginning to be called the Colfax Massacre was the largest racial killing in American history.

Two white men were killed, and an unknown but small number were wounded.

A day later a hundred and twenty Metropolitan policemen landed in Colfax. They found sixty-five corpses on the ground, some of those remains still smoldering. Everywhere they looked they found more bodies. The police reported "The ground was thickly strewn with the dead."

The papers spared none of the horrific details in describing the killing frenzy. The *Republican* cited the official report from Colonel T. W. DeKlyne to General Longstreet: "when forced by the fire to leave the courthouse they were shot down without mercy... Under the warehouse...were the bodies of six men who evidently crept under there for concealment and were there shot like dogs. Many were shot in the back of the head and neck; one man still lay with his hands clasped in supplication; the face of another man was completely flattened by blows from a gun, the broken stock a double-barreled shotgun being on the ground near him; another had been cut across the stomach with a knife after being shot and almost all had three to a dozen wounds. Many of them had their brains literally blown out..."

The massacre settled nothing. Ward and Nash had both escaped harm—Ward was safely in New Orleans when the fight began—and both men continued to claim the sheriff's office. Governor Kellogg, meanwhile, did what was necessary for his own political survival: he blamed McEnery. He sent a letter to the state attorney general and a copy to the newspapers, in which he wrote the massacre in Grant Parish was "if not directly planned and ordered by this man [McEnery and his associates] [it] was the result of their treasonable acts against the State government."

It was an extraordinary charge, based entirely on political calculation rather than fact. In his demand Kellogg pointed out that McEnery had broken the law by "openly referring to himself as Governor of the State...appointing people as public officers and in order to do so has forged the seal of the State." Then, citing the attempted coup of March 5, he directed the attorney general to indict "McEnery and all others implicated with him, for treason."

The penalty for treason was death by hanging. Making this

accusation was a highly dramatic way of diverting attention and perhaps responsibility.

The massacre proved a new weapon to hammer home a political point. Even before all the bodies had been buried, the national media was assigning blame. *The New York Sun* knew whose fault it was: President Grant. The massacre was "a natural result of the lawlessness…encouraged by President Grant in order to give a member of his own family predominance…"

Fusionists placed the blame squarely with "the Kellogg–Casey [President Grant's brother-in-law] party and the Administration," which, the *Picayune* claimed, had encouraged Ward and others to take possession of offices to which they were not entitled.

Once again, Louisiana's failed electoral system was on front pages throughout the country. As *The Nation* magazine wrote, this was what happened when confidence in that system was lost. "A state of things better fitted to produce explosions of violence…could hardly be imagined."

The magazine placed at least some blame on "the disgraceful connivance at Washington at the state of things which has converted Louisiana into a South American banana republic and destroyed all confidence on the part of all classes, not only in the law, but in a popular vote which produces the law."

As Warmoth had threatened weeks earlier, chaos had come to America.

11

The killing done, the law came to Colfax. It was a woefully belated effort to reassure people that the rules of a civilized society still applied, that good people were protected and criminals were punished. But by the time the police and the army got there, Nash's men were long gone. Almost all the participants rode away, waiting to see what the legal outcome would be. Some went far, four hundred and fifty miles to Texas, where they settled, while others lived in the woods a short distance from their homesteads. Women in the area created a code, hanging different colored tablecloths to warn their men when lawmen were nearby.

The long, twisting legal pursuit of the killers, one that eventually would land in the United States Supreme Court and alter American history for a century, began on May 9, when federal prosecutor James Roswell Beckwith convened a grand jury. Because murder is a state crime, Beckwith had to bring charges under the federal government's 1870 Enforcement Act, claiming the victims had been deprived of their constitutional rights. It was a complicated legal maneuver with no guarantee of success.

Beckwith was a northerner by birth, having been raised in Upstate New York, but had settled in cosmopolitan New Orleans with his wife, an author, to practice law. Grant had named him the federal prosecutor after the incumbent was found with his throat slit in his Custom House office.

Beckwith knew he was making himself a target: the Colfax killers had a lot of support in the white community and many people felt strongly that any man who prosecuted them was their enemy.

Especially a white man.

But Beckwith had been appalled at the reports from the town. These were atrocities, he wrote, they were barbaric, and he intended to prosecute every person involved. If America was to be a lawful nation, these men had to be punished.

Assisting him in his investigation was John J. Hoffman, an agent for the Treasury Department's eight-year-old secret service. Posing as a traveling salesman, Hoffman had spent weeks listening in feigned amazement to stories from men who had been in Colfax. He provided evidence against dozens of them, in addition to finding survivors and white men brave enough to testify to the grand jury.

To simplify matters, Beckwith focused on only two victims: Alexander Tillman, who had been shot and killed a distance from the courthouse, and Levi Nelson, who had been taken prisoner and shot by Bill Cruikshank, who was attempting to prove that he could kill two men with one bullet. The indictment was a hundred and fifty handwritten pages long and included sixteen counts. It claimed that Nelson also had been killed—which was to cause the prosecution great embarrassment.

On June 17, a federal grand jury indicted ninety-eight men "of evil minds and dispositions."

The State of Louisiana had an easier case to prove: under state

The Colfax Massacre became front-page news, shocking the nation.

law murder was murder. State prosecutor J. Ernest Breda took charge of the case. Like Beckwith, he willingly made himself the target. In early July, a grand jury met in the warehouse right next to the ruins of the Colfax courthouse and indicted a hundred and forty men. Although Breda tried to keep those indictments secret until the accused could be arrested, the news spread throughout the parish, and no arrests were made.

When Breda returned to Colfax several weeks later, an armed mob confronted him. Some of them, he knew, had taken part in the Easter morning slaughter. At least one shot was fired: it was enough to convince Breda to get out of town before sundown.

The violence that *The Nation* had warned about was spreading. According to President Grant, the Colfax Massacre's "bloodthirstiness and barbarity is hardly surpassed by any facts of savage warfare" and demonstrated "a spirit of hatred and violence that is stronger than law." Inspired by that attack, similar uprisings took place in St. Helena, Tangipahoa, Livingston and several other parishes. Kellogg sent small militia detachments to put an end to them. But by far the biggest and most dangerous resistance took place in St. Martinville.

The center of St. Martin Parish, St. Martinville was the stronghold of Alcibiades DeBlanc's White Camelia organization. DeBlanc had established his own fiefdom: his six-hundred-man militia ransacked newspaper offices, threw Republican officials out of office and initiated a tax boycott. In essence, he had refused to accept the central government and instead set up his own.

The state was on the edge of open rebellion. DeBlanc had to be stopped. On May 3, Kellogg sent a hundred and twenty-five well-armed Metropolitans to St. Martinville to protect his appointed officials; they brought with them the twelve-pound Napoleon that had proved so effective in New Orleans. The men had no idea what was waiting for them there, but every one of them knew what had happened at Colfax and was ready for battle.

After the police had left New Orleans, gangs broke into several gun shops, stealing all the weapons and ammunition. "It is understood," the *New York Herald* reported about the robberies, "a movement is on foot to seize the police stations while the Metropolitans are in the interior."

That turned out to be false. But those weapons would prove very valuable in other coming conflicts.

It took the Metropolitans two days to get transportation to St. Martinville. DeBlanc's men—who were variously referred to as "tax resisters," "citizens" and "McEnery's men"—had the town surrounded when they got there. The Metropolitans marched into St. Martinville without encountering any resistance. The telegraph lines were down, so little news leaked out. On the second day the police began their offensive, advancing about a mile and a half beyond the town, firing solid shot and shell, but in heavy fighting they were beaten back. It was reported that three officers had been killed and four wounded.

DeBlanc's men had trapped them. Reinforcements for his "citizen" army poured into the area from the nearby parishes, while police reinforcements could not get transportation. The town was mostly deserted, all its stores closed. The police had arrested the mayor, charging him with treason. The court was open, presided over by the district attorney and judge appointed by Kellogg. It was a small gesture to demonstrate control. No lawyers showed up, so no business was done.

The whole country was watching with fascination. Reconstruction was falling apart. This seemed like the next deadly event after Colfax. "The Metropolitans are besieged at St. Martinville and cut off from water," wrote the *San Francisco Examiner*. "Their provisions are with them, but otherwise they are in a desperate situation."

There was little doubt who was really behind these insurgencies. As the Vermont *Rutland Daily Globe* explained, "There is enough to show that McEnery and Warmoth have seized upon the occasion to fan the smoldering fires of insubordination in the rebel heart, and to rouse their followers to frenzied deeds."

To relieve the police, Kellogg organized the forty-five-man "Louisiana Cavalry," consisting of both militia and Metropolitans, and told them to get to St. Martinville as quickly as possible. There was a general impression that these men were the more respected—and feared—federal rather than state troops, and nothing was done to dispel that deception.

Kellogg also formally requested assistance from federal troops. In response, two hundred infantrymen were ordered to the parish. A US Marshal went with them, carrying arrest warrants for DeBlanc and several other men, charging them with insurrection.

Transportation remained a problem. When the captain of the steamer *Iberia* refused to carry federal troops, he was arrested. A member of his crew removed the throttle valve from an engine and threw it in the river. Other crew members spent an entire day diving for it but, when it couldn't be found, fashioned a new one.

In desperation, Kellogg purchased a steamship, the *Ozark*, but it took his men half a day's march to meet that boat on the Bayou Teche.

By the time the troops got there the crisis was over. DeBlanc had ended the rebellion when he learned federal troops had been dispatched, admitting, "We did not intend or wish to come into conflict with federal authorities." His men faded back into their normal lives. DeBlanc eventually surrendered to federal authorities and was brought back by steamer to New Orleans.

As many as seven thousand people were waiting on the wharf to greet him with a grand ovation, and many more lined his route to the Custom House. Contrary to reports, it turned out that no law enforcement officers had been killed and very few were wounded, so he was released on $2,000 bail—and within days all charges were dropped.

Rather than DeBlanc, it was Kellogg who came under attack. The Fusionist media was relentless: day after day the newspapers criticized him, reminding their readers he had lost the election and been illegally put in office by Grant, that he had turned the Metropolitan Police into his private army and that his tax policies were unduly harsh. Columns and editorials stoked anger. A failed attempt was made to indict him for sending New Orleans police officers to St. Martinville, leaving the city defenseless against criminals. Murder, rape and robberies supposedly were committed in places usually protected by police officers.

Even the *New York Times* noted, "It is known that assassination has been talked of in New Orleans, and men are known who have been asked to join an organization whose purpose it was to get rid of objectionable men in the community, beginning with the highest."

So it was not surprising that an attempt was made on his life.

On May 7, while the governor was meeting with officials

about a dispute on the docks earlier that day, a hostile crowd gathered around his waiting carriage. When Kellogg appeared, people began shouting insults at him. As he walked to his carriage a man named Charles R. Railey confronted him. "I wanted to tell you that you were a cowardly and usurping scoundrel and that if you have any courage you will stand like a man and I will treat you as the scoundrel you have shown yourself to be."

Kellogg replied somewhat huffily, "I am not acquainted with you, and I don't know that I have done anything to offend you, sir."

As his carriage rounded the corner one shot rang out. Kellogg raised his hand to his neck as his driver raced them away. The story spread quickly: the governor had been shot and "was dangerously, if not fatally, wounded."

For a brief time, it was not known how seriously he was hurt. Several men congratulated the lieutenant governor on suddenly becoming governor. The *Herald* reported Kellogg had been hit in his neck and gravely wounded. It turned out the bullet had missed him completely. He explained, "I heard a shot and simultaneously felt the passage of a shot by my neck. When the ball passed I involuntarily raised my hand..."

He added that Railey had threatened him during their brief encounter, warning him, "You are a dead scoundrel."

The McEnery people showed little sympathy for him. The *Picayune* claimed he had taken refuge in the St. Charles Hotel, only to be told by its proprietor, Bob Rivers, "I'll tell you what I would do if I were in your place, I would pack up my trunk and leave the city at once...

"...[D]on't try to govern a people who hate you. You have escaped this time, but this is not the only attempt which is likely to be made upon your life, and perhaps you may not escape in the future."

This also marked the beginning of a newspaper war, as the *Republican*'s editors wondered in print, "When an American newspaper enters the field as an…advocate of assassination and insidiously cites two or three historical examples to authorize such a crime, it is almost time for us to consider whether it would not be better for us to have a censor established for the press."

Two days later, after learning a warrant had been issued for his arrest, Railey walked into a police station and surrendered. He denied having fired the shot, swearing, "I was as much surprised at the firing of the pistol as Mr. Kellogg could have been." He was released on a $5,000 bond.

Picayune reporter Melvin M. Cohen also was arrested—and charged with actually firing the shot.

Few people gained more from the continuing chaos than New Orleans's lawyers. There were more than one hundred active law firms in the city, and the incredible number of cases resulting from the disarray kept many of them busy—and wealthy. The number of significant legal and constitutional issues spawned by the contested election was astonishing. In some ways it eventually would affect the interpretation of numerous Amendments. While this assassination trial was beginning, for example, a First Amendment libel case against the *Picayune* was concluding. It had been brought by Judge Jacob Hawkins, a member of the Lynch Returning Board who sued the paper after it reported that he had been paid a substantial sum and appointed to a newly created court in return for his support of Kellogg.

Describing the case as "A Lawless Attempt to Destroy the Freedom of the Press," *The New York Sun* suggested that "for the conduct of the trial, perhaps no such case has ever occurred in the history of the legal courts of the country." The case was tried in the court of…Judge Lynch. And among the witnesses for the defense was Henry Warmoth.

Somewhat surprisingly, this civil trial attracted as much attention in the city as a case involving blood or lust. As the attorney for the *Picayune*, H. N. Ogden said the outcome of this case would affect every newspaper in the country. "If this jury fails to do its duty at this critical moment, the result will be not only the suppression of the New Orleans *Picayune*...it will be a large stride toward the suppression of all freedom of speech or thought throughout the country...

"Whenever the attempt has been made to destroy liberty and establish despotism, the very first assault is always made upon the freedom of the press...so as to keep the public from that knowledge which is essential to the proper...protection of liberty."

The courtroom was so densely packed with spectators and other attorneys that in the middle of the first day's proceedings the floor started shaking. Someone yelled, "There are too many people in the room. The floor is sinking." Spectators began rushing to the door. A few of them went to the windows. But within a few minutes order was restored, and the courtroom was quickly and safely evacuated.

Just as the last people left the room a large piece of plaster above the judge's desk came crashing down.

The trial was moved into the larger, more secure Supreme Court room. It lasted six days. When the jury pleaded it was unable to reach a verdict, Judge Lynch refused to dismiss them, insisting in harsh tones that they continue deliberating, and warning they would not be released until they agreed—no matter how long that took. After almost three days of deliberations, they found the paper guilty, and it was fined $18,000—but when the two Democrat members of the jury claimed they had been offered a large bribe to join the majority, the lawyers went back to work.

No sooner was that controversial trial ended than the Railey–Cohen trial began. With feelings on edge in New Orleans, the district attorney asked for and was granted a change of venue. The trial was moved about thirty miles to Jefferson Parish. It began on June 23, with a jury comprised of ten Radical Republicans and two Fusionists. A company of mounted Metropolitans stood guard around the courthouse. Governor Kellogg was the opening witness. On the day of the shooting, he testified, he was a bit apprehensive when he saw the crowd gathered around his carriage. "It flashed upon me that there was a preconcerted attempt to surround me; I had been warned that I might be attacked... I heard reports that there were secret societies for the assassination of prominent Republicans."

He identified Railey as the man who had confronted him but admitted he had not seen who fired the shot. Cohen was asked to stand, but Kellogg could not identify him.

Prosecutors revealed that hours after the assassination attempt a mysterious gold key inscribed with the governor's initials was delivered to his home—supposedly, the prosecution hinted, by one of the defendants!

The jury was sequestered in a locked room each night during the trial. A prosecution eyewitness positively identified Cohen as the shooter, but several defense witnesses provided alibis for him. Another eyewitness told the jury that he had seen Cohen immediately after the shooting—walking in the crowd holding a pad and pencil!

The mysterious inscribed gold key was never further explained.

The jury deliberated for less than two hours before finding both defendants not guilty. No one else was ever charged with the crime.

Kellogg tried to fight the Fusionists with words. Days after the attempted assassination he published a long statement in the *Republican* in which he laid out the situation and asked for cooperation if not understanding. Whatever views people held, he wrote "all must admit it is the only government in the state and must remain so, at least until the national authority shall determine otherwise. Upon myself, therefore...falls the responsibility of sustaining it in the interests of public order and for the prevention of anarchy." If he failed to do that, he continued, the same people who were fomenting the violence would blame him for not stopping that violence they were fomenting.

On several occasions he had been dissuaded from asking the president for federal troops. But the situation was already beyond his control. So he finally made an official request.

Grant had been reluctant to get involved; there was no political gain for him. But Colfax, St. Martinville and several other smaller uprisings had emboldened those people opposed to his Reconstruction policies. The white supremacist organizations were growing. He had waited several months, hoping that Congress would present a plan he could support. Congress was continuing to investigate; it was holding hearings, then holding more hearings, then issuing statements about those hearings. He had to do something to try to calm the situation.

On May 22, the president finally issued a statement supporting Kellogg. It was meant as a warning: "Whereas, under the pretense that William P. Kellogg, the present executive of Louisiana, and the officers associated with him in the State administration, were not duly elected, certain turbulent and disorderly persons have combined together with force and arms to resist the laws and constituted authorities of the State…"

The statement continued, claiming Congress had tacitly recognized Kellogg as the legally elected governor by refusing to take any action to remove him, and that as president he was obligated to protect the citizens of every state and had the right to use military forces to put down any insurgency, therefore…

He wasn't actually going to do anything, instead he was commanding "said turbulent and disorderly persons to disperse and retire peacefully to their respective abodes within twenty days…"

The response was exactly as expected. Grant's proclamation was "infinitely absurd," decided the Fusionist *Picayune*. With peace now in Colfax and St. Martinville, "There is not a single creature in Louisiana to whom the Proclamation has any application."

The statement has little meaning, *The New York Sun* pointed out. "It is out of the rival claims of Kellogg and McEnery to the Governorship that the novelty of this very serious controversy arises, and that the so-called domestic violence in Louisiana springs solely from this source." And settling that "is the first duty of the President."

McEnery, calling himself "the duly elected but deposed Governor," continued to hold out hope for Congressional action. But he was a realist, reminding his supporters "the President of the United States, with the army and navy at his command, has the physical power to coerce the people of this State into any line of policy he may be pleased to dictate, and it would be but folly and madness to interpose any resistance."

Until Congress met again in December when, he was certain, they would recognize his government, he urged that "peace and order may reign supreme..."

Throughout the summer both state and federal law enforcement supposedly searched—without much success—for the nearly one hundred men indicted for the Colfax Massacre. No more than ten people were arrested. Their names were not released, and they were held in the secure prison in New Orleans.

When Judge Register, whose claim to the bench helped ignite the killings, attempted to hold a hearing in Grant Parish in late July, sixty or seventy people showed up and made that impossible. Threats on his life were made.

The violence slowed, but it did not end. On September 8, Judge T. S. Crawford and District Attorney Arthur Harris were on their way to hold court in Winnsboro in Franklin Parish when they were ambushed and killed. The evidence indicated that they had been shot from both sides of the road. This wasn't an attempted robbery, this was a planned assassination. Crawford's body was so badly mutilated that "the number of shots he received was impossible to determine;" Harris was shot in the back of the head.

Law enforcement immediately accused the Tom Winn gang. Winn had been tried and convicted of murder by Judge Crawford, and Harris had been prosecutor. Winn had vowed to get even and escaped from prison. But the judge was a Kellogg

Republican, and rather than being outraged by the murder of a law enforcement official, some Democrats made it clear they believed he shouldn't have been on the bench.

The reaction so startled—and perhaps terrified—Sheriff Dan Shaw that he resigned, writing Kellogg that he was "powerless to do my duty."

Nevertheless, Kellogg posted a $5,000 reward for the capture of the murderers. The inability to capture the leaders of the Colfax Massacre continued to embarrass Grant and Kellogg. Grant, who was considering running for a third term, needed the Black vote—and that meant he had to bring some of those killers to justice. On October 23, heavily armed state militiamen, supported by several infantrymen, boarded the *Ozark* and steamed toward Colfax. They had no idea what type of resistance they might encounter. Just in case, they brought two pieces of artillery with them.

The hunt for the killers was beginning.

G. W. Hadnot's farm was the first stop. The law came riding hard and fast. Hadnot saw them coming and slipped out the back door into the woods, making good his escape. But he had no chance to spread a warning. A mile up the road his brother was arrested. The posse surprised Bill Cruikshank, who was just sitting on his porch. The troops had information that more than two hundred men were camped in the piney woods, "the rendezvous for all who did not care for being in their homes while the *Ozark* remained in this neighborhood." Skirmishers crawled through the deep grass, trying to surprise the camp. But it was deserted. While the posse was searching the Cruikshank place, those men had been warned and took off for Catahoula Lake.

Law enforcement chased them for twenty-five miles before finally catching up to them. But there wasn't a single man among them for whom they had a warrant.

The big prize was Christopher Nash. The posse got a tip that he had made camp north of Colfax on the east bank of the Red River. They hightailed it after him. Nash heard them coming and made good his getaway, racing across the river, outrunning their bullets. His narrow escape made him into an even greater local hero: the story was told that when he reached the west bank he turned and saluted his pursuers with a grand wave of his hat, then disappeared into the woods.

The militia roamed through the area for three weeks. They rode from parish to parish, making raids day and night, but as a reporter embedded with them wrote, "as the news of our approach had been heralded by the underground telegraph, the men for whom warrants were held had fled, seeking hiding places in which militia, police or soldiers cannot find them. The village is a dull place, not a murder within a week. The lively men had gone where the woodbine twineth in solitude."

After the law had left, the white supremacists returned in several towns and punished people who had provided information to the troops.

The *Ozark* returned to New Orleans with less than a dozen prisoners.

Those men were locked up in a single large cell in the Orleans Parish prison. As they were being taken to jail they had an opportunity to speak with reporters. They were innocent, all of them, they insisted. Bill Cruikshank said he had been scared off his farm two weeks before the massacre, "when thirteen armed n——s, who in passing by my residence threatened to shoot with buckshot my four children." The next day he moved his family to Alexandria "until affairs quieted down in Colfax." When he learned his storehouse had been broken into and five barrels of pork had been stolen, he obtained arrest warrants and, "I went to the proper authorities...both the Kellogg and McEnery sheriffs [both acting at the same time...]. The Kellogg sheriff refused to serve on the grounds it was a trick to get him in a scrap, and the McEnery sheriff endeavored to summon a posse to go but did not succeed." He had not been near Colfax for thirteen months, he said.

Johnnie Hadnot claimed he had taken his family and left

home days earlier, after being shown a note that William Ward had put a $250 reward on his uncle James's head.

Prudhomme LeMoine recalled, "On the day of the fight I was at the Catholic church at Cloutierville." And, he added, he had witnesses who had seen him there.

In fact, each of the accused said they could produce numerous witnesses to support their alibi, whatever that alibi happened to be.

The "Grant Parish prisoners" quickly became heroes. They were hailed as good, decent Southern boys, sons of the Confederacy, standing up for what they believed was right. Every movement needs symbols around which people can rally. The Colfax prisoners became that rallying point. One of New Orleans's most prominent lawyers, Robert Marr, volunteered to defend them. He was the perfect man for the task: a white supremacist, Marr had recently formed a committee of seventy wealthy and successful people to support McEnery. For Marr, this trial was an opportunity to gain attention, sympathy and legal standing for the white citizens whose rights, he believed, had been trampled on by the Reconstruction Acts. Other respected lawyers, among them carpetbagger turned white supremacist William Whitaker, who had served as legal counsel to Warmoth's voter registration effort, joined him.

Although the lawyers volunteered their services, money would be needed to fight for their prisoners' freedom. A lot of money. There were legal expenses. Witnesses would have to be transported and housed while in the city for the trial. The prisoners and their families would need assistance. The Committee of Seventy launched a fundraising campaign to support the men. "There has not been, in the history of Radical oppression in Louisiana, a more flagrant instance than that...it should be at least our pleasure to mitigate the sufferings of the unfortunate men..."

In the ensuing months thousands of dollars were raised. A performance of Frederick Schiller's *The Robbers* by the Orleans Dramatic Association raised $1,229. At the Varieties, the Shakespeare Club presented "the ever popular comedy *Money*…a promise of intellectual entertainment and thus enjoyment will happily be subservient to benevolence…" An entertainment at the Opera House raised hundreds. At the Exposition Hall a magician offered a Grand Prestidigitation Performance. A benefit by the Thespians in Alexandria included "good music, fine scenery, well selected pieces, good acting," assuring "that our poor and persecuted citizens, yet in the Bastille will feel grateful…" At that benefit "an elegant watch" was auctioned in a raffle which raised additional funds. The ladies were encouraged to go door-to-door to solicit for the welfare of the prisoners.

While preparations for their defense were being made McEnery remained a pretender to the governor's office. In December, from his "Executive Office" in New Orleans, he advised members of the General Assembly that his government remained in place "ready to be put in motion" the moment it received Congressional recognition. He remained optimistic that would take place during the next session. Meanwhile, although the law required the assembly to meet, "it would be useless" to do so "as no practical benefit could flow from any legislation you might enact." But, he urged them, be ready!

McEnery traveled to Washington, DC, in late February. While the Colfax jury was being selected he went to the White House in an attempt to meet with President Grant to discuss the case. Not surprisingly, the president was unavailable. It was not known when he would be available. McEnery departed, leaving behind a petition signed by several thousand residents of Grant Parish asking for executive clemency—and laying blame for the massacre on the Radical Republicans.

Also not surprisingly, Grant ignored it.

12

No one would ever know precisely how many men were murdered that day in Colfax. The newspapers estimated a hundred and fifty. Weeks later bodies were still rising to the surface of the river, and limbs were poking out of their shallow graves.

But the defendants would not be tried for murder. By law, the case was far more complicated. The federal government can bring murder charges in an extremely limited number of situations; for example, the killing of a federal judge or a crime committed on federal property. These murders did not fall under those statutes. The indictment charged the defendants with thirty-two different criminal violations which deprived the victims of their legal and constitutional rights granted by the Civil War Amendments as well as the Enforcement Acts. The legal theory was simple: killing someone prevents him from exercising his rights.

The defense didn't accept that argument. Marr, Whitaker and the rest of the defense team felt strongly the federal government was encroaching on state business. This was a state matter, and if there was to be a trial, it should be held in a state court. These

men were being used as political pawns; it was nothing more
than an attempt to extend the reach of the federal government
into the people's lives. They intended to prove that the accused
were law-abiding men who had been attacked while attempting to serve a warrant and therefore had the right to defend
themselves.

Making the situation even more complicated was the fact that
almost a year earlier, in the so-called Slaughterhouse Cases, the
Supreme Court had upheld the powers of Louisiana to regulate its meatpacking industry, narrowing the application of the
Fourteenth Amendment. Ironically, that case had been brought
to challenge regulations imposed by Governor Warmoth. The
Colfax case was viewed as a test of the power of the federal government to prosecute individuals for violations of constitutionally protected rights.

The trial began on February 23, 1874. It had all the trappings
of justice. It was held in the magnificent second-floor courtroom in the Custom House. The majestic courtroom, with
its thirty-six-foot-high ceilings, mahogany railings and darkly
paneled walls, was overflowing with spectators. The majority
of them were Black residents of New Orleans. They filled the
courtroom and the corridors, hoping their presence would help
to ensure their rights were protected.

Coincidently, the day the trial began, the *Picayune* reported
that the fight to determine the winner of two Louisiana Congressional seats—eighteen months after the election—continued
in a different courtroom. Lawyers were requesting access to the
ballots, which presumably were being safeguarded in Washington. The people who held those ballots refused to produce them
unless it was guaranteed that Kellogg's people wouldn't seize
them—and Kellogg remained silent.

Judge William B. Woods presided over the Colfax trial. It was
a good fit. Woods, a Union general who had fought at Vicksburg, had settled in Alabama after the war to raise cotton and

practice law. Grant had appointed him to the federal bench. He was well acquainted with challenges to the Fourteenth Amendment. In a controversial ruling three years earlier, he had upheld the Enforcement Act, which in certain situations permitted the federal government to impose penalties on individuals who violated that Amendment's protections of life, liberty, property and "equal protection of the laws." He also had ruled in the lower court decision in the Slaughterhouse Cases that the state had violated that Amendment, a decision that the Supreme Court had overturned on appeal.

Six years after this trial, President Hayes would name him to the Supreme Court.

The trial began with the selection of a jury pool, from which the twelve-man jury would be picked. That is rarely contentious, but nothing about this trial was normal. Setting the stage for what was to come, the prosecution and defense argued over the method used to choose the pool. In a trial in which race was going to play a fundamental role, the racial makeup of the jury might well determine the outcome. It took Judge Woods two days to sort that out. It took another two days of questioning to finally seat a jury.

The jury consisted of nine white and three Black men. Five of the white men were Democrats. If the case was to be decided on racial grounds it would be almost impossible to get a unanimous verdict. The jury was sequestered in the Custom House for the duration of the trial, prohibited from speaking with other people or reading newspapers.

The trial was a logistical nightmare. More than two hundred and fifty witnesses were called by both sides: most of them transported by steamboat from Grant Parish to New Orleans, put up in hotels and rooming houses and then returned home. They also had to be protected: being involved in this trial was dangerous. Seventy armed militiamen were assigned to protect trial participants. Prosecutor James Beckwith received numerous warnings and death threats. Witnesses were confronted on the streets; one witness was beaten and stabbed.

But still they came to New Orleans, raised their right hands and told of the horrors they had seen. It was a courageous act; most of these people were freed slaves, many of them had never been to New Orleans. Few, if any, had ever testified in a trial, especially in front of hundreds of Black and white spectators. And every one of them knew of the threats.

William Ward testified that he was at home when "a man visited my house late at night and said, 'Do you not know you will be hung tomorrow? Hadnot has been mustering men for several days and says he will hang you all,' naming sixteen of us. We held a consultation and Sheriff Shaw was advised to summon a posse...

"...I at that time counted forty men, armed, going toward Jesse McKinney's house; I heard a gun fire and someone said Jesse was murdered..." That killing had caused frightened people to come into the town for protection, Ward explained. Those people "had no design to attack anyone, or be aggressive. I came to New Orleans to get Governor Kellogg to send troops to Colfax."

Alabama Mitchell, who hobbled to the stand because his right leg had been ripped apart by shot, remembered being in the courthouse when it was set on fire. "We then hung out a paper flag and a shirt sleeve and cried out 'Surrender.' The white men told us to come out, we should not be hurt. Some ten or twelve had come out headed by Tillman, when the white men fired at them. I ran back and hid under the floor." After being captured, the mob took several prisoners "in a field and commenced shooting at us. They called us out, by name, two at a time...the prisoners jumped up and ran for the woods... I ran on until I could run no longer, and then crawled into the woods: there I waited two days and night..."

Day after day the testimony continued. The killers were identified by name: Cruikshank. Penn. Irwin. Hadnot. Lemoine. Hickman. Marsh. Lewis. And more, many more.

Levi Nelson's halting testimony was especially dramatic. He identified several of the defendants, saying, "They kept up the fight all day... Shack White held up a white leaf and asked them not to kill him; Irwin shot him down." After escaping from the burning courthouse, "I asked if I might go; he cursed me, saying he did not come 400 miles to kill n———— for nothing... they took me and another man out to shoot us; one bullet struck me in my neck, stunning and dropping me. The other man was killed. They shot him five times... One man inside the courthouse was shot and disemboweled and he was burned up alive..."

His final words echoed through the large courtroom. "I was a voter."

During several hours of cross-examination, the defense tried to poke holes in his story, suggesting that several brothers who were there looked alike and he might easily confuse them, asking Nelson specific questions about time and distance. In response, Nelson gave an even more detailed description of his experience that day. "The man who was taken out to be killed with me was Mac Brown; he and I were side-by-side; the man who shot us stood about fifteen feet from us; he said he was going to shoot us through our heads. When he fired we both fell. I on my face; laid there until daylight... Mac Brown yelled after he fell. The man shot him five times."

The cross-examination failed. According to the *Republican*, "Had witness been in free command of language it may be that the counsel would have been confused. It was evident that Levi knew exactly what he was saying, although he had a halting way of expressing himself."

Meekin Jones swore he had only gone to Colfax "because I could not work contented. I saw men in arms... I considered that I was unsafe when they were threatening to kill us; felt safer in Colfax than in my field because if we were together we could defend ourselves..."

Benjamin Brim, who had lost an eye when he was shot, said that he had surrendered and was sent back into the courthouse to bring out the men hiding there. They all came with him, he said, except "one under the floor said he would as soon be burned as shot down. The man who had me said he was not going to shoot me, I stepped again and my captor cocked his pistol, I turned around to look at him and the bullet struck my nose close to my eyes. I fell and laid there sometime… I was shot afterward as I lay on the ground; the bullet entered my back and passed out my side… I was on the ground, my nose full of blood, and as I blew it out they heard me and shot me again, saying, 'That will do him.'"

Brim eventually crawled into a ditch and watched men and women searching the bodies for valuables then ransacking the Smithfield homes.

Over the course of a week, witness by witness, Beckwith revealed the entire horrific details of the massacre. Men and women marched to the witness stand and told incredible stories of murder and survival. Some of the details were heartbreaking. A woman named Anna Elzie told the court that several Black women had crept back to the town and watched silently from the bushes. Elzie was only a few yards away from her husband, and she heard him pleading for his life and watched him being shot at close range. There was nothing she could do to help him, she remembered. Crying out would have resulted in her own death.

Other women told their stories. Armed men had asked Charlotte Johnson "if I saw any men not dead." She found her cousin's body "in a sitting position under a pecan tree."

The testimony was so shocking that on several days the Fusionist *Picayune* did not even report on the trial, although they did run a front-page story accusing the governor of granting executive clemency—a pardon—to people convicted of "heinous crimes." The suggestion was made that money was exchanged.

The defense strategy was set out by its first witness, W. L. Richardson, who testified that the defenders at Colfax "were fully organized, had captains, sergeants and all that, and were drilled in front of the courthouse." So rather than them being a ragtag group with limited weapons, he gave the impression this was a small militia, fully capable of fighting and ready to resist law enforcement.

The second defense witness was the town doctor, Dr. Conway, who swore that the intentions of the posse were peaceful. "Six delegates were selected to go to Colfax and try to settle the trouble; they were ordered to go unarmed and make no demonstration." He added that Judge Rutland had sworn out an affidavit against the men who had ransacked his home. Five deputy constables were sworn in, but they were prevented from entering the town. "I saw many armed white men in Montgomery." He finished, "They said they were armed to prevent an invasion by the n———s."

These were dangerous men, W. B. Shakelford said, they were criminals. "Rutland's house was pillaged; I saw trunks broken open in his yard and papers and feathers scattered all around."

Several witnesses reinforced the claim that the men at Colfax were well organized, trained and armed. They had officers and ranks. They had two or three homemade pieces of artillery. They were determined to hold the courthouse. Sheriff Shaw, testifying for the defense, said, "They were regularly drilled... They had two cannons made of pipes: the men practiced with these. Pickets were posted..."

A man named James Terry claimed he heard several men "say that they intended, if they whipped the whites, to kill them and their children. They made several other bloodthirsty threats."

Dangerous, threatening men: James Patton raised the hidden fears of the Santo Domingo revolution, telling the jury that Black men "were forming on every plantation; they came up to the store cursing and swearing at the white people and declaring that the country belonged to them and they would rule it."

Several witnesses provided alibis for men who had been positively identified by prosecution witnesses. Charles Smith swore, "On Easter Sunday I was present with Gibbons and Lemoine the whole day. We were engaged in hog killing and breaking eggs. Neither of them could possibly have been at Colfax."

Lemoine and Austin Gibbons supposedly were seen "several times that day. They were at [a town] thirteen miles from Colfax. They had been staying there for over a week."

Arista Simms, a Black servant working for Tom Hickman, testified Hickman "did not leave the house on Easter Sunday because his wife was afraid to stay at home alone. When Mr. Hickman heard of the fight I heard him say it was a shame to kill so many…" Although minutes later a different witness testified to having seen Hickman at another man's home.

Miss Laura Lewis swore, "My father did not leave home on Easter Sunday."

The *Picayune*, which dutifully reported the details of the defense case, reminded readers that the battle had taken place "to decide a contested election…and to install as the duly elected sheriff a man who in open court declares that he was not elected," and that the defenders at Colfax had a "fierce and unappeasable thirst for war and bloodshed…"

Whatever sympathies the jurors held, the prosecution and the defense had provided sufficient testimony to justify their perspectives. It was up to the jury to decide what evidence could be believed.

For three weeks the mixed-race jury had lived without any reports of strife in the Custom House. The jurors had been allowed out only once, under guard, to watch the annual Fireman's Parade. They had heard more than a hundred witnesses and listened to the impassioned pleas of the lawyers to rise above race to reach a just verdict. Judge Woods had reminded them in his charge that the question to be answered was whether the defendants had deprived the victims of their constitutional rights.

The jury deliberated for almost three days. Its verdict was

only somewhat surprising. One man, Alfred Lewis, had been acquitted outright. The jury could not reach a verdict for the other defendants, although it was later revealed that a majority had voted for acquittal.

Judge Woods declared a mistrial. He stated that the retrial would begin as quickly as possible but then infuriated the prisoners' supporters by refusing to grant bail. Hundreds of businesses and as many as a thousand people signed a petition to the judge, but he would not budge. If he let them loose, he feared, they would fade into the countryside and never be seen again.

The defense's propaganda campaign and fundraising efforts resumed, as did attempts to intimidate witnesses.

The retrial was filed under a different name, a name destined to become part of judicial history, *US v. Cruikshank*. Under a quirk in the law, the defense requested that a second judge join Judge Woods on the bench—and the man they requested was Supreme Court Justice Joseph Bradley.

It was not an unusual request. The Judiciary Act of 1789 had established three regional Circuit Courts and assigned Supreme Court justices to literally "ride the circuit" on horseback, hearing cases in those jurisdictions. Initially there were no Circuit Court justices. The Judiciary Act of 1869 called for a judge to be appointed to each circuit who would have the same legal powers as the Supreme Court justice overseeing it, as well as adding a ninth justice to the eight-man Supreme Court. The ninth man was Joseph Bradley.

Judge Bradley was a brilliant, widely respected jurist who had specialized in patent and railroad law. He was known for amassing a 16,000-volume library, his ability to read Hebrew and hieroglyphics, and his mastery of the law. The defense might have been heartened by his ruling in an 1845 New Jersey case defending slavery, his publicly stated opinions opposing abolition and his vote to overturn the state's slaughterhouse law. He accepted the invitation to hear this case, fully aware of potential constitutional issues, and was on the bench as the second trial began on May 18.

As with the first trial, the two sides sparred over the composition of the jury pool. This jury again included nine white men, but two of the remaining three members identified themselves as mulatto, causing the *Republican* to state there was only one Black man on the jury.

As soon as the jury was selected Marr asked for a ruling on his motion to quash several indictments "as it related to proceedings which might flow out of the trial, for determination in the Supreme Court." Justice Bradley, rather than rejecting that request, simply said the trial would proceed. Any determination on that motion would be made after the trial, and only if the defendants were found guilty.

The second trial proceeded much as the first. Victims and eyewitnesses described the shootings and executions that resulted in hundreds of dead and wounded. The defense contended the men in Colfax refused an offer of a peaceful resolution and started the fight. Each of the major newspapers in the city reported events in the manner most likely to satisfy and, at times, inflame their readers' loyalties. For example, on its front page the *Republican* wrote, "Gilbert Noble, an aged man, is a new witness for the United States. He was badly wounded at the massacre and his wounds received over a year ago are still apparent. In fact one on his head is still suppurating. In his evidence he gave details of the fight, fully confirming the horrible statements made by the others who were nearly murdered at Colfax."

The *Picayune*, on its eighth and last page, reported, "Gilbert Noble, a very old and very black Negro as called first on the stand and testified: I live several miles from Colfax. There was a great deal of excitement around. I thought it best to go to Colfax and fight for my country. I was there the day of the fight. I fought in the breastworks and afterwards retired into the courthouse. When that was set on fire I rushed out. The white men fired on me. I was wounded in several places. (Here the witness exhibited his wounds.)"

Not surprisingly, the appearances of defense witnesses were treated with equal bias. The *Picayune* reported that Elzine Dubois testified that she had seen Lemoine and Gibbons all Easter Sunday at L'Artigo.

But according to the *Republican*, Dubois "attempted to prove the alibi for Lemoine and Gibbons; she does not attend 'American' churches but occasionally does the 'French' church; when asked the difference between the two she could not tell."

The *Picayune* wrote that M. Lerno, who was aboard a riverboat, saw frequent drilling at Colfax and the day before the fight had carried Eli Flowers, a leader of the defenders who was leaving the town because, he told Lerno, "they were afraid of the n——s, that if they knew they had run away from Colfax they would kill them."

The same man, who somehow became N. Delerno in the *Republican*, "saw Ward drilling...men in Colfax," and testified Flowers told him, "things were too hot for him in Colfax."

By the end of the trial the newspapers had presented such slanted reports that supporters of both sides were confident of victory.

But as a reminder to its readers how little the situation had changed in the year and a half since the election, while the jury was busy deliberating, a front-page *Picayune* headline welcomed "Governor McEnery" upon his return from Washington. He was greeted by several hundred cheering friends and supporters who blocked the streets. In a blatantly racist speech, he urged his followers to organize and "fight for the white people now."

It took the jury a full day to reach its verdicts. Apparently Judge Woods passed much of the day in his chambers playing the popular card game setback euchre with Governor Kellogg.

Given the composition of the jury—and the personal danger

they faced—there was a widespread belief the accused would be acquitted—if the jury was able to reach a verdict. The fact that it arrived at a verdict in a day seemed to be good news for the defense. As the courtroom filled on the night of June 10, the prisoners were described as "looking in very bad condition. The heat and the unhealthiness of their cells in the Parish Prison, the nervous suffering during the long trial…seemed to have broken them down entirely."

The courtroom had filled quickly, many of the spectators prepared to celebrate the expected acquittal. "Gentlemen," Judge Woods asked, "have you agreed upon a verdict?"

The courtroom was absolutely silent. The foreman, McKee, responded that it had, but apparently he was too overcome with emotion or nervousness to read it, so he passed it to another juror.

William Cruikshank, William Irwin and John P. Hadnot were found "guilty of combining and conspiring on the first sixteen counts and we recommend them to the mercy of the court."

The courtroom exploded with shock. Furious spectators began screaming; it was an "injustice," "a folly." But the evidence supported the verdict: the prisoners had conspired and banded together to prevent the peaceable assembly…to prevent their voting, bearing arms, and generally taking away the victims' rights.

No one was found guilty of any murder, however.

The other defendants were acquitted—but Beckwith announced he intended to proceed to try those men for killing William Williams at Colfax. The three convicted men faced $1,000 in fines and as long as ten years in prison. The other men were released on $10,000 bond.

Lost in the excitement was an announcement from Judge Woods that he had wired news of the decision to Judge Bradley. Bradley had left the city before the verdict was announced, but at the beginning of the trial, he had committed to considering a defense motion to dismiss several of the indictments as unconstitutional should any defendants be convicted. Now he would have to come through with that promise.

In the meantime, supporters of the convicted prisoners were irate. Several newspapers printed the names of the jurors. The *Picayune* found it "remarkable that [the three men] should be convicted of offenses which, according to all accounts, they did not commit." The *Bulletin* suggested the prisoners had been "hunted down like wild beasts" and dragged down to the city, and as a reward for this "infamous outrage" Beckwith probably would be handed a judgeship and Judge Woods might be elevated to the Supreme Court.

On a blistering hot day two weeks later Judge Bradley returned to New Orleans to render his opinion. Sitting next to Judge Woods he explained patiently why none of the sixteen counts in the indictment were valid. The third count declared a conspiracy was formed to take lives without due process—well, "All murderers do this. Has the United States jurisdiction of all murderers?" The fourth, fifth and eighth were "too vague and general." When he was done he concluded that, just as Marr had objected, "the indictment is fatally defective."

The federal government had no jurisdiction in this case, he concluded. All the convictions were dropped.

With his carefully chosen words Judge Bradley stuck a dagger into the heart of Reconstruction. In a few minutes, the entire balance of power between the federal government and the state government was fundamentally changed. He returned to the states an enormous amount of power to interpret the application of constitutional rights. Essentially, he concluded, the federal government could not enact or prosecute laws dealing with crimes generally considered to be within the states' rights, among them murder, robbery and assault. The immediate impact of his ruling was to free the final three prisoners, but the greater effect was to change American history for a century.

Judge Woods respectfully disagreed with that decision. He wrote his own opinion explaining his reasoning. The two judges resolved to certify their disagreement, which meant it would go to the full Supreme Court for a final determination. That would take several years, but until then Bradley's decision had become the law.

Despite its stated simplicity the decision was a complex weave of precedent, opinion and interpretation that federal and local courts would have to unravel, but none of that mattered to supporters of the defendants. The celebrations began immediately. More than one hundred of New Orleans's wealthiest and most prominent citizens gleefully offered to post bail for the prisoners.

Governor Kellogg recognized the racial implications of the decision; it was his belief that it established "the principle that hereafter no white man could be punished for killing a Negro."

That belief was tested within days. The freed prisoners steamed to Colfax, where they were greeted by a large, cheering crowd which included, according to an observer, several of the unindicted men who had participated in the killing spree. A day of raucous celebration became a night of violent retribution. A group of emboldened riders, rumored to include the three Hadnot brothers, rampaged through the Black living quarters, tearing up crops and gardens, firing pistols in celebration —and warning.

At one point they encountered a Black man named Frank Foster on a road. Alone, in the dark, confronted by a group of white men who possibly had been drinking all day, Foster tried to run. His bullet-riddled body was found the next day, a dagger in his throat.

People also discovered the body of an elderly Black man named Jim Cox in the doorway of his cabin. He had been shot, and his throat was slashed. A tough new sheriff, with the support of army troops, detained two men for the murders, but when they were brought in front of Judge Register, not a single man dared speak out against them.

They knew they no longer were protected by the law.

Whatever chances that there might be at least some racial harmony in Louisiana ended with Bradley's actions. Throughout Reconstruction there had been at least a smattering of Black Democrat and white Republican voters; there had even been men of both races on the opposing sides at Colfax. After the massacre the color line was strictly enforced.

There had been ongoing conversations for a long time about forming a new political party to fight the civil rights laws and the abuses of northern carpetbaggers, a party to represent the Southern white race. "Their career [as carpetbaggers] is ended," warned the *Shreveport Times*, "and if they care for their infamous necks they had better stop their work right now… If a single hostile gun is fired between the whites and blacks, every carpetbagger and scalawag that can be caught will in twelve hours be hanging from a limb."

The conviction of the three Colfax killers might have been the spark that ignited the movement. But rather than a traditional political party, it became a militia-like organization consisting of elements of the Democratic party and the Knights of the White Camelia.

The White League had been founded in the spring. Its organizers, in addition to John McEnery, included Colfax defense lawyers Robert Marr and E. John Ellis. Meeting in Opelousas in late April, its officers stated flatly that all efforts at conciliation had failed, and they therefore resolved "that we recognize the necessity of union among ourselves upon one white man for each office, and we earnestly invite all white men, without regard for former party affiliation to unite with us under the banner of the White League, which alone can rescue us from dissention and defeat."

Threats of violence were not incorporated in this charter, but no one doubted the intent. The League immediately either founded or gained control of several newspapers to spread the message. While there had been multiple white militias formed, all variations of the Klan, this was the first effort to create a regional organization with both a rural and urban presence. For many people, the Confederacy was rising again.

Newspapers spread threats and propaganda from the League. In late June the *Picayune* reignited fears of a Black uprising, warning on its front page, and without citing any evidence, that there was "a determination on the part of the colored people now in our city to seize the occasion of the coming Fourth of July for a grand coup on the white people to enforce their 'civil rights' if need be at the point of a bayonet." The paper claimed that the mostly Black Metropolitan policemen marching in the holiday parade were planning to go into bars and restaurants and demand drinks and food. If refused they intended to break everything. If there was resistance, they were "to at once fire and kill the proprietor and as many whites as possible…" and eventually "kill all the men and keep all the women."

They even revealed the secret signs and passwords of this organization. Members would greet each other by using their thumb to exert pressure on the other person's thumb. They would announce themselves by rapping three times, then pausing, and rapping one more time. The answer would be the same. The danger signal was the shout "Ho! Ho!" to be acknowledged with "Hey! Hey!" And the password was "Lost oh found."

The *Republican* dismissed the threat under the ironic headline "A Black League." The story was a "canard instilled in the brain of impressionable young men… The idea that a riot could possibly occur…no one, not even the conductors of the *Picayune*, would entertain for a moment… It would perhaps fire the hearts of White Leaguers…" In other words, it was nonsense.

But it was effective. The threat of a coming race war proved to be a compelling recruiting tool. The White League concept spread rapidly. Large picnics were held in rural parts of the state, where white people could come together and share their dreams of a Southern revival. Men joined by the thousands. By the summer there were more than fourteen thousand members in the countryside and at least fifteen hundred in New Orleans.

In the city the League was run by Frederick Nash Ogden, who a year earlier had led the failed attempt to take over the Mechanics Institute. Members formed "clubs" and drilled regularly in private ballrooms. Former Democratic organizations became White League clubs.

Christopher Nash, whose exploits at Colfax and ability to avoid capture had made him a legendary figure, was among the leaders in the countryside. Many months after the massacre Nash still contended that he was "endeavoring to preserve peace at Colfax" by serving a warrant and, having been fired upon, "summoned a posse comitatus of citizens, both white and c——d and with these [125 in number] succeeded on Easter Sunday in dispersing the 250 rioters and preserving peace... I deemed it was necessary to preserve peace at all hazards, and therefore, I resorted to the measures taken."

Incredibly, Democrats still supported the electoral system as the best way to choose leaders. It was not the system that they blamed but rather the people who had manipulated it. Certainly, there was a racial element to the violence; a large number of white people believed Reconstruction had gone too far. Living separately but equally was one thing—like it or not they tolerated it—but being cheated out of policymaking leadership positions was something entirely different. That no longer was acceptable.

It was their belief that they were righting an illegal wrong. The year 1874 was an election year. The Fusionists, Democrats, White Leaguers—whatever they chose to call themselves—were determined they would not be cheated again. "The white men intend to carry the State election this Fall," wrote the *Natchitoches Vindicator*. "This intention is deliberate and unalterable from the fact their very existence depends on it..."

If they could not win at the polls, they would take power by force.

Fittingly, it started in Natchitoches.

13

A scandal was spreading in New Orleans! A series of published letters revealed that President George Washington, with the assistance of Secretary of Treasury Alexander Hamilton, had overdrawn his $25,000 salary for several years. Washington, who had boldly told admirers he would accept no compensation other than reimbursement for expenses, in fact was thousands of dollars in arrears to the treasury. "He doubtless spent all he received," it was reported, "for he had lived in almost regal pomp, riding in the streets of Philadelphia with four horses to his coach."

The brewing scandal was a brief, amusing diversion from hard times. Governor Kellogg had reined in some of his predecessor Warmoth's spending by imposing strict budget cuts, so services and school support already had been curtailed, while the world-wide Panic of '73 made the economic situation far bleaker. The financial markets had been flooded with railroad bonds, and when they lost value, America's leading bank Jay Cooke & Co. collapsed, triggering a national depression. Louisiana's ports and cotton industry had been severely impacted, thousands of jobs disappeared, working men had their salaries cut, budgets were even further reduced. Politically, Kellogg had essentially forced a bill through the legislature giving him total power to appoint Registers of Election for the entire State—registrars who had the authority to determine who was eligible to vote, and to prevent others from voting.

To make matters worse, a yellow fever epidemic was raging through the rural Red River Valley.

People were angry and scared. They needed scapegoats.

The White League provided them. The League, which by then had become known as "the armed wing of the Democratic party," had become increasingly active in the heat of the Louisiana summer. In mid-July four League members forced their way into the home of an immigrant named Manuel Manos, supposedly to investigate the claim that he had supplied smuggled guns to freedmen, and during the confrontation shot him to death.

About a week later in Natchitoches, Louisiana's oldest settlement, a mob of at least seven hundred white men demanded the resignation of four Republican officials: a Black judge and a white judge, the white tax collector, and the parish attorney. They claimed they all were corrupt and that one of them had stolen "all the school money." Judge Bouilt previously had sworn his arms would have to be cut off before he would agree to resign, but he quickly changed his mind when confronted by seven hundred determined people. Although there was no violence, a witness admitted that had Bouilt refused to sign "it would have been difficult to restrain the crowd."

All four men immediately left the town, at least two of them traveling to the safety of New Orleans to plead with Governor Kellogg to reinstall them, even requesting he send Metropolitans to protect them. Kellogg declined.

News of the coup spread faster than the fever. "If these things can be done in Natchitoches they can be done elsewhere," the *Shreveport Times* proposed. "There is scarcely a parish in the

State where they cannot be done more easily…" The paper then added a far more dangerous suggestion: "There is no reason why Kellogg himself should not…be an outcast from a land he has turned into a desert."

The message spread. Weeks later in St. Martinville, five hundred White Leaguers, led by Alcibiades DeBlanc and armed with double-barreled shotguns and rifles, forced all the parish officers to resign. Any reluctance those officials might have had disappeared one day earlier when vigilantes in nearby New Iberia lynched two Black men suspected of theft.

In Lincoln Parish, an official submitted his resignation after being informed, reported the *Republican*, that "an armed mob of desperate characters…lay in wait for him…with the purpose to assassinate and murder him…"

The rebellion spread. In town after town elected Republican officials and appointees—the majority of them white—were forced from office. In Bossier, Rapides, DeSoto and Caddo; in Avoyelles, Webster and Winn; in Catahoula, Richland and Grant; and in other towns and villages throughout the Red River Basin, governments were overthrown, officials fled for their lives and local white Democrats were installed in their place. Incredibly, until late August in most instances this had been accomplished by intimidation rather than actual violence. But that was about to change.

The town of Coushatta lay on the banks of the Red River, about fifty miles south of Shreveport. A majority of its residents were freedmen, but a good number of northerners had settled there after the war. The local government was led by a popular carpetbagger named Harvey Twitchell. Captain Twitchell, who had commanded Black soldiers during the war, had come to the valley as a Freedmen's Bureau agent, married the daughter of a wealthy landowner and made his fortune. By 1871 he owned the largest plantation in the region. As a state legislator the Republican Twitchell had sponsored the creation of Red

River Parish that same year. Several members of his family, including his brother, Homer, had been appointed to official positions by Governor Warmoth.

Under Twitchell's leadership Coushatta had prospered. It had sawmills, gristmills, a cotton pickery, a machine shop and other local businesses. A courthouse and schoolhouse were built, and there were schools for both Black and white children. The levees had been strengthened. People got along. Coushatta was described as the closest thing to a settled New England town in the South. When Red River Parish was created, Coushatta was the obvious choice for its capital.

During a July 17 meeting in the Coushatta courthouse, Red River Parish White League members resolved to convince Twitchell and his supporters to voluntarily surrender their offices and leave town, although they did not immediately act on it. Twitchell responded by going to New Orleans to plead for federal troops. From the city he wrote a note to the Red River Parish sheriff, Frank Edgerton, advising him, "In case a demand is made for your resignation...be certain first that violence is to be used if you do not, and to save your life, resign.

"The Government will not allow a mob to govern the State."

That wasn't quite true. There was nothing Kellogg could do. In the first weeks of August, men presumed to be White Leaguers made a sustained and determined effort to prevent Black men from registering to vote. They used a variety of threats: if they registered they would lose their jobs or their land or no one would sell them supplies. They also offered bribes and promises. At the same time, they warned any man thinking about running for office as a Republican that he would be putting his life in danger.

It was just a matter of time before the threats became reality. "The incendiary teachings of the White League orators and newspapers have had their effect upon the country people," the *Republican* wrote. "No matter what denials they may make now, it is too late, their followers have received their cue, are told that the Federal Government will not interfere and thus emboldened they will not stop short of human blood to accomplish their purposes."

Like so many other horrors, these murders started with a simple argument. On August 25, White Leaguers James Williams and R. S. Jones were meeting with their Black neighbors Thomas Floyd and Dan Wynn in the village of Brownsville, about ten miles from Coushatta. Wynn apparently made it clear that he was not interested in supporting Democrats, insisting he owed his allegiance to the party of Lincoln, the party that had given him his freedom.

Not the party that had fought a war to keep him in chains.

The conversation escalated into threats. The White League later claimed that Floyd and Wynn had threatened Williams. Whatever happened, Williams quickly packed up his family and moved into Coushatta.

A night later, according to the local newspapers, four armed freedmen went to Williams's home. Whatever their intent, the story spread that they had gone there to assassinate him. Those men searched the place, then left.

Neighbors watched them going through the house. They knew who they were; they knew their names; they knew where they lived.

Within hours the White League had organized a posse. It split into two groups, one going to Wynn's house, the other headed to Floyd's. They later claimed they planned to arrest them. There were several versions of what happened in the next few hours, but all of them ended the same way: one white man was shot and survived, while Floyd, Wynn and a third man who had been in Williams's house, Tom Jones, had been shot and killed.

According to one widely published account, after Floyd was caught he pleaded, "Gentlemen, let me speak one word to my wife before you shoot me."

To which they responded, "'G-d d—n you, we have got no words for you to say.' His own gun was then pressed to his head and his brains blown out by one of the white men."

The story continued that Wynn saw Floyd being shot and fired at the intruders, wounding one of them. The vigilantes caught him and killed him.

Newspapers reported different versions of the event, but there was one fact no one could dispute: three Black men had been murdered.

Both sides raised their militias. White Leaguers were told that as many as a hundred armed Black men were gathering in Brownsville, and that they had declared they would not leave a white man, woman or child alive in the parish, or that they would kill the white men and take the women.

Several white men, led by Sheriff Edgerton, rode to Brownsville to investigate the murders and see for themselves what was happening.

They found Floyd's body lying in a field. The sheriff attempted to calm the situation, promising Black residents the murderers would be punished and telling white men that he saw absolutely no evidence that a Black militia was gathering.

That didn't stop newspapers from turning rumor into "facts."

"Blacks had risen against whites and threatened extermination!"

"Coushatta is guarded by hundreds of white men, who call for help!"

"Conflict is inevitable!"

On the night of August 27, a dance party was held in Coushatta to celebrate the opening of a new brick storehouse owned by White League leader Thomas Abney. Just in case, though, all the men brought their weapons, and pickets were put out on all the roads approaching the town. As they danced into the night, there were whispers that a large number of Black men were gathering at Homer Twitchell's place, preparing to attack the party. No one seemed troubled by the claim that this "Black uprising" was being led by a white man.

The dance ended peacefully about ten o'clock. Within minutes a scouting party set out to patrol the area. Johnny and Joe Dickson rode out to Homer Twitchell's place. They said later they saw armed freedmen in the area. Minutes later the two brothers spotted a man walking on the road and called for him to stop. Instead, he ran into the fields. One of the Dickson boys took several shots at him.

About a half hour later, as the brothers were riding back to town, someone opened fire on them from a cotton field. Joe Dickson was hit five times, in his left arm, leg and side. His horse was also hit and took off. "In this utterly helpless condition," it was reported, he made an extraordinary effort to save his life, somehow managing "to remain in the saddle until he grasped the reins in his right hand, and with the assistance of his teeth, checked, at length, the career of the mad brute."

Dickson made it home in critical condition. The shooting had started.

Tom Abney spread the word: seven hundred freedmen were coming to town to kill men and rape their women.

Within hours a thousand white men raced to Coushatta, ready for the coming fight. They had come from all the surrounding parishes and from as far away as the Texas border towns. They brought their guns.

At just about the same time, people in Brownsville also were being warned: hundreds of armed white men were gathering in Coushatta. Planning on another Colfax.

In an effort to prevent bloodshed, or perhaps, as White Leaguers claimed, for their own safety, a twenty-five-member "Committee of Safety" arrested six white Republican town officials: Homer Twitchell, Sheriff Edgerton, the tax collector Dewees, parish attorney Howell, Supervisor of Registration Clark Holland and Justice of the Peace M. C. Willis. In addition, six or seven freedmen were taken into custody. All the men were held overnight in the Coushatta town jail.

With their leaders imprisoned, freedmen returned to their homes. The confrontation ended.

After a brief public show trial, during which not a bit of evidence was produced tying any of the men to an uprising, the six Republican town officials were offered a deal: in return for safe passage, resign and leave the state immediately, promising never to come back. Eventually, reluctantly, they signed the agreement. "We propose on our part to leave the State of Louisiana and surrender to the people the offices we hold, and here request an escort to protect us out of the State."

Their only stipulation was that they would pick the men who would ride out with them. They planned to go to Shreveport, and from there into Texas. Once they got to the city, they believed, they would be safe. Captain Abney delayed their departure another full day. A lot of men had come to Coushatta ready for action. And many of them were mighty unhappy that Twitchell and the others were just being let go. It was hard for them to accept the fact that armed Black men had come to Brownsville, threatened to attack Coushatta, shot and nearly killed a young man, and paid a very small price for it. Somebody had been responsible for organizing it. Somebody had to pay. And if it didn't get stopped here once and for all, that threatened attack was going to happen down the line.

They needed time to calm down.

The prisoners rode out of town very early Sunday morning, August 30. Twitchell had picked about twenty men to escort them, led by a trusted local citizen named John Carr. They had tried to keep their route secret. Rather than staying on the main road, they took a path along the river. They rode hard toward Shreveport.

They rode through the morning, slowing when they got near the Hutchinson Plantation, about thirty-five miles from

Coushatta. They intended to cross the Red River there, then destroy their flatboat to ensure nobody could follow them.

They never made it.

Once again, there are different versions of what happened next. Some people said that soon after the officials and their guards left Coushatta, a group of forty to fifty men, Texans supposedly, took off after them. Others claimed that a large group of men, as many as one hundred, coming from Texas to join the fight, ran right into them. There were even some stories that members of the guard had arranged a rendezvous with a gang from DeSoto Parish led by a hard-core killer known as "Captain Jack" Coleman. Any of those scenarios are possible, and several years later Carr was identified as a White League captain responsible for at least two deaths in Bienville Parish. People noted the prisoners were attacked right after they entered Bossier Parish, which was known to be far friendlier to white supremacists than Red River. But everyone agreed that when the prisoners saw the posse coming, they made a run for the river. But there was no escape.

The outgunned guards were told, "Git outta the way or share their fate."

Supposedly, Homer Twitchell begged for a gun to protect himself, screaming, "I don't want to die like a dog." Seconds later he was shot in his face. Edgerton and Dewees were murdered where they stood. Howell, Holland and Willis were taken a short distance into the woods and killed.

All of the victims were stripped of their valuables and their money stolen. A large bankroll was taken from one of them. Their bodies were described as "horribly mutilated," one of them "so gashed and perforated with bullets that it could scarcely be moved."

It would be several weeks before anyone was arrested for the Coushatta Massacre, as people had begun referring to it. By late October several hundred warrants had been issued for the Red

River murders as well as for threatening freedmen and Republican officeholders. Cavalry troops swept into Shreveport and neighboring parishes to make arrests. The troops put on a great show but accomplished very little.

Most of those men they were looking for had been warned and either fled "to take shelter in the woods under the canopy of heaven" or simply couldn't be found. Only thirteen men were apprehended, Captain Abney among them. They were taken under guard to New Orleans. All of them were released on $5,000 bond. From time to time, through the next months, other warrants were made public, and several additional men were arrested—and just as quickly bailed out.

No one was ever prosecuted for those crimes.

But those six murders were only the beginning. White Leaguers remaining in Coushatta must have felt cheated. They had gotten no satisfaction. But there was still the Dickson shooting to be resolved. Someone had to pay for ambushing the kid. Two freedmen, Paul Williams and Lewis Johnson, had been arrested and charged with the shooting. Williams supposedly confessed, although obviously under duress: "I shot Mr. J. R. Dickson; I did; now gentlemen you can take me and shoot me or hang me as you please."

In his confession he conveniently implicated Homer Twitchell, claiming Twitchell had ordered them to fire on any white people who came to his house. It was Twitchell who warned that if they did not kill the white men, the white men would kill them. Williams had no choice, he pleaded: Twitchell, Sheriff Edgerton and Robert Dewees, the DeSoto Parish tax collector, had threatened, bullied and terrified men into following them.

Williams's confession did not save him. As Williams and Johnson were being taken to jail, as many as seventy-five men "some mounted and some on foot came up, took them from the guard and swung them to a limb." When reporting it, Republican newspapers pointed out that normally suspected criminals are tried first, then hanged, as opposed to what took place.

According to a federal committee that later investigated these killings, a third freedman, Eli Allen, "was taken from his house by the White League, slowly tortured to death by being shot first in one limb and the others until all were broken, and after being rendered helpless, a fire was built upon his head."

The whole episode was a terrible tragedy, Abney solemnly admitted, but the blame lay with Homer Twitchell. He wanted a violent confrontation. By starting this uprising, he was going to force his men to fight to protect themselves, then "proclaim white people were venting their hatred...and that it was necessary to put down the 'new ku-klux' by Federal power." That would force President Grant or Governor Kellogg to send soldiers into the parish to protect Republican government officials. It was his way of putting an end to the insurrection. The rebellion would stop there.

If that actually was a plan, it nearly worked.

News of the massacre stunned the country. By now northerners were used to reading stories in which Black Southern men had been murdered. It happened every day. But this...this was different. These were white government officials just doing their job. Other white people could identify with them. This seemed an attack on democracy.

In response, Governor Kellogg sent a furious telegraph to President Grant, informing him that "a more wanton outrage was never committed in any civilized community," and asking for federal assistance. Kellogg also declared martial law and offered an extraordinary $5,000 reward for the capture and conviction of any of the participants. There was little else he could do, though: his political enemies were closing in on him.

White League supporters loudly argued that race had nothing to do with the killings: the victims had been corrupt white officials. Democratic newspapers reminded readers that all of the freedmen who had been arrested in Coushatta had been released without any harm. League leaders issued a statement denying any involvement in the murders, placing the blame on those unidentified Texans. Their fight, they claimed, was against all Republicans, especially the northerners who had despoiled their State. It wasn't the color of their skin; it was the way they voted.

The people who really bore the responsibility, they insisted, were Ulysses S. Grant, William Pitt Kellogg and the rest of the thieves who had stolen the election. Even Henry Warmoth deserved a share of the blame.

President Grant moved cautiously. Every decision had a political impact. He responded to Kellogg's request by instructing the secretary of the army to move troops already in Louisiana to places where their presence might make a difference. But he made sure to add that those soldiers could not be used to prevent any legal political or party actions. In reality, all that happened was that the few companies of soldiers were moved into more visible positions.

The attacks on Republican officials continued. Congress would eventually report DeSoto Parish was so lawless that "No prominent Republican can make a speech or openly act with the Republican party...except at the extreme risk of his life. Cases of persecution, destruction of crops and driving from their homes by White League desperadoes are almost without number..."

The White League continued to grow in numbers and power. No other organization since the beginning of Reconstruction had been as successful in fighting Republican rule. What made it especially effective was that rather than having central leadership dictating their actions, it remained a loose association of smaller groups, each of them acting independently in responding to their local issues.

If there was a leader, it was their "Governor," John McEnery, who had maintained his hold on his supporters since the disputed election. Every drop of blood could be traced directly back to his refusal to concede. But McEnery was more their representative, keeping the debate alive, than someone who exercised active control.

The Republican media tried to tie McEnery to the "Coushatta outrage," writing that he had been in that town two days before the uprising and had made a fiery speech, adding that even after the killings he refused to rebuke the murder of defenseless men. The *New York Times* reported that McEnery "in set speeches advised the white people to organize, arm and drive Republicans from the State...to resist even United States troops. McEnery going so far as to say that Grant would not dare to use United States troops against them."

In a letter to the editors of the largest newspapers McEnery angrily denied the accusation: he had made no such speech, he wrote, he had never even been in Coushatta. He had never "counseled or advised our people to deeds of violence and lawlessness." All he had done was point out the crimes committed against the good people of the State, try to assume the post those people had given him and, when that was denied him, "protect society against the ravages of official plunderers and spoliators."

There was one last piece of the tragedy to be played out. State Senator Marshall Twitchell finally returned to Coushatta two years after the murders of his brother and brother-in-law. On May 2, 1876, Twitchell and his other brother-in-law, tax collector George King, were coming to the town to attend a grand jury meeting. While most of the men in town were at the courthouse collecting their mail, which had just arrived, a stranger rode into town. He was well disguised, wearing a false beard, black goggles and an India rubber longcoat, which was closed at the collar and came down to his shoes, covering up his clothing.

He stopped at the blacksmith's to have his horse shod. He sat there for two hours, watching the river landing. As the skiff carrying Twitchell and King across the river came closer, he wandered down to the bank. Just as the boat was landing, without a word he pulled a sixteen-shot Henry rifle from under his coat and opened fire. His first shot hit Twitchell in the thigh.

King pulled a pistol and got off two shots that went wide. The stranger fired again, hitting King in the head, killing him instantly.

Twitchell leaped into the river, grabbing hold of the skiff with his left arm, trying to hide behind it for protection. The stranger shot him in that arm. Twitchell pulled himself around to the other side and held on with his right arm. The stranger shot him in that arm too. Too much: Twitchell let go and began floating helplessly down the river.

The ferryman, Old Dennis, rowed to him and tried to pull him back into the skiff. The stranger kept shooting, taking off one of Old Dennis's fingers.

A townsman on the other side of the river fired several shots at the stranger, missing him completely. Another man approached, but the stranger pointed his rifle at him and warned, "G-d d—n your soul. Get." He did.

The stranger mounted his horse and rode down the river. Chasing the drifting boat. Pulling a Remington six-shooter, he fired several more shots. Old Dennis screamed at the shooter to stop; the deed was done, Twitchell was dead. The shooter turned his horse and rode out of town. He had fired twenty-two times.

Several people watched him go. He was in no hurry. No one followed him.

But with his lie, Old Dennis had saved Twitchell's life. He managed to get the wounded man to land. An army surgeon amputated one arm right away; his other arm was taken off twenty-eight days later. Somehow, he survived.

Although the usual $5,000 reward was offered, the assassin's identity was never learned; although, many people remarked how unusual it was that the man had been in town several hours before Twitchell's arrival without anyone approaching him. Also, he was allowed to calmly ride out of town, and the sheriff proved reluctant to pursue him. The conservative papers named a suspect and a motive, claiming the shooter was a Radical Republican to whom Twitchell had offered a $1,000 bribe to fix the returns in DeSoto Parish—who had ambushed Twitchell because he had reneged on the deal.

That accusation was immediately disproved, as several people had seen the accused man in New Orleans the day of the shooting.

Congressional testimony eventually suggested the shooter was the notorious "Captain Jack" Coleman, but that was never proved. Twitchell told reporters "although he cannot shake hands with friend or foe and that doctors have to feel in odd places for his pulse, he will hereafter give more attention to his brain, his only source to earn a livelihood." Eventually, he was appointed a government consul, assigned to Kingston, Canada.

The White League continued to act with impunity: the list of threats, attacks and killings was long and seemingly endless. John Wesley, a white man who taught Black children, was run out of Coushatta the same day the doomed town officials were arrested. Jack Cawton was pulled out of his house and shot for voting Republican. Richard Bonner, soon after being elected constable, was poisoned. James Williams was shot by "Captain Jack." Officials were run out of towns and villages throughout the state. Few people were arrested. No one was ever tried or convicted.

However, for months the uprising had been restricted to the countryside. Republicans retained control of the cities, especially New Orleans. But slowly the noose was tightening. The White League had officially announced its presence in the city in June 1873, when the Crescent City Democratic Club was officially reorganized as the Crescent City White League. Fred N. Ogden was elected president.

Every public document proclaimed this to be a nonviolent

movement. It was a political organization. It had no secret handshakes or passwords; its members didn't dress in distinctive clothing. No one hid his identity. Republican newspapers noted cautiously that the club was not a danger "so long as its operations are restricted to drumming up voters." Supporters compared it to "The League and the Covenant," a document written and circulated exactly one hundred years earlier by Samuel Adams and Boston's Committee of Correspondence which proposed citizens join together to protest British oppression.

But its stated purpose was far more ominous: it intended to wrest the state from Republican control. After the '72 election debacle, and with the continuing presence of a heavily armed, well-trained Metropolitan Police force and state militia defending Kellogg, they knew this could not be accomplished at the ballot box.

As club membership swelled into the thousands, the League adopted a more military structure. It organized into dozens of companies and appointed officers; its members marched and drilled in private clubs and ballrooms and through the streets of the city. Flags and banners were held high. Bands played "Dixie" and the other songs that lived in their hearts. White women and children cheered as their men marched by torchlight. Veterans marched alongside boys too young to have served in the war. And all of them, the young and the old, men and women, felt the stirrings of lost pride. It was time to seize control of their lives, of their state, of their country.

Secretly, they began buying surplus Civil War weapons.

No one dared stop them. The rebellion had come to New Orleans.

14

In the parishes, small towns and villages throughout rural Louisiana, the White League had sharpened the tools needed to overthrow the Republican government. It had used violence, intimidation, pride and propaganda to inflame an already-angry populace. It had been emboldened by the impotence of President Grant's administration to stop them. Rather than defending local governments, federal troops had been withdrawn from the state. When challenged, Republican officials were resigning, often leaving town rather than offering any resistance. Kellogg's control had been reduced to the cities.

In Washington, committees continued meeting regularly to try to resolve the election confusion, or to place blame for Colfax and Coushatta and numerous other despicable acts of violence. After almost two years of investigation and debate, the Senate still refused to seat Pinchback or anyone else.

Grant's declaration months earlier in support of Kellogg's administration had made little real impact. Words were meaningless. The White League heard a very different message in his inaction: the president was unwilling or unable to provide the military support the governor needed to retain power.

Two years after the contested election, after all the political maneuvering, after all the intimidation and the endless violence, it all came down to New Orleans.

In 1874 New Orleans was America's ninth-largest city. It was the leading port in the South. It arguably was the most success-fully integrated major city in the nation, the home of Thomy Lafon, the country's wealthiest Black merchant. It was widely considered America's most exotic city: a wondrous mélange of cultures and races and religions, the home of Mardi Gras and voodoo; poker had been invented in New Orleans, opera had been introduced to America there. It was a place of fine restau-rants and smoke-filled joints, a place where plantation society met the newly arrived Sicilian Mafia, where One-Eyed Sal and Brick-top Johnson walked the streets and any desire could be fulfilled.

And now it was to stake another claim on American history.

It was all about the guns. The state militia and the Metropoli-tan Police were outmanned, but until now they had not been outgunned. They were well equipped with rifles and cannon. But throughout the summer the White League had quietly been buying cheap surplus weapons and ammunition. It had been arming its men for what was to come. By late May steamboat crewmen were whispering that just about every boat leaving New Orleans was delivering guns to Leaguers in river towns.

The Second Amendment had granted Americans the right to bear arms, but exactly what that meant continued to be de-bated. It was widely agreed that people needed guns to hunt and, in dangerous places like the frontier, to protect their families. The concept that ordinary people needed guns in their homes to defend themselves had taken hold after the war. But Ameri-cans also recognized that guns were inherently dangerous, and it benefited society to limit ownership. Politicians were trying to determine which gun laws made the most people safe, while not abrogating their constitutional rights. Different states had interpreted the Constitution differently and passed unique laws. Gun ownership had always been regulated—and restricted. As early as 1619, Virginia passed laws to prevent felons, foreigners— and Native Americans—from owning firearms. In 1637, Massachusetts Bay barred outspoken members of the colony whose opinions "seduced and led into dangerous errors" from possessing "guns, pistols, swords, powder, shot and match." Through the ensuing decades states had tailored laws to fit their needs; in different places guns had been legally confiscated, registered and even taxed. Even the definition of a gun varied: in some states it referred only to a long gun, musket or rifle, while in others it included pistols and derringers. Various court decisions found that *arms* referred specifically to weapons that might be used by the military or generally to any firearm.

The only restriction on which all states agreed was that slaves could not be allowed to have guns. The danger of an armed uprising was deemed too great. But during the war the North had enlisted, trained and armed almost two hundred thousand Black troops. In fact, Louisiana's 73rd Regiment of the United States Colored Troops were the first Black troops to engage in combat in American history. The postwar Amendments granted them all the rights of citizenship, including gun ownership. After several states passed black codes to prevent freedmen from possessing guns, then General Grant said that those laws were "unjust, oppressive and unconstitutional."

To try to limit the spreading gun violence during the Reconstruction, the federal Department of the South issued regulations prohibiting members of organizations "not belonging to the military or naval forces of the United States"—the Ku Klux and White League, for example—from possessing weapons.

Louisiana had long regulated guns. A law passed in 1813, less than a year after the state joined the union, prohibited carrying concealed weapons and granted police the right to stop and search anyone suspected of being armed. Those laws were tightened in 1855 after a series of murders, making even partial concealment of a firearm a crime. An 1831 New Orleans law made it illegal for anyone to enter "a public ballroom with any cane, stick, sword, or any other weapon."

After the Civil War Louisiana tried to find legal means of preventing freed Black men from possessing guns. The state's 1868 constitution, acknowledging that the Second Amendment begins with the phrase *A well regulated Militia, being necessary to the security of a free State*, declared that the right to bear arms applied specifically to members of the state militia. Therefore, only weapons that might be used by those people were entitled to constitutional protection. A pistol, the state Supreme Court ruled, "was not an arm for war purposes" and therefore could be regulated by the legislature. In 1870, to further limit gun ownership Warmoth instituted a tax, which made it even more difficult for the poor to keep weapons—although, it appears pistols were not included.

These laws ensured the state militia and police would not be outgunned. Beginning with the earliest settlements two centuries earlier, local governments had provided weapons and ammunition to militiamen—who often could not afford to buy their own guns—for the protection of all its citizens. The fact that a majority of Louisiana's state militia were former slaves and war veterans terrified white supremacists like McEnery, "Lieutenant Governor" Penn and White League leader Frederick Ogden. If they were to rid the state of the Kellogg regime, they had to arm their men. Legally or illegally, they had to put guns in their hands.

Buying the weapons was not difficult. The country was flooded with readily available, cheap rifles after the Civil War. Belgian rifles could be bought for as little as two dollars apiece. While Louisiana was still reeling from the Coushatta Massacre, the first shipment of surplus weapons arrived, smuggled in aboard the New Orleans, Jackson and Great Northern Railroad in crates marked *Machinery*. They were delivered to a local foundry building and distributed to League members, who took them home and hid them.

It was impossible to keep the operation secret. The whole city was trembling with anticipation: a revolution was brewing. It was just a matter of when. The White League was going to rid the state of the carpetbaggers and scalawags. And equally important, they were going to teach a memorable lesson to those former slaves who had risen to power. They were going to take back control of their lives and their futures. They were going to be Southerners once again.

As soon as they got the guns.

An audacious plan was discussed. With luck, Kellogg could be overthrown without a single shot fired. Several White Leaguers would take positions near the State House. When a prearranged signal was given they would rush the building, capture Kellogg and other administration officials, put them aboard a waiting steamer and carry them out to sea. They would be kept incommunicado long enough to allow McEnery to assume office. Decent white citizens would take to the streets, they would support the new governor in such great numbers that Grant would have no choice but to recognize the new governor.

It seemed like a reasonable plan. It would require few men, could be done quickly and could be accomplished without shedding blood. But McEnery finally decided against it, fearing it left too much to chance.

Meanwhile, more guns arrived. Early on the morning of September 8, Metropolitans in citizens' garb watched from the shadows as a shipment of seventy-two Prussian and Belgian rifles was delivered to Olivier's Gun Shop at 80 Canal Street. At three o'clock that afternoon, a wagon stopped in front of the store, and three crates were loaded onto it. Two blocks later Metropolitans swarmed the wagon and took the boxes of guns to police headquarters. Hours later two crates filled with ammunition were seized.

In a statement to the press, Metropolitan Police Superintendent Badger said that the weapons were banned as White League ordnance, they were intended for irresponsible parties, and an entirely legal warrant had been issued and enforced.

Few people had seen the actual seizure, but as news spread that the police had confiscated privately owned guns, an angry crowd gathered outside the gun shop to protest. This could not be allowed! It set a dangerous precedent. The Second Amendment protected the right of private citizens to own guns. If they let the police take these guns no one knew where they would stop.

And if their guns were taken away from them, the only people who would have guns served the government. And they did not trust the government.

The Metropolitans did not back down. The next morning several detectives burst into Mr. Olivier's shop, grabbed three more crates of rifles marked "boots, shoes and dry goods" and arrested Arthur Olivier for aiding and abetting certain persons in obtaining arms to be used for riotous purposes.

The raid lasted only a few minutes: the police were gone with the guns before protestors had time to organize. The rumor spread that there would be an attack on the police to recover the guns. General Badger kept several hundred officers on alert inside the stations through the night.

Innocent actions assumed a darker tone. On Sunday evening two Black officers arrested an elderly white man walking home carrying a musket. The policemen, the *Picayune* reported on its front page, "wanted to know what he meant by carrying a gun in the streets of New Orleans." He was detained "on the frivolous charge of carrying concealed guns; frivolous because it being impossible…to carry a musket concealed." While the man was released his gun was added "to the monstrous collection of stolen guns that now fill the police station."

The story concluded, "The negro policeman stated that the carrying of guns would no longer be tolerated in the city."

The meaning was obvious: the government was coming for your guns.

Governor Kellogg tried to defuse the tension, telling the media, "No attempt has been made, or will be made to interfere with the buying, selling, keeping or bearing of arms for private purposes or self-defense…"

Those people claiming the government was violating their Second Amendment rights were troublemakers, he said, men who had "garbled" the meaning of the constitution: "Look at the whole article—the entire sentence—for the extract quoted is only half a sentence. The article reads, 'A well regulated militia being necessary to the security of a free State, the right of the people to keep and bear arms shall not be infringed.' In other words, Congress shall make no law inhibiting the states from maintaining a militia—the right of the people to bear arms as constituent members of the militia of the State shall not be infringed. This is all any candid man claimed this clause meant."

He was seizing guns, he maintained, "to maintain law and order; the citizens are to be protected... It is preposterous to suppose for a moment that the government can allow political bodies to arm themselves in defiance of State laws while openly avowing their intention to war upon the constituted authorities."

As for McEnery and his supporters, "These troubles are generally fomented by designing politicians who have axes to grind and want the masses, who are their dupes, to turn the grindstone; and when they have pushed the unthinking and inexperienced into the breach, these fomenters of political disturbance will generally be found in safety or protected by some subterfuge."

His explanation made no difference. The situation had gone too far to be calmed by the words of a widely despised politician.

The next shipment of White League guns was scheduled to arrive in New Orleans aboard the steamer *Mississippi* on September 12. Two hundred and sixty-four new muskets and twenty-five cases of ammunition, enough to equip an entire company, had been shipped from New York. If the delivery was intended to be secret, that had failed. Kellogg and Badger had learned all the details, and an order was issued instructing the Metropolitans to seize it.

The leak might have been intentional. Kellogg's order was an outrage! An insult! It was exactly what the White League needed to rouse its supporters. It was the provocation for which McEnery and Ogden had been waiting. On Sunday, September 13,

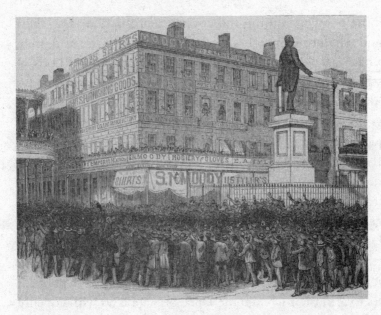

Thousands of armed men gathered at the Henry Clay statue in the morning and were ordered to attack.

sympathetic newspapers published an appeal to the CITIZENS OF NEW ORLEANS. It was the long-awaited call to arms. "For nearly two years you have been silent but indignant sufferers of outrage after outrage—heaped upon you by an usurping government!... Your rights have been trampled upon until...this mockery of a Republican government has dared even to deny you the right so solemnly guaranteed by the very Constitution...

"In that same sacred instrument...it also was declared that even Congress shall make no law abridging 'the right of the people peacefully to assemble and to petition the Government for a redress of grievances.' It now remains for us to ascertain whether this right any longer remains to us."

The announcement called for people to close their businesses "without a single exception" and gather at the statue of Henry Clay on Canal Street "and in tones loud enough to be heard throughout the length and breadth of the land, DECLARE THAT YOU ARE, OF RIGHT OUGHT TO BE, AND MEAN TO BE FREE."

Placards announcing the time and place of the rally were posted in every part of the city. The details were printed on long narrow strips of paper which were pasted to the wooden curbs at every intersection.

The revolution was scheduled to begin at eleven o'clock.

No one doubted what was coming. Kellogg sent a telegraph to the president requesting "aid to protect Louisiana from domestic violence."

Grant responded by ordering the 3rd United States Infantry, stationed in Brookhaven, Mississippi, to proceed immediately to New Orleans. General John Brooke requisitioned a train; if he moved quickly enough, the troops might get to the city in time to prevent the coup.

The White League had to delay them. Penn recalled Henry Warmoth's epic race with Pinchback. As the former governor had done, he wired supporters at the railroad asking for assistance. He got it: while Brooke's train was stopped at a way station, problems suddenly developed in the locomotive's driving gear—problems that could not quickly be repaired. By the time a replacement engine reached them, it was far too late.

Protestors began filling the streets early in the morning. By eleven o'clock a massive, boisterous crowd had gathered around the Clay statue. Speakers addressed them from the balcony of the Crescent Billiard Hall. They told the people what they had come to hear: Republicans in Washington had imposed their government on them; that government was taking away their constitutional rights, especially those granted by the Second Amendment.

The crowd loved every minute, every word. They cheered as newly-appointed Judge Robert Marr told them that McEnery had been elected governor by more than 10,000 votes and Penn lieutenant governor by a 15,000-vote margin. Therefore, Marr shouted, "the existing government of the state is a usurpation, the result of violent abuse of judicial functions and sustained by force!" In such a situation there is nothing more loyal and legal than the people rising to reclaim their rights.

By acclamation they adopted a resolution demanding Governor Kellogg's immediate resignation. A five-member delegation was authorized to present it to him. They proceeded to Kellogg's quarters in the Hotel Royal, but he was gone, having taken refuge in the heavily guarded Custom House.

The committee instead met with Judge Henry Dibble, who relayed Kellogg's response: the governor would be delighted to speak with the representatives of "peaceful citizens" but would not meet with anyone while "large bodies of armed men" were menacing the city.

Judge Marr returned to the balcony. The crowd quieted. This was the moment for which they had been preparing for two years. Kellogg had refused to meet with the committee, he reported. The crowd roared in response, "Hang him! Hang him!" Over and over, "Hang him! Hang him!"

There were no options left. Go home, Marr told them, get your guns. Come back. Fight.

John McEnery was waiting in Vicksburg, Mississippi, where he had gone supposedly to "visit friends." That left Penn in charge of the rebellion. Penn issued a proclamation. "Through fraud and violence the government of your choice has been overthrown and its power usurped," it read, concluding, "The right of suffrage is virtually taken away from you by the enactment of skillfully devised election and registration laws... I do hereby [call] upon the militia of the state...to arm and assemble under their respective officers for the purpose of driving the usurpers from power."

Victor Hugo's stirring story of the French Revolution, *Les Misérables*, had been published in the United States in 1862. It created a national sensation. Soldiers on both sides had carried cheap editions in their knapsacks throughout the war, passing it from hand to hand. Confederates even began referring to themselves as "Lee's Miserables." Hugo's tale of patriots manning Parisian barricades to fight for freedom had captured the imagination of the oppressed, making it the bestselling novel of the time.

In the early afternoon of September 14, 1874, more than six

Most of the main streets were barricaded with carriages, streetcars and timbers and were heavily patrolled.

thousand White League supporters began barricading streets in the city of New Orleans. Camp Street was blocked with logs and barrels. A wall of horsecars stretched across St. Charles, the pavement in front of it pulled up to create a formidable ditch. Whatever materials could be found were utilized: lumber, wagon wheels, broken glass and advertising pillars. Iron guttering was weaved into a twisted barrier at Carondelet Street. Guards were stationed at the main intersections, and only people replying to a challenge with the correct countersign were permitted to pass. Heavily armed White Leaguers hid in buildings along Canal Street. General Ogden set up headquarters on Poydras Street.

Kellogg, Casey and other government officials remained secure in the Custom House. They were protected by a company of federal troops, who took defensive positions behind a barricade made from boxes of floor tiles. State militia commanded by General Longstreet and two Metropolitan battalions dug in on both the north and south sides of the massive building. Several hundred more policemen were stationed inside the Third Precinct station. They were supplemented by dozens of civilian "volunteers," many of them just released from prison and issued guns and ammunition.

By early evening General Brooke's 3rd Infantry was back on track, chugging toward the city at full speed, but still hours away.

All told, more than fifteen thousand armed men were getting ready to fight for control of the city, and with it the entire state of Louisiana.

They also had an audience. Hundreds of excited, curious spectators had turned out to see what was going to happen. Many people still refused to believe it had come to killing. As troops began maneuvering, they rushed to find safe places from which to watch the fighting. It was an astonishing moment, comparable only to the first days of the Civil War. This time, though, American citizens were taking up arms against American law enforcement officers and state militia.

Slightly after two o'clock, General Ogden dispatched a company to seize City Hall. At about the same time General Badger ordered a hundred and eighty infantry and twenty mounted troops, armed with two twelve-pounders and a Gatling gun, to clear Canal Street.

The first shots of the Battle of Liberty Place were fired about two hours later.

The battle raged through the streets of New Orleans for several hours.

Sharpshooters hid behind cotton bales on the levees.

Several dozen White Leaguers had advanced along the levee, hidden by bales of cotton and hay, intending to outflank the Metropolitans' battle line. When they were in place, about three hundred men began moving toward the Custom House. Badger waited patiently, willing to let them come to him. When they got within range, he gave the order: fire. His men opened up with their Gatling gun and artillery.

Seconds later the White Leaguers behind the bales on the levee returned fire.

In an instant, downtown New Orleans had become a battle-field.

Badger was stunned. Where did those men come from? The gunfire devastated his ranks. In the first minute eighteen men went down. He called desperately for reinforcements, then boldly stepped forward to rally his troops. Three bullets tore into his body.

Ogden ordered his men on Canal Street to press the attack. The Metropolitans were in disarray. Leaderless, they began retreating, many of them dropping their weapons and running. With a great rebel yell, the battle cry of the Confederacy, White Leaguers raced forward; the defenders were driven back, beaten, fleeing through the Custom House and out the rear doors down Decatur Street.

General Badger was left lying desperately wounded in the street. While the fight still raged, he was surrounded by angry Leaguers. Suddenly, an officer stood over him, protecting him. Badger was a well-respected man, honored by soldiers for his "cool self-reliance and unflinching courage." The officer waved his sword, threatening to kill the first person who touched the general. Soon other men came running up with a mattress and carried him off the battlefield. He was taken to his home, where his leg was amputated.

General Longstreet was far luckier. His horse was shot out from under him, but he was not seriously hurt.

The entire battle lasted several hours; the shooting ended when Brooke's 3rd Infantry finally arrived and formed a line on Canal Street, driving back the insurgents. But the body count was high: twenty-one White Leaguers had been killed, and at least several dozen had been wounded; eleven defenders were dead, and at least sixty wounded. Several innocent bystanders also had been shot; newspaper reporter J. M. West was killed.

The fighting was done, but the siege had just begun. The White League occupied City Hall, the arsenal, the parish prison, as well as recovering the crates of firearms taken by the police from the *Mississippi*. Two thousand guns stored in the arsenal were handed out to the militia. The last defenders of the State House abandoned the building after being warned by Penn that if they were still there at sunrise "he could not be responsible for the result."

His men also seized telegraph lines, cutting off communications between US Marshal Packard and the attorney general in Washington, while allowing the White Leaguers to spread their version of events to the rest of the country. There were some holdouts. Federal troops protected Kellogg and several hundred other people who had found refuge in the Custom House. About a hundred and twenty-five members of the state militia, led by the wounded Captain Lawler, occupied the Third Precinct station house. They were heavily armed, with guns, two cannon and a plentiful supply of ammunition. Lawler was determined to hold out.

Early in the evening Penn wired McEnery "I am in complete possession of the city and State government. Come down."

Penn also issued a reassuring statement to the city's Black residents. "Rest assured," it read, "that no harm is meant toward you, your property or your rights... We war against thieves, plunderers and spoliators of the State, who are involving your race and ours in common ruin..."

The night passed peacefully. Armed White Leaguers patrolled the city. The barricades were removed from the main thoroughfares, and streetcar service resumed.

On the morning of September 15, newspapers throughout the South proclaimed, "The war is over. Louisiana is free and peace reigns throughout the city. The arsenal, with 5000 stand of arms, fifteen pieces of artillery, Statehouse and all police strongholds, with the entire police and militia forces, surrendered to the citizens this morning. No blood today." Kellogg's defenders were granted amnesty; they laid down their arms and went home.

But Kellogg, General Longstreet and several other Republican leaders remained in the Custom House, protected by federal troops, trying to figure out how to proceed. Kellogg's only hope, he knew, was support from President Grant.

The White House remained silent.

For McEnery's victorious supporters it was a day of celebration. Thousands of jubilant people wandered through the streets, sharing their joy. No one wanted to go home. When it was announced early in the morning that the troops inside the State House had surrendered without a shot, they responded "with a

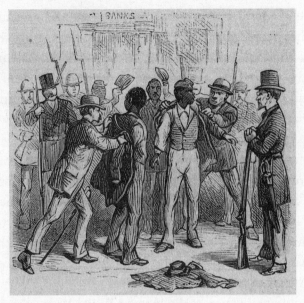

Metropolitan Police officers were captured, stripped of their weapons and uniforms, and released.

show of rejoicing that went heavenward that will never be forgotten."

Inside the besieged Third Precinct station house, Captain Lawler accepted the impossibility of his situation. Throughout the night, as his wounds were treated, men had slipped out of the building. When he surrendered his sword to White League Colonel Angell only five men were with him. The once-vaunted Metropolitan Police department had been defeated.

"The Day of Riot and Blood," as the *Republican* referred to it, was done, but with ten thousand armed men, two-thirds of them, according to the media, "illiterate roughs, boys and irresponsible men brought in from the country and plentifully supplied with whisky," roaming the streets, maintaining the peace was difficult. A cordon of soldiers with fixed bayonets took positions in front of the governor's mansion, where Mrs. Kellogg had stayed alone, and were serenaded by "drunken rowdies yelling filthy imprecations."

Late in the afternoon, an estimated twenty-five thousand people turned out to watch Lieutenant Governor Penn publicly inaugurated as acting governor on the State House gallery. Bands played, flags waved, and fifteen hundred men, displaying some of the artillery captured in the armory, paraded through the streets, from Bourbon to Chartres, from Court to Toulouse, before a wildly cheering crowd. Some of those men had even taken their Confederate jackets out of storage for the occasion. After being sworn into office, the new governor began naming supporters to official positions: within an hour every office was filled. General Ogden was named attorney general, Detective Tom Boyland became superintendent of police, and there was a new auditor, new superintendent of education and new fire chief. New judges were appointed, and plans were announced to convene the McEnery legislature, perhaps as early as the following week.

The leading citizens sent a telegram to Grant, asking for his approval. "Kellogg government completely deposed. Perfect confidence restored... Not a single case of lawlessness. The c——d population and all other citizens perfectly secure in their lives and property... As loyal citizens of the United States, we confidently rely on you for the recognition and guarantee of the government under McEnery and Penn..."

The *Picayune*, essentially the official organ of the insurgents, warned Kellogg supporters not to try to organize or demonstrate. If any of their white leaders tried to instigate riots, "Let them be shot down like dogs and brutes they are."

Outside the city the reaction was not as peaceful. In Grant Parish, one of the men released on bail after the Colfax Massacre killed two Black men. In other areas the remaining Republican officeholders were warned to resign or be forced out—just like Kellogg.

Kellogg finally spoke publicly. Meeting with a reporter from the *Vicksburg Herald* in the basement of the Custom House he spoke frankly, with only a hint of defeat in his words. He regretted not asking for federal assistance a week earlier, he admitted, but he had never believed the citizens would rise up against him. "I did not want bloodshed," he pleaded. "I wanted this trouble left to the ballot box; I intended to give the people a fair election at every hazard…throughout the State.

"I will abide by the decision of the people of Louisiana, in this matter—if a fair and equitable election can be had…" Claiming he had directed the occupants of the State House to surrender rather than risk more blood, he added, perhaps wistfully, "I think if the people knew and understood me there would be no animosity felt against me." As for dealing with the insurrection, "I will now abide by the decision of the President… I am going to remain in this city. My estate is here: I like the people, soil and climate, and I want to dwell here.

"I have done them [the citizens of Louisiana] no wrong, and I want to tell them so."

The funerals began the next day: Frederick Mohrman, shot through the heart while leading his section in the gallant charge… A. M. Gantier, the first man to fall… Sam B. Newman Jr., whose funeral train stretched several squares in length… Major William Robins, cut off at the early age of thirty, battling for the redemption of the state… As some of the families of the fallen men lacked the funds to properly bury them, people were urged to offer donations.

The details of how men died depended on which side of the fighting the teller was on. According to the Fusion *New Orleans Times*, for example, the well-known reporter J. M. West was standing innocently on a corner taking notes when he was shot by someone firing from the Custom House. The *New Orleans Republican* claimed West, who had previously been imprisoned for treasonable conduct, saw a man killed in hand-to-hand combat with a Metropolitan and tried to grab the wounded policeman's gun. As he did, the officer stabbed him with a bayonet and fired at point-blank range, and both men died.

Slowly, the city resumed its natural pace. Its leading industry, the Cotton Exchange, closed at noon in an expression of support for the new government and sympathy for the heroes of Liberty Place. Some of the courts opened, watched over by armed White Leaguers; in the Third District Court, Judge Monroe ascended to the bench, replacing Jerome Meunier, "who had been occupying the court for the last year." The Eighth District Court, which the legislature had closed, was revived, and Judge Elmore was appointed to run it. The churches were filled with parishioners offering thanks. At the Academy of Music, Sheridan and Mack gave a blackface performance, although admittedly the theater was barely filled as most women did not yet feel safe on the streets.

The takeover of the government proceeded mostly peacefully and orderly. No one had even touched the filled money boxes on the streetcars. The only visible destruction was at the governor's office: the windows were thrown open, and records, papers and documents were flung onto the streets and trampled by the revelers. And while some of the surrendered Metropolitans were treated roughly, the only major crime took place in the Sixth District, where people broke into the office of the tax collector and blew open his safe; fortunately, he had given the money to the auditor several days earlier, and the safe was empty.

Almost lost in the celebration was the somber news from Washington. Penn had wired the president pledging "unswerving loyalty and respect" for the federal government, promising property and officials would be protected, and asking Grant "to withhold any aid or protection…from the enemies of Republican rights and of the peace and liberties of the people."

His plea was ignored. This was a national crisis. The entire front page of the *New York Times* was filled with news of the insurrection. "It is considered in official quarters that the extraordinary proceedings in Louisiana do not concern that State alone, but all the States in the Union...if countenanced by the General Government might become a precedent in other sections of the country...and might introduce a system which would substitute military power for legal forms in the conduct of State Administration."

The president and his cabinet met for several hours. Grant finally decided he could not allow Kellogg's administration, which had been recognized as the legally elected government by the judicial system, to be violently overthrown. He issued a proclamation acknowledging "that turbulent and disorderly persons have combined together to overthrow the State government of Louisiana..." and citing his constitutional obligation to "call forth the militia of any other State or to employ such part of the land and naval forces...for the purpose of suppressing such insurrection," he commanded "such turbulent and disorderly persons to disperse and retire peacefully to their respective abodes within five days and to submit themselves to the laws and constituted authorities of said State."

Five days. Grant ordered General Emory to proceed to New Orleans with an estimated five thousand troops to enforce this decision. The president also dispatched three gunboats to offer assistance if needed. Emory was ordered that under no circumstances was he to recognize the insurgent government. He also was informed that about $750,000 owed to the state's creditors was being held by the Louisiana National Bank, and the Penn government was not permitted to withdraw any funds.

John McEnery got to the city at nine o'clock the night of September 16. More than a thousand people were waiting at the Jackson Railroad depot when his train pulled in. He knew exactly how charged the situation was: these supporters were ready to do whatever he commanded. He made a few restrained remarks from the caboose platform, urging them to demonstrate their newly gained freedom by showing moderation and justice in their actions. Additional crowds lined the streets as his carriage took him directly to the State House.

There was great pressure on him to resist Grant's decree. This wasn't an insurrection against the United States, his supporters emphasized, they were putting in place the government that had been elected two years earlier. They were righting a terrible injustice. White Leaguers claimed a hundred thousand men from North Louisiana, Mississippi, Arkansas, Texas and Alabama had pledged to "rule or ruin," many of them already on their way. That force was sizable enough to hold the State against the US Army, maybe even sufficient to ignite another war. Kellogg supporters warned ominously, "A very few hours will decide whether the United States flag will be fired on once more or not." Even Jefferson Davis, the former president of the Confederacy, recognizing the possibility that the violence would spread, refused to comment.

Several of McEnery's closest advisers urged him to move quickly, to capture Kellogg and occupy the Custom House before Grant's army arrived in force. But his military commander Ogden was firmly against it. Penn remained neutral. McEnery had used force in the past—he had directed the March riots, for example—but this time he hesitated. There was little doubt his supporters were willing to fight; if the leaders of the rebellion were to "get up a statement declaring that the moon was made of green cheese," the *Times* wrote, "and that the sun revolved around the earth, half the bankers and merchants of the city could be dragooned into signing it."

General Emory reached the city the same night. He set up headquarters at the St. Nicholas Hotel. Early the following morning he began a steady stream of meetings with McEnery, Penn, Ogden and city business leaders. Those men asked for some recognition of their grievances, suggesting new elections or a constitutional convention. Emory listened politely to their pleas, then flatly demanded they comply with Grant's decision: surrender all the State property, disband their forces and go home.

He gave them no hope of any compromise. Surrender. Go home.

Throughout the day, troops continued pouring into the city. Infantry, cavalry, artillery and three gunboats began taking up positions. Any brief edge the insurgents might have had disappeared completely.

McEnery knew his supporters would fight for their cause. He also knew they would lose. Almost a hundred thousand good Southern boys had been killed in the recent war; there was no reason for more men to die in a hopeless fight. He told General Emory, "We have neither the power nor inclination to resist the Government of the United States."

The insurrection was done. All that was left was formality and logistics. At precisely six o'clock on the evening of September 18, General Brooke walked into the governor's office. McEnery and Penn stood to welcome him and shook hands. According to witnesses, "The Governor then stated to General Brooke that he gave him the possession of the State Capitol and all other State buildings...

"General Brooke merely bowed in acceptance."

McEnery, who was described as trembling and nearly overcome with emotion, then read his statement defending the rebellion, making sure reporters wrote down every word, telling his men to stand down. "Our people could bear the wrongs, tyranny, annoyance and insults of the usurpation no longer," he read, "and they arose in their might, swept it from existence and installed in authority the rightful government..."

But the fight was done, he concluded. Go home. Then he added ominously, take your weapons with you.

The attempted revolution ended quietly. After finishing his statement, the governor, lieutenant governor and the several other prominent citizens in the room quietly withdrew, "leaving the Capitol of Louisiana in the possession of the United States Government."

Outside, reported the *Picayune*, "Not a cheer or groan was heard" from the large crowd who had assembled. Instead, "Every face wore a look of bitter disappointment and the citizens of our downtrodden state turned away in sorrowful silence to seek their homes."

Perhaps if they had known what was to follow, they might not have been so downcast.

15

In May 1869, during the debate over ratification of the Fifteenth Amendment, which granted Black men the right to vote, a large crowd gathered in New York's Steinway Hall to demand it be expanded to include women's suffrage. Escaped former slave Frederick Douglass defended the Amendment's limitations to members of the Equal Rights Association—among them Susan B. Anthony and Elizabeth Cady Stanton. "With us," he told them, "the matter is a question of life and death. It is a matter of existence…

"When women, because they are women, are hunted down through the streets of New York and New Orleans; when they are dragged from their houses and hung upon lamp-posts; when their children are torn from their arms and their brains dashed out upon the pavement; when they are objects of insult and outrage at every turn; when they are in danger of having their homes burned down over their heads; when their children are not allowed to enter schools; then they will have an urgency to obtain the ballot equal to our own."

THE HISTORIC NEW ORLEANS COLLECTION, 1974.25.9.226

The contested election of 1872 led to an insurrection known as the Battle of Liberty Place.

Black Americans, Douglass explained, were risking their lives when they cast a vote.

And as the election of 1874 approached, that right was being challenged not just in Louisiana but in Alabama, South Carolina, Texas and Mississippi. This election would be a referendum on Grant. On Reconstruction. On states' rights. On the use of federal troops to enforce federal law. And ultimately, on the expansion of civil rights.

Republicans had won the Battle of Liberty Place. A day after McEnery's surrender, Kellogg walked back into the governor's office, accompanied by General Brooke, and without fanfare resumed his duties. But the war would continue at the ballot box. Ironically, while the White League had been defeated in the streets, it had emerged stronger than ever. Its bloody resistance had captured the imagination—and the hearts—of people throughout the state and far beyond its borders. In New York, Chicago, Cincinnati, St. Louis and all the great cities of America, newspapers wrote about the League and quoted its lead-

The fighting ended with the White League in control of the government, and its leaders addressed the crowd from the balcony of the St. Charles Hotel.

ers. And in the South, membership was booming. Republicans may have controlled New Orleans, but the White League had expanded its domination of rural Louisiana. In those parishes, they would decide who would vote.

Governor Kellogg tried to limit the League's growing power by appointing loyal Republicans to supervise the registration process. As part of that effort, he challenged the right of Louisiana's six thousand to eight thousand naturalized citizens—many of them Democrat-conservative voters—to vote. He suggested providing two ballot boxes, the second one specifically for that group, isolating their ballots until the court could decide their eligibility. The chairman of the Democrat/Conservative Registration Committee, Edward Burke, was furious. The longtime feud between the two men finally erupted a few days before the election.

Late in the afternoon of October 30, as Kellogg's carriage was proceeding slowly up Canal Street, it was hailed by Burke near Basin Street. According to the *Republican*, Kellogg leaned

out and extended a friendly hand; according to the Democratic *Picayune*, Kellogg "smiled sarcastically and with his finger
made a gesture of derision." Then Major Burke either grabbed
Kellogg's hand and tried to pull him from the carriage, striking him with his whip as he did, or climbed into the carriage
and hit Kellogg with a cowhide whip. In response, all the papers agreed, the driver whipped the carriage forward, throwing Burke to the ground. Kellogg drew his pistol and fired one
shot, while Burke fired five wide shots at the governor as his
carriage raced down Canal Street.

If it was an assassination attempt, rather than a nasty alterca-
tion that went out of control, it failed. Burke voluntarily surrendered to police. Within an hour Kellogg sent word that Burke
should be released and the incident forgotten.

Once again, election day in Louisiana reportedly was calm.
Reportedly. The White League had been preparing for months,
warning Republicans in general and freedmen specifically what
might happen if they tried to vote. The lack of violence on election day—and in the days following—was evidence that intimidation had succeeded. There was no way of calculating how
many hundreds or thousands of Black voters were too fearful to
go near the polling places not guarded by federal troops.

The spirit of Liberty Place had spread throughout the former
Confederacy. Democrats, after being thoroughly defeated in several postwar elections, were poised to make a massive comeback.
Local campaigns around the country focused on the financial
crisis of 1873, Grant's Reconstruction policies and, in several
regions, unhappiness over the new Amendments. For the first
time in almost a decade Democrats sensed victory—and nothing was going to stand in their way. In Eufaula, Alabama, for
example, after a minor confrontation at a polling place, White
Leaguers opened fire on Black voters. Within minutes more
than seventy-five freedmen had been wounded, seven had been
killed, and hundreds more were driven away from the polls. In

town after town across the South there was widespread intimidation, ballot boxes were stolen or broken open, and votes were
thrown away or burned.

The result was a massive Democratic victory. Democrats
flipped an incredible ninety-four seats in the 293-member US
House of Representatives, gaining control for the first time
since the beginning of the Civil War. Republicans managed
to retain control of the seventy-member Senate, whose members were appointed by state legislatures, though the Democrats
won nine seats.

Throughout the South this extraordinary result was celebrated as the end of Reconstruction. Northern domination was
done! Finished! It had taken a decade, but the South had risen
from the ashes that Sherman's army had left in its wake. The
series of events that had begun with the contested election two
years earlier—which included the political maneuvering, the
uprisings, the massacres, the coup attempts, street battles and
finally the founding of the powerful White League in Louisiana's ironically named Grant Parish—had culminated in this
political earthquake.

After all that, it seemed improbable that the situation could
get even worse. But it did, creating a contradictory and seemingly bizarre situation that might accurately be described as a
military-enforced democracy.

In Louisiana, Democrats gained two Congressional seats; incredibly, though, Opelousas native Charles Edmund Nash was
elected the state's first Black member of Congress. But once
again the makeup of the state legislature would be determined
by the Returning Board. Although an attempt had been made
to create a reasonably neutral Board, it was faced with the same
issues—fraud, intimidation, cheating, and disputed, missing and
illegally added ballots—that had plagued the Board during the
election two years earlier. This time though, the Board members'
lives were in danger. They were, wrote the *Republican*, "The

object of constant and unjust attacks...absolute threats, meant to intimidate them into making their returns, not according to the facts and the law, but as the Democratic party and the press have predetermined."

The Returning Board acknowledged it had an impossible task. If it followed election laws strictly, it reported, "so many of the polls would have been thrown out that there would have been no election in the State."

Perhaps for their personal safety its members finally decided there was only one possible outcome: a tie. It declared fifty-three Republicans and fifty-three Democrats elected, with five disputed seats to be decided by the legislature when it convened in January.

For President Grant, the election was a personal as well as political disaster. A united Southern bloc could derail his dream of a third term in office. Anticipating that this confrontation in Louisiana would lead to more violence, Grant sent General Sheridan on a tour of Southern states. It was Sheridan who had originally been in command of Reconstruction in Texas and Louisiana, so it was fitting that he would try to hold it together. For the media, this was described as much as a pleasure trip as a political one, but the hope was his presence would temper passions.

Former governor Henry Warmoth had spent the entire campaign in Washington, away from the headlines, but actively involved in the process. He helped plan strategy and advised Democratic candidates. Looking ahead to his own political future, Warmoth had strongly opposed White League attempts to resegregate the races, particularly in education and public transportation. As a result of Warmoth's public statements, the editor of the conservative *Bulletin* challenged him to a duel. Warmoth later contended the real cause of the editor's bitterness was the fact he had awarded the state printing contract to the *Republican* rather than the *Bulletin*. Whatever the reason, Warmoth accepted the challenge; it was to be pistols at ten paces. As dueling was illegal in Louisiana, they agreed to meet in Mississippi the following Monday.

American politics had been reduced to a duel to the death.

Two days before the scheduled fight, Warmoth was walking on Canal Street, having been to his lawyer's office to make out his will. As two women passed, he raised his hat in salutation—and suddenly was brutally attacked. Without warning, Dan Byerly, the *Bulletin*'s manager, began beating him with a thick walking cane. Byerly was a large man with a gray beard who, despite losing the use of one arm in the war, was still stout and strong. His first blow opened a horrid gash on Warmoth's head, and blood began flowing. Byerly hit him again and again until the cane split. He tossed it away and threw Warmoth down on the raised wooden sidewalk, then jumped on top of him.

"Seeing him endeavoring to draw what I thought was a pistol," Warmoth later said, "I drew out my pocket knife." It was a four-inch spring knife, which snapped open. Warmoth began stabbing his attacker over and over, in his side, in his gut. Three times, four times, five times—until a Metropolitan Police sergeant pulled the men apart.

Byerly got to his feet, then collapsed. He was rushed to the hospital.

Warmoth was arrested and taken to Parish Prison on Orleans Street. The former governor was covered with blood—his own as well as his assailant's.

Byerly was mortally wounded, his spleen pierced with two large gashes. He died later that night.

Warmoth spent four days and nights in prison. The former governor's cellmate was a gambler who had been convicted of killing a woman and was sentenced to be hanged.

A steady parade of politicians and the leading businessmen of the city visited him. An estimated five hundred people paid their respects to the accused murderer, among them Kellogg, McEnery,

Penn, Lieutenant Governor Antoine and Judge Dibble, as well as Louis Wiltz, the White League mayor of New Orleans.

Many of those same people also attended Byerly's funeral.

The media could not help comparing this to the historic 1804 duel in which Vice President Aaron Burr shot and killed Alexander Hamilton. Burr was charged with murder in New York and New Jersey but fled to the safety of Washington, DC, where he became the first indicted murderer to preside in Congress.

At the coroner's inquest, witnesses testified Byerly had planned the attack. Several men testified that before buying the cane he had tried to borrow one. "He took hold of my cane," a man named John Vairen told the prosecutor. "I said, 'You do not want that cane.' He said, 'Yes, I do. I want to give a damned rascal a caning with it.'"

After hearing numerous witnesses, the judge ruled that Warmoth had acted in self-defense, and he was released without consequence.

When the Louisiana legislature met in January, it seemed like events were repeating themselves, like the State was stuck in a political conundrum for which there was no solution. Once again, the question was which candidates would be seated. The only difference between the previous election and this one was the numbers; rather than the entire House, there were only five disputed seats. But with those five seats came control of the otherwise evenly divided chamber—and the State.

This time, though, the Democrats had guns.

The battle for the House began on January 2. Republican A. J. Cousin, the elected representative of St. Tammany Parish, was kidnapped. He was seized by two men, held briefly in prison then forced on board a steamer. To his friends and family, it appeared he had simply disappeared. He was seen standing on a New Orleans corner, and then he was gone. No one heard a word from him.

His kidnappers treated him well, he later told reporters, telling him nothing would happen to him—unless there was an attempt to rescue him. In that case they would kill him.

He was held under armed guard in the woods a few miles outside the town of Covington. His captors told him that he had been taken to prevent Republicans from gaining control of the legislature. He would be released after that body had been officially organized, they promised.

The legislature convened on the fourth. Fearing violence, Metropolitans guarded all the entrances to the State House while more than a thousand army troops occupied the surrounding streets and the levees. A sea of curious people surrounded the building, filling streets and squares; among them were an unknown number of unarmed White Leaguers, supposedly there to preserve the peace. Only state officials and men claiming seats in the legislature were admitted. The Senate organized without difficulty.

General Sheridan set up headquarters in the St. Charles Hotel; "Governor" McEnery established his own headquarters only a few yards away, in Antoine's Restaurant.

When the House was called into session, fifty-two Republicans and fifty Democrats were present. The first order of business was electing a temporary chairman. The clerk called for nominations—and the Democrats put their plan into action. Seconds after someone on the floor nominated former mayor Louis Wiltz, a Congressional investigation reported, "As quick as thought upon the putting of the motion...[Wiltz] sprang to the Speaker's desk where the Clerk was standing, seized the gavel from his hand and pushed the Clerk violently off the stand and declared himself temporary Speaker."

The chamber erupted in bedlam! Men began screaming to be recognized, one louder than the next until no one voice could be heard. It didn't matter; Wiltz simply ignored them all. A justice of the peace appeared as if magically and swore him into office.

As the din continued, Wiltz swore the members into office—

among them all the Democratic candidates for the five disputed seats! That gave him a clear majority. With the gavel in his hand, Wiltz bullied his way through several appointments, utilizing or ignoring parliamentary order as it suited his purpose.

Furious Republicans refused to accept the Democratic takeover; instead, they decided to deny Wiltz the necessary quorum by walking out. Their intention was to organize elsewhere, establishing a second legislature that would be recognized as legitimate by Kellogg. But as they began leaving, doors swung open and about thirty-five strong, young men, presumably White Leaguers, entered; Wiltz welcomed them, announcing they were the new sergeants at arms. He swore them in, then ordered them to prevent Republicans from leaving. He intended to keep the House in session all day and into the night.

Republican legislators trying to escape from chamber were blocked by these men, but some evaded them, making it to the lobby where they were pulled outside by police officers. The tug-of-war between the White Leaguers and police continued for several minutes. A mob of supporters and protestors crammed into the already-crowded lobby. Supposedly guns and knives were drawn, and there were rumors that punches were thrown, but there was no serious violence.

While the situation was still boiling, Wiltz asked General Regis de Trobriand, in command of the federal troops in the building, to clear the lobby. The general reluctantly agreed. For a few minutes, at least, Wiltz had his quorum and began conducting business, primarily appointing Democrats to government positions.

Meanwhile, a group of "escaped" Republicans appealed to Kellogg for assistance. The governor ordered General Emory to take action. Minutes later General de Trobriand reappeared in the House, this time following Republican orders. He was alone and showed Wiltz his orders to remove those Democrats who had not been declared elected by the legal Returning Board.

Wiltz refused. "I cannot instruct members to leave the hall," he said defiantly. "You must use force to compel them!"

If necessary, the general responded, he would do exactly that. Then he left. Minutes later he returned, now accompanied by about two dozen armed troops. Each disputed member was pointed out, and two soldiers, bayonets fixed on their rifles, went to that desk and escorted him out of the now-silent chamber.

Wiltz was the last to go. As he was being removed from the speaker's rostrum he protested "against the invasion of our hall by soldiers of the United States with drawn bayonets and loaded muskets. We have seen our brother members violently seized by force of arms... The officers of the House are prisoners... I solemnly declare that Louisiana has ceased to be a sovereign state..."

He was escorted out, followed by all the Democrats and conservatives. They reassembled in a nearby hotel. Once again, they organized an impotent legislature and began meeting.

The State House remained surrounded by soldiers. A cannon was placed at each entrance. Wooden planks were nailed across doors and windows. Other troops remained stationed in nearby streets to prevent an attempt at mob rule.

Inside, Republicans elected a speaker, swore in their chosen members and went to work.

Somehow, Democrats had managed to turn an embarrassing defeat into a victory. The specter of the army occupying a state legislature was devastating for President Grant. The details may have been disputed and confusing, but what Americans read about was the national government once again imposing its political will on a state government. Since Lee's surrender to Grant, nothing had done more to unify the South than the use of soldiers to impose political objectives. Legislatures in numerous states voted to censure or condemn the action. The *New York Herald* wondered if Grant would "decide who shall belong to the next Congress and enforce his decisions with five or six regiments of United States troops." The *Nation* suggested, "At this pace...the President has the right to inflict capital punishment with his own hand." The great orator William Cullen Bryant had been a founder of the Republican party and a strong supporter of Lincoln, but this was too much for him. Speaking in New York several days later, he warned the nation "...when it is done in one state, it is done in all!"

In this type of sensitive situation, a careless word or phrase can be picked up, amplified and become a rallying cry. While the army was still protecting the State House, General Sheridan sent a telegram to Grant: "I think that the terrorism now existing in Louisiana, Mississippi and Arkansas could be entirely removed and confidence and fair dealing established by the arrest and trial of the ringleaders of the White Leagues. If Congress would declare them banditti they could be tried by military commission. The leaders of this banditti...should be punished..."

It was the banditti who had been behind three or four thousand murders, he claimed.

Banditti! It was a rarely used word that carried an ominous tone. It was an insult—and when the telegram leaked the contents to the public, the Democrats considered it a badge of honor. They embraced it: we are all banditti!

Rather than Sheridan's intended meaning, White Leaguers, Democrats and conservatives gave it a far different meaning: people who had been fighting against the usurpation of political power—especially the use of troops to impose a government on the people. They were fighters for democracy!

Sheridan was vilified for his remark. His life was threatened. At least one newspaper suggested he should be hanged from a lamppost. When he dared appear on New Orleans streets, people shouted curses at him. Friends ignored him. He tried to backtrack, telling a *New York Times* reporter, "I don't suppose there is a sensible man in the State who really imagines I mean all the people were banditti, for they are not blunderers and robbers!"

But it was much too late. The Grant administration was struggling against a resistance that had the support of many white Americans. If the president had any chance of being reelected

in 1876, he had to end this mess. In December, the US House
had created the seven-member Committee on the Condition of
Affairs in the South, headed by Republican abolitionist George
Frisbee Hoar, to find a solution. A three-member subcommittee
was dispatched to New Orleans to investigate the 1874 election.
They happened to be there to witness the disastrous attempt to
open the newly elected House.

After interviewing ninety-five witnesses, their fifteen-
hundred-page report concluded the actions of the Returning
Board in 1874 were "arbitrary, unjust and, in our opinion, illegal." The election was fair and peaceful, the report continued,
and the result was "a clear conservative majority was elected to
the lower house."

For Republicans, this report was a disaster. A bipartisan Congressional committee was telling the nation the election had been
stolen. As far as Republican legislators were concerned, there was
only one possible solution: appoint another committee. Claiming
the first committee was only investigating to determine if the
election was worth investigating, a second committee, this one
headed by Hoar, went to New Orleans. Not unexpectedly, this
group reached the completely opposite conclusion. It described
a climate of intimidation and bloodshed, citing numerous acts
of threats and violence, concluding the '74 election was fraudulent at the ballot box rather than with the Returning Board.

The recommendation? Accept the Kellogg government.

In March 1875, the House passed a resolution recognizing
Kellogg as "the governor of the State of Louisiana until the end
of the term of office fixed by the Constitution of that State."

Two weeks later the Senate approved a similar resolution; although, rather than simply upholding Kellogg's election, it acknowledged that President Grant, "in protecting the government...
and the people against domestic violence and in enforcing laws of
the United States in that State," had done the right thing.

Those resolutions had little meaning. Nothing significant
had changed. No member of either party trusted any election

returns. Holding political power had become a matter of who could best manipulate the system—and who had the guns. Republicans controlled the cities, with the support of the military and police, while Democrats and conservatives dominated the rural areas of the State.

The situation may have been best summarized during a debate in the US Senate. Republican Senator John Logan, from Illinois, said that there had been such extensive fraud in 1872 that neither Kellogg nor McEnery had been legally elected, then asked Maryland's Democratic Senator William Hamilton if he endorsed the overthrowing of Louisiana's government.

Hamilton had a ready answer. There was no state government to overthrow.

His remark was greeted with laughter on the Senate floor and cheers from spectators in the gallery. Hamilton continued, reminding Logan that "American freedom was born in revolution and rebellion and the sympathies of the American people were always with those whose rose against oppression and tyranny."

The cheers from the gallery were so great that the spectators were told to leave.

After more than two years, there still was no agreeable way to settle the situation. The debate continued on the floor and in committees of the United States Congress. The search for a compromise continued without success. Among the casualties of the stalemate was the nomination of P. B. S. Pinchback to the Senate; the divided Senate refused to seat him, and his nomination was eventually withdrawn.

The consequences had been incalculable. General Sheridan estimated more than thirty-five hundred people had been killed. The State was essentially bankrupt: taxes were high, collections were low. Property values had crashed. There were vacant storefronts on every block. Vital government services had been curtailed or ended. Countless men were unable to find work. Banks were not making loans. A huge increase in crime had made city streets unsafe while vigilantes controlled the countryside. Efforts at integration had stalled, and the State was slowly fading back into separate Black and white societies.

There was no leadership, no respect for government, no trust and, perhaps most devastating, no hope.

It would still be several decades before a new type of music they named *jazz* emerged from the streets of New Orleans; it could not have been born anywhere else. No other place had the soul for it. The word itself supposedly derived from the slang term *jasm*, meaning a special level of energy, drive, vitality, vim; or, as a dictionary notes, "a zest for accomplishment." But defining or describing jazz is far more difficult. It's music not bound by conventional structure. It's the musical expression of freedom, played from the heart rather than written notes.

It was born as a reflection of life in New Orleans, with its lack of predictability, its constant surprises and its shifting focus; in jazz, every player has their moment. And that accurately described the state of politics in Louisiana in 1876. Warmoth, Kellogg, McEnery, Penn, Pinchback, Antoine and even Sheridan all were playing their own tunes. Each one of them had taken the lead for moments, but no one was really in charge. Several proposals had been made to restore some structure to the system, and for a brief time there was a semblance of harmony, but eventually all attempts to forge some type of compromise failed.

Having tried just about every other tactic to oust Republicans from state government, in March 1876, Democrats in the divided House collected enough votes to impeach Governor Kellogg. Among the fourteen articles, Kellogg was accused of making illegal appointments, failing to conduct regular inspections and sending armed police into the State House. There was no real intent to remove Kellogg from office; this was an attempt to weaken him politically. In fact, the House intentionally waited until the last possible moment before voting to impeach him, believing the Senate had adjourned, meaning Kellogg would remain suspended until it reconvened. The governor rebuffed that effort by recalling the State Senate for an extra ten-day session.

In anticipation of that ploy, the fourteenth article of impeachment charged Kellogg with illegally convening the Senate, but not the House, in an extra session—beginning the day after the House voted to impeach him!

The *New Orleans Bulletin* admitted the real strategy. "We do not believe the impeachment would succeed; but it is nevertheless the duty of the House to proceed as it would, and thus throw the blame for the failure on the Senate."

The *Republican* responded in defense of Kellogg. "No Governor of a State has ever been so maliciously persecuted by a minority from his induction in office..."

Kellogg dutifully answered every charge as this political charade played out. The Senate quickly acquitted him, then rebuffed a series of complicated parliamentary maneuvers to reinstate the charges.

This was pure politics; it marked the beginning of the 1876 presidential election campaign, one destined to become among the most contentious in American history. Until then the nation had watched Louisiana's political struggles with some combination of fascination, curiosity, astonishment and perhaps even amusement, but it had remained a state problem. No more.

The State's once-local difficulties were about to explode nationally and would come perilously close to destroying the American electoral system.

President Grant had equivocated about running for a third term. Several scandals had weakened his administration, and his controversial decision to send the army to Louisiana had cost him significant support. Finally, a House resolution declaring it would be "unwise, unpatriotic, and fraught with peril to our free institutions" for a president to run for a third term had convinced him to stay out of the election.

He would not be a candidate for reelection, he said, claiming,

"I do not want to be here another four years. I do not think I could stand it."

To replace Grant on the ticket, in mid-June Republicans nominated Ohio governor Rutherford Birchard Hayes. A strong abolitionist, Hayes had worked his way up the Union ranks, wounded five times during the war, to become a brevet major general. Hayes was considered so honest that for the first time, Mark Twain became actively involved in politics, explaining, "In truth I care little about any party politics, the man behind it is the important thing."

Weeks later, while the nation was stunned by reports that young, charismatic General George Custer and about three hundred men of his 7th Cavalry had been massacred by a coalition of Sioux, Cheyenne and Arapaho tribes at Little Bighorn River, the Democrats met in St. Louis and gave their nomination to New York governor Samuel J. Tilden. While Democrats lauded Tilden for his honesty and integrity, Republicans immediately portrayed him as a lawyer who had made a "colossal fortune" representing the unpopular railroad interests.

A key issue in the campaign was the fate of Reconstruction. While both candidates had fought for the Union, Tilden's supporters believed that after sixteen years of Republican control of the White House, a Democratic president would help bring an end to Grant's postwar policies.

In Louisiana, Kellogg's decision not to run for another term had thrown open the race for governor. Among the leading candidates to replace him? Henry C. Warmoth, who immediately began maneuvering for the Republican nomination. "His followers are those who crave for the lavish times of his former administration," the *Picayune* reported.

As the United States prepared to celebrate its centennial on the Fourth of July, Louisiana Republicans spent a week battling for the gubernatorial nomination. Essentially, the race pitted Kellogg's nominee, federal marshal Stephen Packard, against both

Warmoth and Pinchback. The rivalry between Warmoth and Packard was especially personal and bitter because years earlier the marshal had been among the leaders of the effort to impeach the former governor.

The convention immediately dissolved into a shambles; within the first hours men were screaming to be heard, jumping on chairs, throwing things at the podium and literally wrestling in the aisles. When pistols were produced the police had to be summoned to prevent violence.

And that was just to elect a temporary chairman.

It took five days and one seriously wounded delegate before they agreed on a compromise that allowed the convention to proceed. The first ballot was won by Packard, with Warmoth second. But by then it had become clear to the former governor that he could not win the nomination. On Independence Day he told the convention, "When I go into a fight I mean to keep it up until I am licked. I entered this fight with the purpose of succeeding... I will suffer no humiliation that I did not succeed in all."

Reporters noted that contrary to Warmoth's "gay and nonchalant air, a deep under-current of feeling [was] welling up from the springs of disappointment and crushed aspirations."

The convention nominated Packard. Democrats immediately tried to link him to Grant, blaming him for the presence of federal troops in the state.

Candidates for the Democratic nomination included McEnery, Ogden, Penn, Wiltz and Francis Redding Tillou Nicholls, an attorney, former slave owner and West Point graduate who had literally lost an arm and a leg fighting for the Confederacy. What also set Nicholls apart was the fact that, unlike the other candidates, he came from the countryside, from rural Assumption Parish in southern Louisiana, and had not been involved in the political fighting. What made him further different from all the others was his claim that he did not especially want to be governor. There is little more appealing to voters than a politician who claims not to want their vote.

He was nominated on the fourth ballot.

The two candidates were as different as blue and gray: Packard was a city man, a US Marshal as comfortable with the bigwigs in Washington as he was in the French Quarter, while Nicholls represented the forgotten white working man.

Although the future of Reconstruction was not officially on the ballot, it was the subtext of the election.

In the cities, the parties held big, colorful, raucous rallies offering food and lots to drink, with brass bands and banners and earnest political promises. But in the country, the campaign was marked by terror, night riders, warnings and killings. Democrats acknowledged the violence but claimed it was a Republican attempt to provide the necessary excuse for Grant to send in troops—and provoke a response.

The vilest attack took place in Ouachita Parish the Saturday night before the election. As many as thirty white men broke into the cabin of former slaves Henry and Eliza Pinkston. Henry's crime was attending a recent Republican rally. "He votes no Radical ticket here," one of the raiding party shouted. "He may vote in hell!" The men then shot Pinkston seven times. When Eliza tried to stop them she was slashed, shot, raped, hit with an axe, her teeth knocked out and shot again. Somehow, she survived to later testify that after killing her husband, his killers had cut her baby's throat and thrown its body in a lake.

Although Eliza Pinkston was rumored to be a troubled woman with a dark past, a woman whose word too often was doubtful, the bodies of her husband and child were real. As was the blood that soaked her clothing.

This was the horror story that led America into the election of 1876. It was an apt beginning.

16

On November 7, 1876, in a celebration of American democracy, almost 8,500,000 men went to their local polling stations and cast their ballot for either Rutherford B. Hayes or Samuel J. Tilden. Countless thousands of people traveled long distances or braved winter weather; in many places they waited patiently in unusually long lines. They did it because they believed in the system of government and wanted their say.

The election had been bitterly contested. As a result, the highest percentage of eligible voters in the nation's hundred-year history had made their opinion known. The actual voting process went smoothly. America sent a message to the rest of the world: This is how a democracy functions. One man, one vote!

But then they started counting those votes.

The system collapsed. The fire that had been sparked in Louisiana four years earlier had spread and engulfed the entire nation. In several states it was impossible to determine which candidate had won, which votes counted or how many people had been frightened away from the polls. The outcome in those states

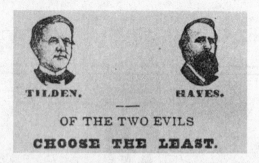

Louisiana's collapsed government played a significant role in the bitterly contested 1876 presidential election.

would determine the winner of its electoral votes, and with that the next president. All of the still-unresolved issues that had thrown Louisiana into turmoil were now a national problem.

As a result, rather than being elected by voters, the president of the United States would be selected by a Congressional committee.

In the days following the election Tilden was reported to have a 260,000-vote lead. Democrats were celebrating. The numbers told the story: Republican rule of the postwar era was finished. Even Hayes acknowledged his loss, admitting, "I think we are defeated... I am of the opinion that the Democrats have carried the country and elected Tilden."

Tilden was on the verge of becoming the first man in history to lose the presidency with a majority of the popular vote. But even with his substantial lead, he was guaranteed only 184 electoral votes—one short of the 185 needed to become president. He had to find one more electoral vote.

Hayes was far behind with 165 electoral votes. He was prepared to concede the election—until *New York Times* editor John Reid convinced Republican leaders to wait. Incredibly, due to a quirk in the electoral system, there was a slim chance Hayes could become the first person elected president with a minority of the popular vote. Four states, with a total of twenty electoral votes, had not declared a winner. If he were to win them all, he would become president—by that one, elusive electoral vote. That certainly was possible, Reid noted; each of those Southern states had a Republican governor. So while most newspapers in the nation were declaring Tilden the winner, Reid's *Times* ran with a different message: The Battle Won. Governor Hayes Elected.

The election would be decided by Florida, South Carolina, Oregon and, of course, Louisiana.

Four years of negotiating, debating, arguing, compromise and violence had settled absolutely nothing in Louisiana. Both parties claimed victory. Republicans announced that Hayes had won the state's eight electoral votes, Packard had been elected governor by 3,500 votes, and they had elected three members of Congress while keeping control of the state legislature. Conversely, Democrats claimed Tilden had carried the state, Nicholls had been elected governor by about 8,000 votes, they had won four Congressional seats and a majority in the state legislature.

Even in 1860, when the election of Lincoln led to the Civil War, voters had accepted the results. Southerners did not question the results of the election, they objected to the policies of the Republican majority being imposed on them. In fact, the constitution of the Confederate states established an electoral system derived from the United States Constitution, including an electoral college rather than direct election by popular vote.

It wasn't said very often, but in addition to an established structure, described by written rules and regulations, the American electoral system required an element of trust. It had worked, at least until 1860, because people trusted that the outcome was fair, that the will of the majority was respected, and that if their candidate or party lost this time, within a few years there would be another election, and the opposition, should the outcome be reversed, would grant the winner the same respect.

In Louisiana, the loss of that trust had resulted in the establishment of two governments, massacres at Colfax and Coushatta,

numerous other acts of violence and Gatling guns in the streets
of New Orleans.

It was easy, and chilling, to imagine what might happen if
the entire nation lost trust in the electoral system.

The reported vote totals were ignored as both parties accused
the other of rigging the presidential election. The accusations
were the same as they'd been in the state but magnified: Republicans claimed threats and widespread violence had kept thousands of freedmen from the polls in the countryside.

Democrats protested that thousands of legitimate votes for
Tilden had been miscounted, discarded or mutilated, and that
ballot boxes in heavily Democratic areas simply disappeared.

Republicans countered that Democrats had stuffed those ballot boxes, allowed supporters to cast multiple votes and in some
places had even printed Democratic tickets bearing Lincoln's
picture, tricking illiterate voters into believing they were supporting Republicans.

The "official" totals were incredibly close. Of the 47,000
votes cast in Florida, for example, Republicans claimed Hayes
had won by 922; meanwhile, Democrats reported Tilden had a
razor-thin 94-vote margin.

According to South Carolina election officials, an incredible
101 percent of all eligible voters had cast ballots; one county reported 2,000 more votes than it had registered voters.

Oregon's Democratic governor dismissed a Hayes elector for
a minor technical violation, replacing him with a Democratic
Tilden vote—the one vote he needed. He was replaced yet again
before casting what would have been the deciding vote.

And Louisiana? The *Times* reported from New Orleans, "The
feeling here today is that the national contest has narrowed down
uncomfortably close to five debatable parishes...it comes to a
question of counting or rejecting the votes of several parishes."
Kellogg told reporters that returns should not be counted because the parishes had been heavily guarded by White League

members, who had been "reinforced by armed bodies from Arkansas and Mississippi, [and] most of the Republican leaders had been driven away or murdered..."

In those parishes, the report continued, no one could vote Republican "without the danger of exile or assassination. There is no law there, and no order, except the law of the revolver." The intimidation worked: in one of those places, East Feliciana, more than two thousand freedmen were registered—and not a single vote for Hayes was recorded.

No one knew how to resolve the Louisiana conundrum. Grant notified his military leaders to be ready to "preserve peace and order," using force if necessary, then dispatched a committee to New Orleans to monitor the work of the Returning Board. These were men, Grant said, "of irreproachable character and respectability, whose opinions and judgment would carry conviction to the whole American people." Among them were the Civil War general Lew Wallace, who was just beginning to write the classic *Ben-Hur*, and Congressman James A. Garfield. The Democratic National Committee also sent representatives to the city to watch the counting. Newspapers around the country began referring to the observers as "the national jury."

The state's gubernatorial election was just as confusing and contentious. Just as Kellogg and McEnery had done, both Packard and Nicholls claimed victory and began setting up their administrations.

Newspapers were filled with the most recent results of the national and local elections, which bounced back and forth day-to-day, morning to afternoon, sometimes hour by hour. A *Republican* note claimed, "The customary salutation each morning now is: 'Well, who is elected today?'"

The Louisiana Returning Board consisted of four men, two white, two Black, charged with reading reports, hearing evidence, tallying ballots and interviewing witnesses to try to reach a fair conclusion. Should they limit their count to votes actually cast, which clearly included fraudulent ballots, or should they rely on registration numbers to estimate the number of votes Republicans would have received in a different atmosphere? The impossibility of that task was reinforced by the very first letter the Board opened, which threatened, "If you swindle us again your lives will pay the forfeit... We are armed, organized and sworn to do our duty..."

The Board was not above reproach. Each of its four members had some questionable dealings in their past. There were some reports that the Board had put itself up for sale, supposedly asking the Democratic National Committee for $1,000,000 in return for certifying Tilden's victory. One member of the Board later claimed that it actually was the Democrats who had offered a bribe, and when it was rejected, party officials maliciously instituted criminal proceedings against Board members. In fact, one member eventually was sentenced to two years at hard labor, although that sentence was never carried out, and another member's once-profitable stable business essentially was destroyed. As Henry Warmoth explained, "Corruption is the fashion."

Similar rumors concerning bribes and threats surfaced in Florida and South Carolina as those states struggled to count votes. A South Carolina elector, for example, said he had been offered $10,000 to vote for Tilden.

As those Returning Boards, or *canvassing boards* as they were known in the other states, plodded through claims, records and eyewitness testimonies, trying to find order in chaos, supporters of both candidates began to fear they were being cheated out of the presidency. Anger escalated. Newspapers began reporting "Plain Talk about a Political Civil War," in which "The will of the majority would be expressed by firearms." Militias began girding for action. Several Democratic commanders contacted Tilden, volunteering to support any effort he mounted. Indiana claimed to have five hundred thousand men ready to fight for him. Iowa Republicans informed Hayes that they had a hundred-thousand-man army ready to respond.

As the race tightened even Hayes became more aggressive. After the Civil War, a fellow member of the 23rd Ohio Volunteer Infantry, William McKinley, recalled how Hayes's demeanor changed completely in combat. "From the sunny, agreeable, kind, generous gentleman's gentleman…he was, once the battle was on…intense and ferocious."

The battle was on. All thoughts of concession had long ago disappeared. Hayes threw himself into the fight.

By this point it had become obvious that this election was not going to be decided by the numbers. The system had failed. It could not be modified to fit the circumstances. No matter who was finally declared the winner—in both the federal and state elections—a huge segment of the population was going to be disillusioned and disenfranchised. Too many of them owned guns, and as had been seen, they were not hesitant to use them. The goal became finding some acceptable means of keeping the country from descending into chaos.

In early December, the Louisiana Returning Board declared Republicans had carried the state: the electoral college votes would go to Hayes. The Board also ruled that Packard had beaten Nicholls and would become governor and Republicans had won four of the six Congressional seats and both houses of the state legislature. That legislature presumably would send two Republicans to the Senate.

It was a resounding victory, even if few people believed it.

To justify that result, the Returning Board had to throw out or modify the count from ten parishes—eventually 15,000 votes were rejected, 13,000 of them for Tilden. The entire returns from Grant Parish and East Feliciana were declared invalid. In Grant Parish "not one form of law was observed…the vote taken was as informal as votes taken on a railroad train…

"Evidence as to intimidation by murder, hanging, whipping

and other outrages as affecting the vote at other polls was so conclusive that the returning officers unanimously rejected the votes cast at those polls..."

Results from eight polling stations in Ouachita were rejected for various reasons, among them "the United States Deputy Marshal in charge of the ballot box was shot..."

Democrats fought back. A state senator claimed that the Returning Board had acted illegally, stating that Democrats "were in possession of certain clues, which, in time, would lead to important revelations, intimating that some of the members of the board would be put on a rack so excruciating as to force confession from their unwilling lips!" Tilden's supporters believed that, even if no such evidence was ever produced.

Believing the action of the Returning Board to be illegal, *de jure* Governor McEnery certified a slate of Democratic electors to vote for Tilden. When those men met in the State House on the morning of December 7 to actually cast those votes, Kellogg ordered police to clear the hall. The Democrats refused to leave, forcing Kellogg to back down. The electors chose a representative to take their McEnery certificates of election to Washington.

Nicholls remained calm as the election wound its way through the legal system, expressing confidence in the outcome—and setting up his own new administration.

The canvassing boards in Florida and South Carolina were also finding creative ways to justify giving their electoral votes to Hayes. A Democratic congressman, upon being told Florida would go to Hayes, threatened, "There is nothing for Democrats to do except to buy muskets."

A Democratic party leader predicted that "within a hundred days people would be cutting each other's throats."

Republicans warned, "Any attempt to defeat this will be followed by the tramp of armed men—men who have marched before and are no mere holiday soldiers."

The Congressional investigations continued into the new

year without resolution. It was a fine political show: the hearings generated a lot of headlines, a lot of promises were made, suggestions were offered and nothing of consequence got done. Meanwhile in New Orleans, to thwart a threatened Democratic takeover of the State House, Governor Kellogg stationed a hundred and fifty Metropolitans in and around the building.

In preparation for the new session, which was scheduled to begin at noon on January 1, Republican legislators occupied the building on December 31 and spent the night there. Supper with a wine selection was served.

The legislature went into session just after twelve o'clock. Minutes later several hundred Democrats, among them both elected and defeated politicians, marched up to the front door and demanded to be admitted. A police officer blocked their way, keeping a steady hand on the butt of his gun. Too many men had been shot recently not to take precautions.

The Democrats eventually left to organize their own legislature elsewhere. The situation was a repeat from four years earlier: Louisiana had two men claiming to be governor, two legislatures, two courts and two officials in numerous state posts. One newspaper even suggested Kellogg remain in office until the dispute was finally settled, which would have given the state three governors.

On January 8, a dull and gloomy day, Packard was sworn into office in the barricaded State House, "notwithstanding the threats against my life which are freely bandied about." At the same time, on the balcony of St. Patrick's Hall, as a band played "Hail to the Chief," Francis Nicholls was sworn into the same office, promising that his administration would promote kindness, sympathy, confidence and justice.

The only trouble that day came from a group of street toughs who cut the reins and harnesses of carriages in front of the St. Louis Hotel. Governor Kellogg's carriage was badly damaged.

Governor Nicholls issued an order that the mob disperse, which was instantly obeyed.

It was as if time had stopped; years had passed but nothing had changed. The next day ten thousand Nicholls supporters clogged the streets and closed down the city. They took control of the Supreme Court building and swore in Democratic judges, who opened the Court and began hearing cases. They took control of the Third Precinct station house and then one by one every other station surrendered without a shot fired. They occupied the arsenal. They cut telegraph wires. By early in the afternoon Nicholls's men occupied every government building in the city other than the State House, which was completely encircled.

Three hundred Metropolitans armed with Winchester rifles took defensive positions in the hallways and at the doors and windows inside. There were hundreds more people in the building, and every one of them was armed, including the senators and representatives. Late in the afternoon several Democrats knocked on the State House door. They were answered by three shots, fired well above their heads.

Kellogg and Packard pleaded with army commanders for help from troops waiting in the nearby Orleans Hotel. That help was never given. Governor Packard told reporters his men would resist any effort to capture the State House.

Governor Nicholls, hoping to avoid bloodshed, urged his supporters to go home peacefully.

President Grant refused to recognize either man as governor, although his secretary of the interior, Zach Chandler, wired Packard telling him, "Make an attack if you have to die in the street." Packard, who essentially was trapped inside the State House, politely declined the suggestion. The situation in New Orleans had reached an impasse. There was no government. Once again, people simply chose which man to follow.

The fact that Nicholls had not been legally elected governor made little difference. His supporters occupied all of the essential

buildings in the city, as well as government offices in most parishes. Just about the only building of importance that remained
in Republican hands was "Fort Packard" as Democrats began
referring to the State House. Democrats appointed a citizens'
group to collect advance payments of taxes and, surprisingly,
announced that enough people had voluntarily paid a portion
of their taxes to pay outstanding debts.

Privately, Nicholls's takeover was supported by city business
interests, especially the Cotton Exchange, which enabled his
government to function.

Gradually, Louisianians began to accept the reality of the
Nicholls administration.

The national situation continued to deteriorate. The media
reported every threat. An armed insurrection seemed almost
inevitable. A Congressional committee released copies of wires
sent to several Southern states by Interior Secretary Chandler
days after the election, "evidently intended to incite fraud and
tampering with the returns." There was some evidence that
Florida Republicans had offered the secretary a substantial bribe
to "deliver the state to Hayes." That committee demanded the
Louisiana Returning Board come to Washington with all the
materials it had used to determine the outcome of the election.
When the four members of the Board refused, the committee
charged them with contempt of Congress and ordered them
arrested.

Congressional Republicans objected, arguing that the Constitution specifically gives states the right to appoint its presidential
electors, and Congress had no power to interfere with how they
did it. Senator James A. Garfield noted that beyond the rights
mentioned in the Constitution, the federal government has no
more rights to investigate State elections "than they would have
to inquire into the conduct of an election in England."

Garfield was firm in his words: it is entirely up to each State
to determine how its presidential electors would be chosen and

what restrictions—if any—were placed upon them. The federal government had no power to interfere with that process.

The Founding Fathers had given the new nation a constitution that had worked extraordinarily well for the first hundred years...until it didn't. It had created a foundation on which to grow and build but in too many places lacked necessary details. It had been left to politicians and judges to do the patchwork.

Just to further confuse the situation, a group of Democrats in Congress decided it might be a good time to impeach Grant for "misuse of the army and other offenses."

The president responded to that threat by warning the leaders of the effort he would have them arrested.

The government that Lincoln had only a decade earlier lauded as "of the people, by the people and for the people" had lost its legitimacy. The electoral system had collapsed, leaving the United States on the edge of anarchy. This situation had never been anticipated; there was no legal mechanism for dealing with it.

Congressional committees investigating the legitimacy of the returns also demanded that Western Union produce copies of all telegrams relating to the election from the contested states. Company officials resisted initially but after being threatened with subpoenas agreed to comply. Congress specifically wanted to see a telegram sent to Florida by the Democratic national chairman which said, according to the *Times*, "Florida must be held and counted for Tilden at all hazards, and any money which was necessary to secure that end would be furnished."

The same question that had paralyzed Louisiana now threatened to rip open all the national wounds. Who would count the electoral votes? Republicans insisted Article II Section 1 clause 3 of the Constitution stated clearly "The President of the Senate shall... open all certificates and the votes shall then be counted," meaning that leader could decide which returns to accept. Senator Thomas Ferry, Republican of Michigan, had become the acting vice president of the United States more than a year earlier upon the death of Grant's vice president Henry Wilson. Republicans were confident he would accept the Hayes returns.

Democrats countered that the vice president's role was largely ceremonial, that it was constitutionally limited to opening the return certifications and that he was given no discretion to make any determination about their validity. They cited another article of the Constitution which stated that if no presidential candidate received a majority of the electoral votes, "then the House of Representatives shall immediately choose by Ballot one of them for President." Given the situation, the Democratic majority in the House contended, this was the applicable clause.

Considering the complexity of the situation, Americans were fortunate that Democrats held the House and Republicans controlled the Senate. It allowed for the possibility that a solution would appear to be bipartisan, which made it slightly more likely Americans would accept it.

Congress wrestled with reality, trying to convey an appearance of competence and confidence, to make it seem as if they were following some sort of established parliamentary path. In fact, they were stumbling in the dark. Nothing like this had ever happened. There was no precedent, not only in America but anywhere else in the world. As usual, Congress continued to do what it did best. Committees met, conferences were held, ideas were floated, resolutions were debated, somber-sounding statements were issued and political games were played until they finally achieved the ultimate objective: they rid themselves of the ultimate responsibility by appointing a commission.

On January 29, 1877, days before they were to open the electoral ballots, Congress created the Electoral Commission to determine which ballots to accept. The commission consisted of five senators, five representatives and five Supreme Court justices: by agreement it would be made up of seven Democrats, seven Republicans and one supposedly impartial independent.

One independent. Inevitably, that man would cast the deciding vote. No one believed the charade that any of the seven Democrats and seven Republicans on the commission would vote to put the other party in the presidency. The independent appointee would cast the deciding vote. He would pick the president of the United States. It was the ultimate one-man, one-vote situation.

By mutual agreement, that one vote would be Justice David Davis, who had been Lincoln's campaign manager in 1860 and subsequently was nominated by him to the Court. But Davis had a reputation of being fair-minded and as honest as any politician.

In an attempt to sway his vote, Illinois Democrats offered Davis one of that state's two Senate seats. He accepted the obvious bribe, but then, rather than voting for Tilden as he was expected to do, Davis recused himself. He was replaced on the commission by Judge Joseph Bradley, a Republican activist selected for the Court by Grant. Bradley had been the judge who essentially overruled the convictions of the Colfax killers. But after their bribery fiasco, Democrats had lost the moral ground to protest.

One Republican. The deciding vote.

On February 1, more than eighteen hundred people filled the House chamber to witness the electoral count. Minutes after one o'clock, Acting Vice President Thomas Ferry opened a rectangular wooden box containing the certificates issued by each state. As was his constitutional duty, he withdrew the envelope holding Alabama's certificate, broke the seal and handed it to one of the appointed tellers, or vote counters. Alabama's ten electoral votes were cast for Tilden.

Arkansas, six for Tilden. California, six for Hayes. Colorado, three for Hayes. Connecticut, six for Tilden. Delaware, three for Tilden. Florida...

Florida submitted three sets of returns. Rather than accepting any of them, the counting was stopped, and these papers were sent to the Electoral Commission to decide which return to certify. South Carolina was treated the same way. And, of course, Louisiana.

The Electoral Commission met daily for weeks. The rumors were endless: Tilden, Hayes, Hayes, Tilden. Newspapers reported every rumor. Louisiana Democrats boasted to reporters, "We cannot tell why, but we know that everything is alright for Tilden."

It wasn't. In every decision the Board voted 8–7 for Hayes. He was handed the presidency by a single electoral vote, 185–184. His inauguration was scheduled for March 4—unless the Democrats could stop it. They did everything possible. They forced debate on every issue, fighting for time. House Obstructionists, as they were referred to, announced a filibuster would begin. A Democrat senator was quoted in a New York paper "in a violent appeal," warning "he was to stop the progress of the count by any means in his power." Supposedly a hundred thousand men were preparing to descend on the Capitol to prevent the inauguration of the man they called "Rutherfraud" or "His Fraudulency."

Given the twists and turns so far, it seemed hard to imagine that something even more unexpected could take place. But in Louisiana there was always another surprise coming. This time, an attempt was made to assassinate Governor Packard.

On the morning of February 15, as the Electoral Commission was hearing witnesses in Washington and two governors with two legislatures were trying to conduct business in New Orleans, Governor Packard was working in his office at the St. Louis Hotel. Several other people were in the room with him.

A neatly dressed, handsome young man later identified as William Weldon had been drinking at the Ville de Luxembourg with a one-armed man and a one-legged man. Weldon announced he needed to see Packard and convinced the one-armed man to accompany him. It was reported he locked his arm in the other man's stump, and they walked the few blocks to Packard's office. When they reached the hotel Weldon presented a card identifying himself as Frank Hudson, correspondent for the *Philadelphia Press*, and was admitted.

Weldon took a seat several feet behind the governor. After patiently waiting a few minutes he pulled a revolver and said loudly, "Governor, how long do I have to wait to see you?" Packard turned—and saw the muzzle pointed directly at his head. He responded instantly. In one swift movement he pushed the gun away with his left hand and slugged the would-be assassin with his right. Some witnesses swore Weldon pulled the trigger, but the gun misfired; then he fired again, and this time the gun boomed.

Packard's punch knocked down Weldon. In the melee several men drew their pistols. Police Superintendent W. F. Loan fired one shot at the assailant. Packard reportedly stepped in front of Weldon, saving his life. Then the governor was hustled out of the room to a safer upper floor.

Packard was fortunate: Weldon's bullet had barely grazed his right leg. Loan's shot smashed into Weldon's left arm; he bled profusely. For a brief time, it appeared the wound was fatal. But Weldon was equally lucky and survived without serious damage.

"The most notorious man in the nation," according to the *New York Times*, the twenty-five-year-old Weldon was described as a clerk at Pepper's dry goods store in Mobile, Alabama. The paper suggested this attempt was part of a larger plot, reporting that Louisiana Democrats had advocated Packard's assassination "as a means of ridding the state of Republicans distasteful to the White League community." The doctor who bound Weldon's wound believed he was under the influence of opium and alcohol and was carrying a bottle of absinthe. He had intended to kill both Hayes and Packard, he admitted, "to save the country."

Not surprisingly, the *Times-Picayune* quoted him as saying, "I am a Republican," while the *New Orleans Republican* reported he told police he was a Democrat.

When informed Packard had saved his life he said, "Tell him I want to see him."

Weldon was charged with crimes that would have locked him away for decades. Instead, his father, a Lutheran minister, came to New Orleans and appealed personally to Packard. Other character witnesses sent letters. Packard agreed to release the young man on $5,000 bond and allow him to leave the state. When a grand jury met to consider an indictment, no one appeared to testify, and the case was dismissed.

By that time Louisiana's new governor had taken office. Incredibly, it was Francis Nicholls.

It had taken an astonishing turn of events to reach that resolution following a historic conference that never officially took place.

Democrats had refused to accept the electoral college result from Washington. One man was not going to name the president. Republicans knew the outcome hadn't been fair. Hayes supporter Mark Twain admitted, "Even with the disputed states counted as Republican, Tilden had a plurality of 250,000 votes over Hayes. There is no longer any doubt that this election was stolen."

The problem was how to deal with it. Democrats would do whatever was necessary to prevent Hayes from being inaugurated. Several members of Congress floated the idea of a new election, calling it "a peaceful appeal to the ballot." But the lessons of Liberty Place had not been forgotten. This was no longer a political conflict. Guns ruled the streets. In Columbus, Ohio, shots were fired into Hayes's home as his family was enjoying dinner. In New Orleans, even after surviving Weldon's attempt on his life, Packard was warned "that an attack would be made upon the fort," meaning his headquarters in the St. Louis Hotel, and the mercenaries were "fully equipped with death-dealing Winchesters," awaiting "only a slight touch to make it explode..." The governor repeatedly pleaded with Grant for fifteen hundred men, claiming he needed that many troops to maintain Republican control of the state.

Nicholls tried to restrain White League troops, fearing an attack would give Grant the excuse he needed to send the army. It was uncertain if Nicholls would be able to prevent them from taking action against Packard.

During the waning days of February, in a last-minute effort to prevent a violent confrontation, party leaders met secretly at Wormley House in northwest Washington, DC. The prestigious hotel and restaurant had been developed by Black businessman James Wormley; it was a popular meeting place for powerful political leaders, celebrities, wealthy executives and military officers.

Representatives of Hayes and Tilden tried to work out a deal to give both parties what they needed to prevent bloodshed. No records were kept of the meeting, no notes were made, there were few discussions with reporters. The people attending the meeting had no legal status, no one had appointed them or given them any direction. They had no official power to make or enforce any agreement.

But they negotiated as if they did. Democrats agreed to end their filibuster and concede the election to Hayes in return for his pledge to withdraw all remaining federal troops from the South, share patronage, appoint at least one Southern Democrat to his cabinet and support substantial appropriations for railroad construction and other projects. Democrats also agreed to guarantee equal rights and safety for all citizens.

The deal was simple: the presidency in exchange for the end of Reconstruction.

It carried a high price, effectively eliminating federal protection for Black rights in the South. No one ever publicly admitted that, but as details leaked it became obvious.

Neither Hayes nor Tilden ever acknowledged this agreement. Hayes later pledged to restore "wise, honest and peaceful local self-government" to the Southern states. Tilden, who believed his options were limited to accepting this agreement or watching the outbreak of a second civil war, said, "I can retire to public life with the consciousness that I shall receive from posterity the credit of having been elected to the highest position in the gift of the people, without any of the cares or responsibilities."

Few newspapers carried any reports of this meeting, and even those papers that hinted at it provided few details. No one knew for certain that there was a "Wormley Compromise" or "Bargain of 1877." But something had changed; it was as if a derailed train had been put back on the tracks and suddenly there was forward movement.

Still there was no unanimous agreement. A large group of Democratic holdouts in Congress was determined Hayes would not be anointed president, while a large group of Republicans held out against handing the South over to Democrats. At one thirty in the morning March 2, during a remarkable joint session of Congress, a Democratic filibuster in the House collapsed after fourteen hours, and any semblance of order disappeared. The Congress of the United States descended into bedlam.

In an extra edition that hit the streets within hours, the *Times* described "An exhibition of rowdyism which would have disgraced a Democratic ward convention." Members of both parties were screaming for attention, arguments had broken out everywhere on the floor and women in the galleries, "fearful of a free fight," were escorted out. Acting Vice President Ferry, presiding over the joint session, pounded his gavel over and over, trying desperately to restore some sense of decorum. As he did, New York congressman George Beebe "mounted his desk and running over the tops of four desks in front of him, denounced the rulings of the Speaker unlawful and unjust... The noise and confusion which was caused by Beebe's disgraceful performance exceeded anything ever known in Congress."

Sufficient order was finally restored to move forward with

the business of selecting a president. At 4:10 a.m., the electoral college vote was approved, and Rutherford B. Hayes became the nineteenth president of the United States. Hayes was asleep on a train en route to Washington. An aide opened his stateroom door and told him quite anticlimactically, "It's all right, Your Honor. You have been voted in… The thing is decided and you've been declared elected President."

"Is that so?" Hayes replied. After being assured the news was accurate and he was to become the next president, he said, "Well, I declare," thanked the man for delivering the news, then turned over and went back to sleep.

Despite losing the presidency, Southern Democrats were elated. "Louisiana Republicans are completely disheartened," the *Picayune* wrote. "It is authoritatively stated that President Grant will withdraw the United States troops and leave Packard to his fate, carrying out the States rights doctrine enunciated by the Electoral Commission."

Some Republicans still held out hope Packard could retain power. "A covenant that the new administration shall abandon the Southern Republicans," newspapers reported, "leaving them to be dealt with by their opponents…would be a base surrender, of which no one who knows anything about Mr. Hayes would believe him capable."

They could not have been more wrong. In accordance with the compromise, among the first actions Hayes took after being inaugurated was to order the remaining federal troops withdrawn from Southern states. Packard was a realist: he accepted the fact that his administration would not survive without federal protection. The difficulty was how to legally cede power to Nicholls. Finally, it was decided to follow the national model and appoint a commission to figure it out.

Deals were made to satisfy everyone. Having no alternative, Packard abandoned the State House and told his militia to disband, to go home. He remained convinced that his government, the state's legally elected government, had been usurped. His bitter parting words might have served as a eulogy for Reconstruction. He told the four hundred and fifty supporters who had gathered there in the middle of the night to witness his surrender, "Louisiana, the first state rehabilitated after the war, is the last State whose government thus falls."

Packard was appointed American consul to Liverpool, England. Liverpool was a major international trading center, and this was among the most prestigious and lucrative appointments in the entire foreign service. Among his predecessors in the position was the author Nathaniel Hawthorne. State Supreme Court justices got new offices, clearing the way for a Democratic majority on the Court. Members of Packard's Republican legislature slid easily into the Democratic State House and Senate, giving Nicholls a majority in both.

For Democrats, April 24, 1877, "was a gala day for New Orleans, indeed for the whole State. It witnessed the triumph of law and justice over wrong and oppression... At 11 a.m. the streets were absolutely jammed with a living mass of humanity," there to witness "the final deliverance of the State."

At eleven thirty, the 3rd Infantry, clad in dress uniform and accompanied by the regimental band, proceeded to the levee and boarded the steamer the *Palace*. About twelve thirty, to the roar of one hundred guns and deafening cheers, the *Palace* left its moorings, leaving behind the debris of the election of 1872.

EPILOGUE

As the United States military sailed out of New Orleans, Jim Crow came marching in. The origin of the name Jim Crow was a buffoonish, dancing blackface character created by white performer Thomas Dartmouth "Daddy" Rice in the 1830s. The popularity of his demeaning caricature laid the foundation for the minstrel shows which became a staple of American stages for decades.

Far more importantly, *Jim Crow* became the catch-all phrase encompassing all the laws, regulations, customs and traditions that robbed Black Americans of their constitutional rights. With the withdrawal of the troops that had been enforcing Reconstruction, Jim Crow almost instantly turned African Americans into second-class citizens.

Even if President Hayes had wanted to protect the rights of Black citizens—and there is little evidence that he did—the Supreme Court had made that impossible almost a year earlier. The Court's decision in *US v. Cruikshank* was among the most significant ramifications of Louisiana's 1872 election and the Colfax Massacre; the ruling would play a significant role in shaping American history and impacting millions of lives for nearly a century.

Following the Colfax Massacre, the federal government had brought charges against William Cruikshank and eighty more white men, claiming they had violated the Enforcement Act of 1870 by conspiring to deprive freedmen of their constitutional rights. Specifically, they cited the First Amendment freedom of assembly, the Second Amendment right to bear arms and the Fourteenth Amendment, which guaranteed citizenship to all Americans. The Enforcement Act had been passed to give the federal government the power to take action against the Ku Klux Klan and other marauding white vigilante groups who used violence—including murder—to prevent Black men from voting.

But the court case focused on the still-unsettled balance between state and federal rights. Which entity had what rights to govern behavior in what situations? How far could Washington go to impose its laws on the citizens of Louisiana? The Civil War had not settled that question.

Eventually seventeen men, including Cruikshank, were tried in federal district court on sixteen charges—notably not murder—and convicted. Their attorneys appealed, arguing that the federal government lacked jurisdiction, that previous Supreme Court decisions had made prosecuting such crimes a state matter.

It took the Supreme Court a year to reach its decision. It threw out the convictions, deciding the federal government had no constitutional right to bring civil rights charges against individuals. "There is in our political system a government of each of the several states, and a Government of the United States," wrote Chief Justice Morrison Waite. "The same person may be at the same time a citizen of the United States and a citizen of a State, but his rights of citizenship under one of those governments will be different from those he has under the other."

Waite wrote that the rights of the federal government were

limited to protecting a citizen from actions taken by the State, not against offenses committed against them by other people. The federal government could bring action against a state government, but not, as was done in this case, against individuals. And even then those actions were restricted to those specifically enumerated and defined.

There also were a limited number of situations in which both governments had jurisdiction; for example, both the federal government and state government could prosecute an individual passing counterfeit money, although the actual cause of action would be different. "All that cannot be granted or secured are left under the protection of the States."

Democrats were euphoric. "The announcement will be hailed with delight everywhere by all friends of constitutional government," the *Picayune* editorialized. "The reserved rights of the States have been recognized by the highest judicial tribunal in the land; the conditions on which the Union was founded have been reaffirmed, and the lawlessness of the party which insists upon what it calls 'the higher law' has received a final and overwhelming rebuke."

The Court also found that the federal government could not infringe the Second Amendment right to bear arms, that any regulation of guns was restricted to "municipal legislation."

The ruling left it entirely to the states to choose how and when civil rights laws would be enforced. It was up to state governments, legislatures and courts to regulate race relations. And so they did, relegating Black Americans to the back of the bus, underfunded and underequipped public schools, and segregated seating in public venues. The Jim Crow laws prohibited them from attending state colleges, dining in white restaurants and cafeterias, or even getting proper medical care. It legalized discrimination in the workplace and trades, and designated where Black Americans could live or shop, serve on a jury or go to the movies, and going full circle, whether or not they could vote.

Louisiana Democrats took full advantage of this opportunity, passing legislation in 1898 that effectively disenfranchised most Black residents. Prohibiting them from voting guaranteed the election of white men committed to perpetuating a racist, segregated society—and there was nothing the federal government could do to rectify that.

Cruikshank affected every aspect of Black life, from before birth to after death. Perhaps most importantly, *Cruikshank* gave states, cities, towns and villages the power to decide what crimes to prosecute or ignore, in some places allowing people literally to get away with murder. As a distraught William Kellogg said, *Cruikshank* "was regarded as establishing the principle that hereafter no white man could be punished for killing a n—o."

This decision became the foundation of Southern segregation.

It seems incredible that a Louisiana gubernatorial election could have this massive, long-lasting impact on the entire nation, but that is precisely what happened.

The consequences of that election weren't limited to legalizing segregation. To prevent the electoral college debacle that took place after the 1876 election from ever happening again, Congress eventually passed the Electoral Count Act of 1887. The electoral college was always an unnecessarily complicated method of selecting a president. There is no easy-to-understand explanation why the Founders created it. No other country in the world had anything like it.

Basically, it was a compromise. The number of electoral votes each state cast was based on its population. The problem faced by the Founders was how to account for the slaves living in Southern states without giving them citizenship or the right to vote. In some Southern states slaves accounted for 60 percent of the population. The result was the notorious Three-Fifths Compromise, in which three-fifths of the entire number of slaves would be counted toward determining how many electoral votes a state would have. Nobody liked it much, but there was little choice. It had to be done to convince several Southern states to join the Union. Drawing it as broadly as possible allowed a wide range of interpretation.

That ambiguity made it potentially a very dangerous document. Problems with the electoral college surfaced almost immediately. Clever politicians might bend it to achieve their own goals. The quest to streamline it began after the 1872 election when the first committee was formed and continued steadily for fourteen years. The goal, according to Delaware Democratic senator Thomas Bayard, was to create a plan that would allow "a quiet, orderly, accepted, lawful method of deciding the vexed and troublesome question" of how the electoral votes would be cast and counted.

The final result, the Electoral Count Act of 1887, was little more than a bandage. It shifted much of the responsibility for determining which candidate had won a state's electoral votes from Congress back to the state, setting out broad procedures a state had to follow to resolve competing claims. It did simplify the task for the House, giving governors the responsibility of certifying results, but left mostly intact a rickety system open to manipulation. While the *Yonkers Gazette* noted after the bill was passed, "It is difficult to imagine a case that can now arise of a disputed election such as agitated the country in 1877," the act did little to close the loopholes that left the electoral system vulnerable to a candidate willing to manipulate them at some point in the distant future.

The appointments in 1877 of Rutherford Hayes to the presidency and Francis Nicholls to Louisiana's State House finally resolved the turmoil that had begun almost a decade earlier, but most of the principal players in the drama continued their political careers. Henry Warmoth, the young architect of the chaos, stayed involved in Republican politics—while becoming a wealthy man.

Warmoth was a complicated man, a fascinating package of

charisma, intelligence, ambition and ruthlessness, tempered by a roguish charm and the commitment to racial fairness, which he apparently never lost. He remained a powerful figure in Louisiana politics after being pushed out of the State House. In 1876 he returned to elective politics, winning a seat in the state legislature, which he hoped might be used as a springboard to higher office.

A year later Warmoth married and settled on a sugar plantation. In 1888 he made one last foray into elective politics, running as the Republican candidate for governor—against Francis Nicholls. Democrats were still scared of him, fully aware that he had strong ties to the Black community. Warmoth was leading the race by a significant margin, he later wrote, until Nicholls offered incumbent Governor Samuel McEnery "the assurance of an appointment to the Supreme Court of the State… He in turn promised to see to it that every ballot box should be stuffed to the limit in favor of General Nicholls…"

Sam McEnery, the younger brother of Warmoth's former opponent, actively campaigned against him, stoking old fears by warning that if Warmoth was elected, he would bring Black leaders back into power with him. "Before I will consent to such a calamity I will wrap the state in revolution, and I now proclaim that I suspend the law until the danger is over, from the Arkansas line to the Gulf of Mexico."

Sam McEnery also instructed local political leaders to "see that a large Democratic majority is returned from your Parish." He also advised, "Don't let n——s register or vote, but always count them for the Democratic ticket."

The political machine that Warmoth once controlled was now in Democratic hands, and it was turned on full force against him. As a result, Nicholls was returned to office by a massive majority—and to eliminate the threat of Black rule for the foreseeable future, a year later he made sure laws were passed that made it extremely difficult for Black men to vote in the state of Louisiana.

That was Warmoth's last, bitterly ironic legacy.

The Republican party rewarded his faithful service, though. In 1890 President Benjamin Harrison appointed him collector of customs for the Port of New Orleans. It was the same desirable post once profitably filled by Grant's brother-in-law James Casey. By that time, the carpetbaggers who had raced south after the war were disappearing into American folklore, having either returned to the North or had lived there long enough to be accepted as Southerners. After serving as collector for three years, Warmoth returned to private life and lived in New Orleans until his death in 1931, three years after Democratic populist Huey Long—the "Kingfish" who would be compared to him—had become Louisiana's governor.

Warmoth's political rival, John McEnery, died in 1891 still convinced he had won the gubernatorial election of 1872 and had been cheated out of the office by the Republican Returning Board. Many thousands of his supporters also believed it. Throughout his life, McEnery remained extremely popular among white conservatives; with his assistance, his brother Samuel became lieutenant governor and then ascended to the State House when the incumbent died in office. Three years later, Sam McEnery was elected governor for a full term.

The year John McEnery died, the city of New Orleans erected a 35' tall monument honoring the Battle of Liberty Place. Years later an inscription was added to the granite obelisk explaining, "McEnery and Penn having been elected governor and lieutenant-governor by the white people were duly installed by this overthrow of carpetbag government, ousting the usurpers, Governor Kellogg (white) and Lieutenant-Governor Antoine (colored). United States troops took over the state government and reinstated the usurpers but the national election of November 1876 recognized white supremacy in the South and gave us our state." The monument became an extremely controversial reminder of segregation, and in 2017, protected by police, city workers removed it. It remains in storage.

After his own political career ended, McEnery returned to his successful law practice and remained one of the state's most celebrated men.

Louisianians who loved McEnery hated William Kellogg with equal passion, believing he symbolized the evils and excesses of Reconstruction. After leaving the State House in 1876, William Kellogg carried his carpetbag into the United States Senate, although Pinchback, who was never seated by that body, claimed bitterly that legislators received $250 each to vote for Kellogg. When Francis Nicholls became governor, he nominated a loyal Democrat to the seat, and the ensuing battle once again left Louisiana without two senators. The Senate eventually voted to give the seat to Kellogg. "A transient victory," Democrats predicted in the *Picayune*, "beyond which is an early plunge to obscure infamy."

Kellogg was the last Republican the state would send to the Senate for almost a century. But he was a survivor: after his term ended he became one of very few former senators elected to the House of Representatives—the only Republican in the state delegation. While in office the carpetbagger was often criticized for the amount of time he spent traveling outside Louisiana; his political career ended after his one term in the House and, fittingly, he lived the remainder of his life in Washington, DC.

Although Pinckney B. S. Pinchback served in office for only six weeks after Governor Warmoth was impeached, that still secured his place in American history as the first Black man to be sworn in as governor of an American state. After Republicans failed to secure his seat in the Senate, he helped create the prestigious, historically Black Southern University and became a member of its board. His various endeavors had made him a wealthy man. At fifty years of age, he decided to attend law school and eventually was admitted to the Louisiana bar, but rather than practicing law he accepted appointment as a federal marshal in New York City. In 1895 he settled in Washington and remained active in Republican politics until his death in 1921.

Louisiana's 1872 gubernatorial election changed American history in ways that could never have been anticipated or predicted, and the consequences of that contest were felt for almost a century. Before its recent removal, in 1993 the New Orleans City Council declared the Liberty Place monument a "nuisance," and it was moved from its very public setting to a more obscure setting between a public parking garage and a wall. At that time, the overtly racist comments were removed and replaced in part by a hopeful but—given recent events—ironic message that summed up the entire political tragedy: *A conflict of the past that should teach us lessons for the future.*

★ ★ ★ ★ ★

ACKNOWLEDGMENTS

We both would like to thank Dan Abrams, who first introduced us to this astonishing, important story and urged us to tell it to a greater audience.

We also would like to thank our editor, Peter Joseph, who has been constantly steadfast in his support and wise with his pen.

We also would like to express our appreciation to our agents, Bryd Leavell at UTA and Frank Weimann at Folio Literary Management, who together helped us navigate the often perilous publishing waters.

We are grateful to author and historian Adam Fairclough, professor emeritus of American history at Leiden University, as well as the author of several acclaimed books, including *Bulldozed and Betrayed: Louisiana and the Stolen Elections of 1876* (LSU Press, 2021), for his guidance and editorial review.

David Fisher: I also want to express my admiration and appreciation to Dana Bash, who has brought her dedication to the truth, her professionalism, her desire to educate, enlighten and entertain, and her respect for her audience to every page of this book. Working with her has been a delight and I share her hope that readers pay careful attention to this cautionary tale.

I have been fortunate to have been a friend and neighbor of Carol Cooper, who with her husband, the legendary Richard Leibner, initiated the representation of journalists and media personalities at Bienstock Associates and later UTA. Among those people she has represented is Dana Bash, and Carol made our collaboration possible. Simply saying thank you to Carol and Richard doesn't begin to express my love and gratitude to them and their family.

I would also like to thank my friends David Stein and Jerry Stern, both of whom served as sounding boards as we uncovered the layers of this complex story and graciously offered advice and suggestions.

Finally, a project of this magnitude could never have gotten done without the continued enthusiastic support of my wife, Laura, who creates and maintains my world. As someone whose professional life has consisted of finding the right words to put on paper, even I fall short finding the right words to properly express my love and gratitude for Laura. I also benefited greatly from the support of my sons, Jesse and Beau, and, this time, Beau's wonderful fiancée, Jeannie Lee, the beautiful turtle-raising dentist! And finally, sitting on my lap as I work, as usual, spreading kindness and love, is our dog, Willow Bay.

BIBLIOGRAPHY

Berry, Jason. *City of a Million Dreams: A History of New Orleans at Year 300.* Chapel Hill: University of North Carolina Press, 2018.

Diamond, Raymond T., and Robert J. Cottrol. "'Never Intended to be Applied to the White Population': Firearms Regulation and Racial Disparity—The Redeemed South's Legacy to a National Jurisprudence?" (1995). LSU Law Digital Commons. https://digitalcommons.law.lsu.edu/faculty_scholarship/281/.

Dufour, Charles. "The Age of Warmoth." *Louisiana History: The Journal of the Louisiana Historical Association* 6, no. 4 (Autumn 1965), downloaded from JSTOR.org.

Dunning, William A. *Reconstruction, Political and Economic 1865–1877.* New York: Harper Brothers, 1907.

Emberton, Carole. "The Limits of Incorporation: Violence, Gun Rights, and Gun Regulation in the Reconstruction South." 2018

PhD candidate thesis, History Department, Northwestern University. Stanford Law School, Stanford, California.

Engstrom, Erik J., and Samuel Kernell. *Party Ballots, Reform, and the Transformation of America's Electoral System.* New York: Cambridge University Press, 2016.

Foner, Eric. *Reconstruction Updated Edition: America's Unfinished Revolution, 1863–1877.* New York: Harper Perennial Modern Classics, 1988.

Gonzales, John Edmond. "William Pitt Kellogg, Reconstruction Governor of Louisiana, 1873–1877." *Louisiana Historical Quarterly* 29, no. 2 (April 1946).

Haskins, James. *The First Black Governor: Pinkney Benton Stewart Pinchback.* Trenton, NJ: Africa World Press, 1966.

House Select Committee Report. *Use of the Army in Certain Southern States.* (1877). OpenLibrary.org.

Keith, LeeAnna. *The Colfax Massacre: The Untold Story of Black Power, White Terror and the Death of Reconstruction.* New York: Oxford University Press, 2008.

Kellogg, William Pitt. *Inaugural Address of Governor Wm; Pitt Kellogg.* Privately printed 1873. Republished 2018, London, Forgotten Books.

Kendall, John Smith. *History of New Orleans.* Chicago and New York: The Lewis Publishing Company, 1922.

Koenig, Louis W. "The Election That Got Away." *American Heritage,* October 1960.

Lane, Charles. *The Day Freedom Died: The Colfax Massacre, the Supreme Court, and the Betrayal of Reconstruction.* New York: Henry Holt & Company, 2008.

Lonn, Ella. *Reconstruction in Louisiana after 1868.* New York: G.P. Putnam's Sons, 1919.

Louisiana Adjustment: Abstract of the Evidence of Governor Kellogg's Election in 1872 and the Frauds of the Fusionists. Originally published 1875, privately printed at Republican office. Republished 2018, London, Forgotten Books.

Luxenberg, Steve. "The Forgotten Northern Origins of Jim Crow." *Time*, February 12, 2019, https://time.com/5527029/jim-crow-plessy-history.

New Orleans Republican, 1868–1880, accessed through Newspapers.com.

New Orleans Times-Picayune, 1868–1880, accessed through Newspapers.com.

Newspapers.com, 1867–1880, various American newspapers.

Nystrom, Justin A. "Battle of Liberty Place." *64 Parishes*, January 3, 2011, https://64parishes.org/entry/battle-of-liberty-place.

Pitre, Althea D. "The Collapse of the Warmoth Regime, 1870–72." *Louisiana History: The Journal of the Louisiana Historical Association* 6, no. 2 (Spring 1965).

Sublette, Ned. *The World That Made New Orleans: From Spanish Silver to Congo Square.* Chicago: Lawrence Hill Books/Chicago Review Press, 2008.

Takahashi, Sawako. "The 1872 Presidential Election in Louisiana." 1974 master's thesis, Louisiana State University.

Waldo, Curtis, ed. *Visitor's Guide to New Orleans.* (1875). Southern Publishing & Advertising House, University of Michigan Digital Library.

Warmoth, Henry Clay. *War, Politics and Reconstruction: Stormy Days in Louisiana.* New York: Macmillan Company, 1930. (Revised edition, new introduction by John C. Rodrigue. Columbia: University of South Carolina Press, 2006.)

INDEX